'67

'67

THE MAPLE LEAFS,
THEIR SENSATIONAL VICTORY,
AND THE END OF AN EMPIRE

Damien Cox & Gord Stellick

John Wiley & Sons Canada Ltd.

Front cover photo: Leaf captain George Armstrong holds the Stanley Cup as (left to right) Ron Ellis, Bob Pulford, Jim Pappin, Brian Conacher, Pete Stemkowski and Larry Hillman join in the celebration of the 1967 Maple Leaf Stanley Cup victory.

Library and Archives Canada Cataloguing in Publication Data

Cox, Damien, 1961-
    '67, the Maple Leafs : their sensational victory and the end of an empire / Damien Cox, Gord Stellick.

Includes index.
ISBN-13: 978-0-470-83850-1 (pbk.)
ISBN-10: 0-470-83400-5 (bound)
ISBN-10: 0-470-83850-7 (pbk.)

    1. Toronto Maple Leafs (Hockey team)—History. I. Stellick, Gord II. Title. III. Title: Sixty-seven, the Maple Leafs.

GV848.T6C69 2004   796.962'64'09713541   C2004-904426-5

Production Credits:
Cover design: Karen Satok
Interior text design: Adrian So
Photo insert layout: Mike Chan
Front cover photo: Frank Prazak/Hockey Hall of Fame

Printer: Tri-Graphic Printing Ltd.

Printed in Canada
1 2 3 4 5 TRI 10 09 08 07 06

To Mum and Dad for encouraging dreams.
— Damien Cox

To Lisa, Jesse and Justin:
My Stanley Cup Team!
— Gord Stellick

Photo Insert Corrections

Photo Insert One:
Page one, top photo, Imperial Oil – Turofsky/HHOF
Page one, bottom photo, Graphic Artists/HHOF
Page three, top photo, Graphic Artists/HHOF
Page three, bottom photo, Graphic Artists/HHOF

Photo Insert Two:
Page two, bottom photo, Graphic Artists/HHOF
Page three, top photo, Imperial Oil – Turofsky/HHOF
Page six, Graphic Artists/HHOF

Contents

Acknowledgements

The idea for this book was formed by decades of memories and the sense the story of the '67 Leafs had yet to be fully told. It was crystallized during a late night marathon phone conversation between Montreal and Toronto in the fall of 2003 and, despite various twists and turns, never lost its original energy. Our thanks go out to the living members of that '67 Leaf team, all of whom, without exception, helpfully co-operated with this book, mostly by being far more interested in talking about their teammates than themselves. They truly were a great team, and in many ways remain that to this day.

The authors would also like to thank John Shannon of Leaf TV for providing helpful video evidence of that spring, and to Hadley Obodiac, the daughter of the late Leaf public relations executive Stan Obodiac, for providing many compelling photographs.

Many people generously contributed their imaginations and ideas, a list that includes Jim Gregory, Trent Frayne, Bobby Orr, Bobby Haggert, Bob Stellick, Anne Barilko Klisanich, Bill Watters and Jim McKenny. The Toronto Star Syndicate provided invaluable research material through its "Pages of the Past," and "The Blue and White Book" by Andrew Podnieks was invaluable in making sure the facts of the story were kept straight.

We also would like to thank Phil Bingley for being the first to tell us this was a great idea, and Vicki White and

Lisa Stellick for continuing to tell us this was a great idea over the months.

Finally, our thanks go to Karen Milner at Wiley, who always, always provided an encouraging voice and more than a few important pointers along the way.

Our goal was to tell a story that, in many ways, hadn't been told fully. We hope we accomplished that task.

Damien Cox
Gord Stellick

September 2004

Prologue

Each player understood the obstacles to winning the Stanley Cup that season, 1967, and some felt the undeniable decay that was already eating at the foundation of their team, the Toronto Maple Leafs. They knew, quite obviously, that theirs was a team of greybeards, one of the oldest clubs to ever pose a serious bid to capture the Cup. They knew, from their shared experience and the very different nature of the individuals in their dressing room, that pro sports was changing in a very fundamental way, moving away from the stiff, patriarchal, dictatorial traditions that had ruled for decades, traditions that their commander, Punch Imlach, clung to like a desperate man clings to a lifejacket. They knew that their team lacked goal-scoring and youth at key positions, relied on injury-prone goalies and included some brittle, erratic personalities that created tensions within the team. They knew they had endured a most difficult regular season, one in which they'd lost 10 consecutive games at one point, and that their team was vulnerable to an opponent willing to meet the challenge of snuffing out the stubborn spirit of a near-dynasty that still had some fight left in it.

But there was also much they didn't understand. That experienced, determined group of Maple Leaf players that would record such a dramatic accomplishment in the spring of '67 could not have known that the men who signed their pay-cheques were also stealing money from the team and its shareholders, and committing crimes that would bring the force of the law down upon the franchise and humiliate the proud club. They might have sensed, but couldn't have fully understood, the manner in which the organization was squandering its heritage and losing its once feared ability to control key sectors of Canada's hockey talent landscape. They didn't know that Imlach, trading on his successes, was involved in a curious series of business transactions and beginning a process of poor management decisions that would see him destroy the franchise's competitiveness not once, but twice, in just over a decade. They sensed with some trepidation that a players union could be in their best interests, but didn't fully understand the aggressive ambitions of the man who would bring it to them or how that union would fundamentally alter the nature of the business. They didn't know, and wouldn't find out for decades, that while they were taping their sticks, nursing their injuries and testing newly sharpened skates within the confines of Maple Leaf Gardens, their home away from home, that a horrifying pedophile ring was beginning to spread its ugly tentacles within the very same walls. They could not have known that some of the most important members of their team would die in tragic ways in the years that immediately followed, while others would become estranged from the club, hopelessly alienated from the group that had seemed so focused upon their common objectives that golden spring. In general, they could not have grasped the beginnings of a destructive process that would unfold over the ensuing decades and bring the team that once had been the pride of English Canada to its knees.

They were hockey players, not detectives or soothsayers. They were sons and fathers, some educated and some not, ambitious heroes and flawed characters, men who sensed the hockey world was not quite what it had been just a handful of years earlier, but were still focused on using their physical and mental skills to achieve their dreams in the game that some loved and others saw merely as a means to gaining wealth and fame. That the '67 Stanley Cup triumph was a mask that covered crime and decay, tragedy and human frailties, nepotism and greed, does not diminish their accomplishments. Rather, the fact that that collection of athletes was able to capture a Cup in Canada's centennial year is enhanced by the hurdles they overcame. Understanding, in retrospect, all that was happening at the time doesn't denigrate the accomplishments of those players, but rather amplifies them. Coming to grips, for example, with the fact that Imlach was, by 1967, a wholly destructive manager and outdated coach accentuates the excellence of the players, giving many the credit for that '67 Cup they have never justly received.

The passage of so much time has mythologized that 1967 Leaf team and turned it into an elusive standard of supposed greatness to which every subsequent edition of the team has failed to measure up. The memory of that team is hearkened back to as though somehow in the legacy of the '67 Leafs there is a model to follow—a blueprint to greatness. But this take on '67 is wrong. That team at that time and place was actually a once powerful club in serious decline, an organization that wasn't ready to meet the challenges of change, both within the business in which it operated and the cultural fabric of which it had been such a compelling element.

The basic question that befuddles Leaf fans is straightforward. How could a team that won an extraordinary four Stanley Cups in six years—1962, 1963, 1964 and 1967—fail to achieve anything close to that level of success in the decades that followed? How can this be explained and understood? The '67 Cup was clearly a turning point in the history of the franchise, an unexpected success that fed the arrogance and greed that had grown within the club over that magically successful decade. Winning fed the sense that championships would always happen because they always had. Indeed, you could make a compelling argument that the franchise might well have been better off had it not won the Stanley Cup in '67, that winning exaggerated all the organization's worst characteristics, allowed internal infections to fester rather than be salved and allowed those who wished to use the Leafs and Maple Leaf Gardens as a shield for their shady designs to operate more freely and effectively. The years of losing on the ice that followed the 1967 championship twisted the character of the club, gradually turning the Leafs into an operation that defined success by profit more than by wins and Stanley Cups. As the years went by and Harold Ballard turned the Leafs into a laughingstock, and as those who succeeded him were eventually forced to admit to inside knowledge of the sexual abuse crimes committed inside Maple Leaf Gardens during the 1960s, Conn Smythe's 1966 indictment of what he saw unfolding, that the Leafs had started to put "cash ahead of class," seems to have been a premonition of startling accuracy. Looking back, winning in '67 allowed the team to blithely continue as it always had, not understanding that the times were changing—and fast. Winning in '67 was important, not because that's when things were right, but because that's when it all started to go so very wrong. This is the story of a remarkable group of athletes who managed to achieve immortality amidst unfolding chaos.

GAME ONE
MAPLE LEAFS AT CHICAGO BLACKHAWKS, APRIL 6, 1967

As the 1967 Stanley Cup playoffs began, an unusual Maple Leaf image from the previous spring's disastrous post-season still lingered.

The image was of Punch Imlach, never himself a player of note, standing in the walkway of Maple Leaf Gardens with his skates on, poised to jump on the ice during Game Four of his team's first-round series with Montreal. The situation was desperate, with the Leafs having already lost the first three games of the series. But it wasn't so desperate that Imlach was poised to become a modern-day legend by actually playing in the game and evoking the legend of Lester Patrick to try and turn the series around. It certainly wasn't a gesture born of a celebratory spirit as would be the case in 2002 when Scotty Bowman, a career coach like Imlach, laced up the blades after his Detroit Red Wings had won the Stanley Cup so he could experience the feeling of skating around the rink with the Cup held aloft. No, Imlach was just mad that night. Fed up. Annoyed in general but, specifically, with the officiating of referee Art Skov, whom he felt had done his team one bad turn after another against the powerful Habs. As photographers snapped his picture, he prepared to jump onto the ice and bring his complaints to the attention of the veteran Skov in what would have been a most controversial manner. He was going to tell Skov of his unworthiness to be an NHL official, how he had aided and abetted the Canadiens in their dominance of his team, a club that had won championships in 1962, 1963 and 1964 but was by the spring of 1966 crumbling under his guidance.

With that fourth game scoreless in the opening minutes, a wild brawl had broken out after Peter Stemkowski crashed ornery Montreal winger John Ferguson into the boards. Within moments, Ferguson was trading punches with Stemkowski, Leafs Eddie Shack and Larry Hillman were battling Habs forwards Claude Larose and Dave Balon and, finally, Montreal defenceman Ted Harris and Toronto forward Orland Kurtenbach squared off. Kurtenbach was a youthful, towering centre regarded as a young but indestructible NHL heavyweight, but Harris flattened him with one punch. Kurtenbach claimed afterwards he'd slipped on the Gardens ice. At the conclusion of the mayhem, Imlach blew his stack when he learned Skov, after handing out 110 minutes in penalties to the two clubs, had given the Habs a power play. As the bickering continued, Imlach donned his skates. "I was going to go out after the referee," said Imlach. "If it was going to cost me $100 anyway to go on the ice, I wasn't going to try to catch [Skov] in my boots. I put on my skates so I could catch him and tell him my opinion on things."

Whether Imlach was overwhelmed by good judgement that night, restrained effectively by assistant GM King Clancy, or whether he never really intended to complete the caper, the Leaf boss didn't follow through. He stayed off the ice while his Leafs went down 4-1 in the game and were swept, managing to score only six goals in the series against the Habs, who went on to win the Stanley Cup. It was an unmitigated disaster for the Leafs, and, given Imlach's frayed relationship with team president Stafford Smythe, it was easy to believe that Imlach's reign with the Leafs might be coming to a close unless he could find a way to recapture the glory of the early 1960s.

One year later, as the Leafs took to the ice at Chicago Stadium to begin the 1967 playoffs, Imlach must have experienced some of those same feelings of desperation, frustration and hopelessness as he walked up the stairs to the rink. His aging team, essentially unimproved since the Hab Sweep, had just finished a very difficult season, one fraught with internal problems that seemed to have left the team uncertain of its abilities and individual players utterly dispirited. A player like Jim Pappin had enjoyed a strong second half to the season, but only because he hoped one of the six new NHL teams would pick him in the upcoming expansion draft and end his misery under Imlach.

The Leafs had big names, sure, but some of them couldn't stay healthy and others were past their due date. Elsewhere in the sports world, Jim Brown had stepped away from the gridiron and Sandy Koufax had hung up his spikes, both outstanding athletes departing at the peak of their abilities. Similarly, it seemed likely that high-profile Leafs like Red Kelly, Terry Sawchuk and George Armstrong were at the end. Kelly, in fact, had talked openly of retiring after the debacle against the Habs a year earlier, but had been coaxed back for one more year. Sawchuk had threatened to quit at the previous fall's training camp. Another well-known Leaf, defenceman Carl Brewer, had bolted the club 18 months earlier and was skating for Canada's national team. A sense of foreboding change haunted Imlach, who knew Alan Eagleson and his players union had infiltrated the Leaf dressing room. Eagleson had assisted a players' rebellion in the minor leagues that had brought down Imlach's iron-fisted colleague, the great Eddie Shore. What might Eagleson do to Imlach? What might he do to the Leafs? The outlook seemed so gloomy that Imlach had divested himself of a chunk of Leaf stock partway through the season.

'67

Even the once conservative city of Toronto was changing, madly trying to catch up with Montreal, which was preparing to enchant the world with Expo '67. Yorkville, once a downtown haven for the hippie culture, was out of control, allegedly infested with teenage prostitutes and drug-dealers. The cops were cracking down and fining parents $25 for children under 16 found in the Yorkville area after 10 at night. Former Leaf captain Syl Apps, now a provincial politician, suggested it was time to "get rid of Yorkville." Other news reports cited a case of a group of teens attacking Toronto firefighters trying to do their job. Four youths had been taken into custody after a subway driver had been stabbed seven times. Instead of the Leafs' playoff preparations, an appearance of The Monkees in Toronto for a 46-minute concert at the Gardens on the last day of the NHL season dominated the newspapers. A television cameraman had been booted out of the band's hotel, and 54 fans had been treated for "hysteria" at the concert itself. At least social conservatives could rejoice in the fact the Canadian government had turned away LSD guru Timothy Leary when he'd tried to cross the border and speak in Toronto. Colour television, finally, was all the rage in Toronto and across the country, which to Imlach probably meant his team was about to be ravaged in full technicolour, rather than in old-fashioned black and white.

The Blackhawks, after all, were a fearsome club, a team that appeared even more powerful than the splendid Montreal squad that had plundered the Leafs 12 months earlier. Just days earlier, the Hawks had ended the regular season by destroying the New York Rangers 8–0, a frightening display of firepower that pushed their record total to 264 goals for the season. Bobby Hull and his wicked curved stick had fired home 52 of those scores, and Stan Mikita had led the league in scoring with 97 points while centring the Scooter Line between Doug Mohns and Ken Wharram. Pierre Pilote was an all-star legend on defence, while Billy Reay, who had been fired by the Leafs as their coach nine years earlier and replaced by Imlach, looked to have more than enough weapons to gain a measure of revenge against his former employers. A late season improvement had, it's true, pushed the Leafs to a respectable 32 wins and a third-place finish, and they had looked good in winning their last regular season game in Boston by a 5–2 score. After that game, the Leaf charter plane landed at a military base in Trenton, Ontario, and instead of taking them back to their homes in Toronto, a bus whisked the weary players to the Rock Haven Motel on the outskirts of Peterborough, Ontario. "Who knows why?" recalls Pappin.

For three days, Imlach worked over his players, subjecting them to a ferocious regimen of two-a-day practices, a boot camp atmosphere that was lampooned in a Toronto newspaper as hockey's version of Hogan's Heroes, a popular TV program of the time based on a German prisoner-of-war camp. The Leafs sweated and groaned, and while Terry Sawchuk grumbled and complained and refused to try to even pretend to stop his teammates' shots during practice, Johnny Bower played every rush as though it was Game Seven of the Stanley Cup final. On one sequence, a shot by Stemkowski struck Bower on the unprotected part of his right hand, splitting his baby finger and putting him on the sidelines for Game One against the Hawks. Neither Bower, 42, nor Sawchuk, 37, had managed to stay healthy enough to play 30 games that season, so it was no surprise one was injured to start the post-season. Being exiled from their Toronto homes and forced to suffer through extra workouts after a difficult season, meanwhile, just made the Leaf players hate Imlach a little more. Some just wanted to get the season over with, and the Hawks, even with Hull iffy until the last minute for the opener because of knee problems, seemed ready to oblige.

Opening night of the '67 playoffs was the expected nightmare, a one-sided 5–2 thrashing at the hands of the surging Hawks in the cacophony and craziness that was the Madhouse on Madison, Chicago Stadium. The game was surprisingly wide-open, with both teams managing more than 40 shots on the enemy goal, but the Hawks were far better and Sawchuk was badly outplayed by Denis Dejordy in the Chicago goal. Imlach's mini-camp seemed a disaster as the Leafs looked exhausted and disorganized. About the worst moment for the Hawks came when Phil Esposito had to retire for a new pair of hockey pants after they were accidentally slashed by Tim Horton's skate during a third-period scrap. Only a big hit by Leaf third-liner Brian Conacher on Mikita late in the game served as a highlight for the Toronto side. "We probably should have lost 10–2," says Pappin. "I thought we were going to lose four straight."

It was Toronto's seventh consecutive playoff defeat, stretching back to their ouster from the 1965 post-season. The Chicago crowd serenaded Sawchuk with a sing-song version of "Goodbye Terry" and the sense of impending disaster, the same disaster that had befallen them against Montreal the previous spring, felt nearly overwhelming to the Leafs as they packed their equipment and flew back home. Not all the players, however, felt hopeless after the one-sided defeat. "If that's as good as they can play, and as bad as we can play, then I thought we could beat them," says Dave Keon, looking back. Still, the satisfied Hawks, ousted from Chicago Stadium by an ice show, decided to take two days off. Reay, with vindication in the offing, felt comfortable taking his foot off the gas pedal. This, after all, was going to be easy.

1 Losing the Edge

For Wendel Clark, a treasure of Canada's hockey heartland, it was a glorious day for a wedding. The former Maple Leaf captain and his fiancée, Denise, had gathered hundreds of friends, family, media and members of the hockey glitterati at the Saskatoon Hotel in June 1996. NHL stars like Doug Gilmour and Joe Sakic were on hand. It was a happy moment for the Leaf organization. Clark had been brought back to the club in a trade three months earlier, albeit a trade that had, in the long-established tradition of the franchise, squandered another horde of young talent, defenceman Kenny Jonsson and a draft pick that would become goalie Roberto Luongo.

The long, generous summer days had brought countless hours of sunshine to the western plains, and for Maple Leaf general manager Cliff Fletcher, the man who had repatriated Clark in March, these were also sunny, buoyant times despite the struggles of his hockey team, for he had a stunning surprise in store for Leaf fans across Canada and around the world. He was going to bring The Great One, Wayne Gretzky, to the Leafs.

Three months earlier, the Leafs had been bounced out of the first round of the playoffs after a troubled season in which Pat Burns had been dumped as head coach and ownership had forced Fletcher to delete expensive contracts by trading popular, productive players like Mike Gartner, Dave Gagner, Todd Gill and 50-goal shooter Dave Andreychuk for little in return. Fletcher, with 30 years of pro hockey experience, could live with the disappointing playoff defeat to St. Louis, one in which interim coach Nick Beverley had clumsily labelled his players "a bunch of nimrods" for their lacklustre play. Fletcher figured he'd be able to fix what ailed the team. But the cost-cutting moves forced on him by ownership, specifically chairman Steve Stavro, were worrisome. Stavro, Fletcher remembered, had tried to block the former Calgary GM's hiring by the club in 1991 as part of his political tug-of-war with Don Giffin, who, along with Stavro and Don Crump, had been named the executors of owner Harold Ballard's will after his death in 1990.

Fletcher liked to tell the story of how Stavro had insisted on driving him back to his hotel after Giffin had introduced him to the Leaf board in June 1991. The board had enthusiastically greeted Toronto's newest hockey saviour, but Stavro was not so welcoming and warned Fletcher he planned to fight his hiring. "Look, it's nothing personal," Stavro told Fletcher, tapping Fletcher on the leg repeatedly for emphasis. "But I'm going to be running this operation and I have different people I want to run it." Five years later, Giffin was dead and Stavro had maneuvered himself into a position as Ballard's successor. He had come to respect Fletcher, but that deep sense of loyalty wasn't there, and there were obvious indications to Fletcher and close observers of the club that he was losing support at the ownership level as the team failed to follow up on their playoff successes of 1993 and 1994. Indeed, former Montreal Canadiens goaltending great Ken Dryden was one of many taken into the confidence of influential Gardens directors as Fletcher struggled to maintain the support of ownership. Dryden had a long-standing relationship with Brian Bellmore, Stavro's lawyer, and had been offering his thoughts on the hockey club behind the scenes.

Despite his decaying position, Fletcher was thinking big in the summer of 1996—as big, really, as any Leaf manager had thought since Jim Gregory had unsuccessfully schemed to lure

Anders Hedberg and Ulf Nilsson to Toronto from the World Hockey Association in 1978. Fletcher had been contacted by representatives of the incomparable Gretzky who had made it clear The Great One was interested in finishing his magnificent career in Toronto. Growing up in southern Ontario, Gretzky had rooted for the Leafs as a boy and had always treasured his visits to Maple Leaf Gardens, an arena where, ironically, over the course of his NHL career, he frequently had brilliant scoring nights to damage the chances of the team that he had cheered for in his youth. In Game Seven of the 1993 Western Conference playoffs, for example, Gretzky had put on a spectacular show at the Gardens with a five-point performance that had scuttled the chances for a most appealing Toronto–Montreal Stanley Cup final. "I think that was probably the best game I ever played, anywhere," he later said.

In 1996, three years after that momentous game, Gretzky was an unrestricted free agent. At 35 years old, he was clearly slowing down, and had suffered persistent back problems since being crosschecked from behind by American defenceman Gary Suter in the 1991 Canada Cup. He had been traded partway through the previous season from Los Angeles to St. Louis, recording 23 goals and 79 assists between the two clubs, and had helped the Blues beat the Leafs in a seven-game series just weeks before. But he wasn't interested in staying in St. Louis after a sour experience under Mike Keenan, and the possibility of joining the Leafs fascinated him. His father, Walter, had suffered a brain aneurysm in 1991 and had nearly died. Playing for the Leafs was an opportunity for Gretzky to be closer to his Brantford family and other business interests, including a restaurant in downtown Toronto.

Sitting at a table with his assistant general manager, Bill Watters, and others at Clark's wedding, Fletcher could barely contain his excitement. Gretzky, quite clearly, would bring 10 times the level of glamour and excitement than even the incredibly popular Clark had. More important, Fletcher craved the symbolism of signing Gretzky, of having Gretzky play for him after torturing Fletcher's Calgary Flames for so many years while skating for the Oilers. Signing Gretzky would bring pride to the organization that already owned Doug Gilmour and Mats Sundin. Gretzky would galvanize the enthusiasm of skeptical fans and help fortify Fletcher's flagging support at the corporate level of the Leafs. "I felt bringing Wayne to Toronto would be the biggest shot in the arm for hockey in Canada," recalls Fletcher. "At the time, people were saying nobody wanted to play in Canada, that free agents wouldn't play there, that Canadian teams couldn't compete. I just felt bringing Wayne back would be an unbelievable coup." Even better, the acquisition of Gretzky would cost the Leafs nothing in terms of players, prospects or draft picks. It would not be a short-term fix that sacrificed the future, but rather an attempt to add a layer of quality without giving up anything but the dollars that would be paid out in salary, dollars that would be easily recouped through sponsorships, merchandise sales and increased TV ratings. "It wasn't at all about money," says Mike Barnett, then Gretzky's agent. "It was about something that would be fun to finish."

Incredibly, despite Fletcher's best intentions and Gretzky's keen interest, the deal fell through. Eight years after the fact, Gretzky finally revealed in stunning, explicit detail just how he failed to become a Leaf. In an interview at the 2004 NHL all-star game in St. Paul, Minnesota, he explained for the first time the sweetheart deal he had offered the team of his youth. "We were talking about something between $2 million and $3 million a season," he recalled. "And you know, the ridiculous part is Vancouver was offering me $8 million a season. But I wanted to be a Leaf in the worst way. I told Cliff, 'I'll do whatever it takes to make it work. You can defer my salary for 25 years if you have to. Whatever it takes to get the deal done.' But he couldn't get the deal done." On the Canada Day weekend that soon followed Clark's wedding on the prairies, Fletcher gave Gretzky the bad news. "He said he couldn't get the deal approved," says Gretzky. "He told me that they were channeling their money towards the new arena and were serious about cutting back on payroll." For years, Gretzky and Fletcher declined to give the true version of the story, choosing not to further embarrass the Leafs and Stavro. But Gretzky remembers fervently believing he was going to follow the likes of Syl Apps and Dave Keon and play for the Leafs. "Oh, definitely. I thought that way for a few weeks," he recalled.

The decision of Leaf ownership to dismiss Gretzky was probably about more than just plans to build a new arena. Three months earlier, Stavro had been forced to pay out an extra $23.5 million, plus interest, to the charities that had been named in former owner Ballard's will but, in the opinion of government officials, had been shortchanged through the complicated sale of the team and the famous arena. Declining to sign Gretzky was never a pure hockey decision. "There was an awareness that Gretzky was available to us," said Fletcher. "But I never got any signals to pursue it aggressively." Instead, after his flirtation with the Leafs and Canucks, The Great One was reunited with Mark Messier and went to finish his career with the New York Rangers.

Within a year, after the Leafs had missed the playoffs, Fletcher was fired and replaced by Dryden. Gilmour, the team's best player, had been peddled to New Jersey along with defenceman Dave Ellett in another salary dump. Politics and finances had, once more, won out over hockey interests on Carlton Street. "I'm sure there will always be a great debate whether I did a good job, a fair job or a poor job with the Leafs," said Fletcher. "I tried to restore the image of the team, partly by recognizing former great players. We wanted to merge the past with the present. Bringing in Wayne Gretzky would have topped it all off."

Given where Gretzky was in his career at that time, it's unlikely he alone could have powered the Leafs to a championship. But one of the top three players in the history of the sport would have cost, in relative terms, almost nothing at that time to a team that was about to embark on its 30th season since winning the Stanley Cup. Moreover, it was a kind of philosophical statement on hockey talent that had been made repeatedly over the previous decades of Leaf history, a tradition that had begun with a terrible and far more significant oversight 36 years earlier.

In March 1960, a fateful exchange of letters between the Leafs and a minor hockey organizer named Anthony Gilchrist in Parry Sound, Ontario, changed hockey history. Gilchrist wrote to Leaf GM/coach Punch Imlach advising the Leafs of a young player named Bobby Orr. He suggested Imlach should take a serious look at the 12-year-old "or I feel sure it will be too late." The boy's father and grandfather, Doug and Robert, Sr., respectively, were diehard Leaf fans, and dreamt that the young star, who had grown up learning the game on the frozen beauty of the Seguin River and had been coached by former Leaf defenceman Bucko McDonald, would one day play for the Leafs. Orr's peewee team had played a game at the Gardens earlier that month, posing for a picture in the Leaf dressing room along with his teammates and Leaf players Dick Duff, Larry Regan and George Armstrong. "You sized [Orr] up and made a remark that he was a hockey player," Gilchrist wrote to Imlach. "Well, he sure has the earmarks of a combination of [Gordie] Howe and [Doug] Harvey." Gilchrist suggested to Imlach that he come and take a second look at Orr, and gave him a schedule of Parry Sound's upcoming games.

In what would be his greatest error as a hockey man, Imlach didn't respond himself. Instead, he passed the note on to his chief scout, Bob Davidson. In a letter dated April 7, 1960, Davidson courteously thanked Gilchrist for the information, but declined to follow up on Orr, writing that "the boy is a little too young to be put on any list for protection." Davidson wrote, "I will keep his name on file and when he gets to be fourteen or fifteen we will contact him and, if he is good enough, I would recommend a hockey scholarship for him here in Toronto." Davidson ended the four-paragraph letter with a haunting remark. "I hope that some day Bob Orr will be playing for the Maple Leafs."

The Leafs were loaded with young talented players at the time and they were used to having players directed to them. But while they responded with a condescending, "if he is good enough," the Boston Bruins leapt upon the opportunity. A horde of Bruins officials travelled to Gananoque, Ontario, to watch a bantam tournament, primarily to consider a boy named Ricky Eaton. Instead, Bruin executives like Hap Emms, Milt Schmidt and Wren Blair were captivated by the talent of the white-haired, crew-cut Orr, who was playing against older boys in the competition but always seemed to have the puck. "After that, Wren Blair pretty much lived in Parry Sound," says Orr. The Bruins sensed they'd found a special player and were determined not to let him go.

In later years, Orr laughed when he recalled the letter from the Leafs, but not out of spite or any sense of vindication. "I just wanted an NHL contract," recalls Orr. "Looking back, I knew the Bruins weren't a very good team, so it might be easier to get to play in the NHL. But I'm sure if the Leafs had come up to Parry Sound and convinced my parents that I should play for them, I would have gone to play for one of their teams." By 1962, all of the Bruins' efforts paid off when Orr's parents, Doug and Arva, agreed to let their 14-year-old son, then just 5-foot-6 and 135 pounds, sign a card to play for the new Oshawa Generals in the Ontario Hockey Association, which was then part of the Boston sponsorship chain. Orr was under Bruin control.

The Leafs, meanwhile, probably barely noticed what they'd missed, for they were beginning a run of three consecutive Stanley Cups. Yet the reality was that after carefully gathering and sculpting young talent for years through their ownership of the Toronto Marlboros and tight relationship with the St. Michael's College hockey factory, dismissing Orr as a prospect was an important indication that the focus was changing within the Leafs: A new era, dominated by non-hockey pursuits, was dawning. Sure, other NHL teams had made similar enormous mistakes. The New York Rangers, for example, were the first team to invite Howe to a tryout, and the Rangers sent him back to the prairies with the suggestion that he try some other line of work. The difference with Orr was that the Leafs lost him when they were moving into a period in which they would win four Stanley Cups in six years, capping it off with their surprise Cup in 1967. Their string of success served to mask oversights and mistakes in player development and procurement that would become a lamentable tradition. Missing Orr marked the beginning of that tradition.

The St. Mike's and Toronto Marlboro teams had stocked the Leafs with elite talent in the middle to late 1950s—players like Dave Keon, Carl Brewer, Ron Ellis and, of course, a true superstar, Frank Mahovlich. They'd almost never missed on a defenceman of any significant quality coming out of Ontario. In the following four decades, however, they failed time and time again, through the abilities of their own scouting department and the universal draft, to successfully land another burgeoning superstar of similar dimension to Orr or Mahovlich. During the 1970s, there was a brief period of success when they landed top-flight talents in Darryl Sittler, Lanny McDonald and Borje Salming, all of whom became outstanding players. But none won a major individual trophy like the Hart (MVP), Art Ross (scoring champion), Norris (top defenceman), Calder (top rookie) or even the Lady Byng (most gentlemanly). And no player the Leafs drafted from 1967 to 2002 accomplished any of those feats either. The Leafs failed to acquire excellence in the final years of the old sponsorship system, then were consistent failures at the universal draft system when it kicked in after the 1966–67 season. Players like Jacques Plante, Grant Fuhr, Doug Gilmour, Mats Sundin, Alexander Mogilny, Ron Francis, Curtis Joseph and Ed Belfour would all play for the Leafs, but only after being acquired through trades or free agency and generally when they were well past their prime. When Orr was missed it was as though the franchise that had recruited brilliant talents from Charlie Conacher to Ted Kennedy had become completely impotent in its ability to envision greatness in a young hockey player.

Before Orr, the Leafs had built up a strong collection of young talent that would fuel their near dynasty of the next decade, and much of that talent was acquired through the sponsorship system. Like most teams, the Leafs "sponsored" a group of junior teams, and those teams, in turn, would sign promising players to "cards" that bound them to the Leaf reserve system, and to the Leafs, in perpetuity. Davidson was the club's legendary scout, the only full-time employee of the Toronto scouting department. A former Leaf captain with an agile, analytical mind and friends throughout the industry, Davidson had a fiercely loyal network of 200 or more "bird dogs" throughout the country who were trusted with alerting him to top prospects. A man like Clark Simpson, who ran the Winnipeg Monarch Juniors, would direct young players to the Leafs, and Simpson would have others throughout the province that would in turn supply him with information. A bird dog might get $250 from the Leafs for alerting the club to a talented teenager if that player signed a card with one of their affiliated junior teams, or perhaps a Leaf jacket, tickets to a Leaf game or other tidbits.

All six NHL clubs had similar networks, but the high-profile Leafs had the added advantage of their connection with St. Michael's College in Toronto, a school controlled by Basilian priests. That meant other Roman Catholic priests throughout the country might also steer players to St. Mike's and therefore, the Leafs. Mahovlich, born in Schumacher in northern Ontario, was so highly sought after that the St. Catharines Teepees offered Mahovlich's father a farm property if Frank signed to play for the junior team. Instead, the Mahovlich patriarch, swayed by the life and the experiences of his peers who worked in the mines and stressed education for their children, steered his son to St. Mike's, and the entire Mahovlich clan followed. Hundreds of other young men were attracted by the lure of St. Mike's and a conservative Catholic education, or at least their parents were. "If you lived, say, in Haliburton, Ontario, and Bob Davidson approached your child about playing for St. Mike's, that would give the Leafs an edge over a guy like Baldy Cotton with the Bruins who was offering to place the kid in Niagara Falls and have him live in a board-ing house," said Jim Gregory, a St. Mike's alumnus who moved up through the Leaf system to become the club's general man-ager in 1969. "It was similar to the edge the University of Notre Dame had in recruiting football players back then."

The storied Leafs were a privileged team watched most Saturday nights on *Hockey Night in Canada* from coast to coast. That's how Doug Orr, and his father, Robert, would have fallen in love with the idea of young Bobby one day skating for the blue-and-white at Maple Leaf Gardens. The Leafs controlled St. Mike's and the successful Marlboros as well as teams in Winnipeg, Calgary, Ottawa, Trois-Rivières and Melville, Saskatchewan. The other five NHL teams would occasionally squeeze a player away from the Leafs, but throughout the 1950s the Leafs maintained an iron grip on the vast majority of elite talent coming out of Ontario and particularly Toronto, benefiting from a system based on history, persuasion, patronage and deal-making.

That began to change in the early 1960s for a variety of reasons. First, the Basilians decided they no longer wanted to ice a team, and so the appeal of St. Mike's was lost to the Leafs, who started up a new affiliate at Neil McNeil High School in Toronto, another Catholic institution but one that didn't have the lure and image of St. Mike's. Second, tired of being constantly outbid by the Leafs for Toronto-area prospects, other teams became more aggressive, offering money and cars and gifts and jobs to parents of young players. The Rangers, for example, sponsored a team in the Toronto community of Leaside, while the Blackhawks sponsored the Dixie Beehives on the outskirts of the city, thus gaining control over quality players like Vic Hadfield. Ron Schock, a talented young forward from the small northern Ontario town of Chapleau, was recruited by the Leafs in 1961, but instead opted for the Boston Bruins after the Bruins offered Schock and his family the then outrageous sum of $10,000 to sign a junior playing card with Niagara Falls. To get Orr, the Bruins sponsored the entire Parry Sound minor system, spending thousands of dollars to lock up the young star as other NHL clubs moved boldly into territories that once harvested talent primarily for the Leafs.

Finally, starting in 1962, the NHL began to seriously consider expansion and moved to end the sponsorship of amateur teams and players with the ultimate goal of developing a draft system that would give all of its member clubs equal access to players. When the first such draft was held in 1963 at the Queen Elizabeth Hotel in Montreal, most of the top junior talents were already on the reserve lists of the six teams and couldn't be selected, as would largely be the case until the league moved to a universal draft in 1967. Still, some players slipped through the cracks. Prior to the 1963 draft, for example, the Leafs unsuccessfully tried to convince Garry Monahan and Frank Mahovlich's brother Pete, two youngsters playing for the St. Mike's juvenile team, to agree to sign junior cards with Neil McNeil, thus placing them under the exclusive rights of the Leafs. Without the St. Mike's Junior A program to attract them, however, both Monahan and Mahovlich declined to join Neil McNeil and were the first two players taken in the '63 draft by Montreal and Detroit, respectively. With a new ownership group led by Stafford Smythe firmly in charge, the club was not only being outbid for players, it was even losing control of players it already seemed to possess as the entire system by which NHL teams procured teenage prospects was being restructured.

Moreover, players from the Toronto area weren't being automatically funnelled to the Leafs as they once had been. In the west end of the city, a young Ken Dryden, for instance, grew up playing in the Humber Valley organization, a hockey chain founded by Leaf president Stafford Smythe, who was from that part of Toronto. In fact, Dryden played one year with Smythe's son, Tommy. The Junior B outgrowth of that Humber Valley organization was the Etobicoke Indians, but the entire chain was independent, and therefore none of the players were affiliated with a particular NHL club. Dryden had several years earlier failed to crack the Marlboro organization in a tryout and was happy playing with his community-based team, and when the 1964 NHL draft rolled around his rights were available because the Leafs hadn't previously lured him to one of their sponsored teams. Boston selected him with the 14th pick, and immediately flipped his rights to Montreal. "It was a very, very private draft. I didn't even get a letter from Montreal saying I was their property," recalls Dryden. "In fact, it wasn't until 10 years later that I learned about the trade. I thought I'd been Montreal property all the way along." The Leafs certainly knew of Dryden, who knew members of the Smythe family. But they took two forwards from other teams in the area who never made the NHL before Dryden was selected. It wasn't until Dryden arrived in spectacular fashion in the 1970 Stanley Cup playoffs after a sterling career at Cornell University that it became widely known the Leafs had missed on a local lad. Others teams, it seemed, were now doing a more thorough and efficient job of scouring the Toronto market for talent than the hometown Leafs.

Still, after passing on Orr in 1961, losing St. Mike's and seeing their grip on their primary hockey breeding territories weakened, the Leafs set about winning, capturing the 1962 and 1963 Stanley Cups, their first since Bill Barilko had bagged the winning goal in the 1951 final. Good times were back, Imlach was the toast of hockey coaches everywhere and the club's roster was oozing with mature talent. That said, winning in back-to-back years created more pressure to win a third, and Imlach's relentless drive to stay at the top produced a pressure all its own. In the 1963–64 season Montreal and Chicago had risen to challenge the defending champs, producing a three-team dogfight for first place as winter moved towards spring and the playoffs.

Still, the Leafs were a confident, talented bunch as they prepared on February 22, 1964, to face a New York Ranger team that was destined to miss the playoffs. If first place wasn't to be, Leaf players believed they had more than enough to win a third straight Cup. But one crucial individual did not share the prevailing confidence that permeated the organization—Imlach. Imlach felt a shakeup was needed, a shuffling of the roster to bring in some new bodies and destroy the sense of complacency he believed had poisoned the Leaf room.

That day, the airwaves crackled with the news of a rumoured blockbuster trade between the Leafs and Rangers as Gregory, the general manager of the Junior Marlboros, and

Davidson went about their usual Saturday afternoon routine, driving to watch a Marlie practice at George Bell Arena to get a little extra scouting in before the Leaf game that night. Though both were key employees of the Leaf hockey department under Imlach, neither knew of the trade that was being speculated upon in the urgent radio reports. Imlach certainly hadn't asked them what they thought of any such trade, one that would apparently bring Ranger star Andy Bathgate to the Leafs in a multi-player deal that would involve Dick Duff and Bob Nevin, talented young players who had risen through the Leaf sponsorship system and had become dependable pros. They were, in the eyes of many, true Leafs. What was especially distressing to Davidson, however, was that the names of two young defencemen, Rod Seiling and Arnie Brown, were also included in the radio report. Both were southern Ontario boys who had come up through the Leaf chain, playing for both St. Mike's and the Marlies. Davidson prided himself on his ability to secure the best possible talent in English Canada for the blue-and-white. With a rapidly aging defence corp, these were two of the young ingredients of the future.

Stunned and silent, Gregory detoured to the closest available place where he could get access to a telephone. His brother-in-law's fruit market was close by, and the two men pulled over to call the Gardens. Their worst fears were confirmed. Bathgate, 31, and Don McKenney, 29 years old, had been acquired from the Rangers in exchange for Duff, 28, Nevin, 26, Seiling, 19, Brown, 22, and Bill Collins, 20 years old. While Gregory tried to digest the trade, he felt badly for a clearly disheartened Davidson. The nucleus of the 1962 and 1963 Stanley Cup teams had all been inked to their first Leaf contracts by Davidson, whose imprint on the team was being smudged with not so much as a word from Imlach. Gregory and Davidson weren't the only two shaking their heads over the trade. Imlach's daughter, Marlene, wouldn't speak to her father for weeks after he traded Duff, her favourite player. The speedy winger was widely regarded as a "money" player, an athlete who could come through when it mattered, and Duff was also seen as a player who wore the blue-and-white with enormous pride. Nevin was just entering his prime and was a very popular player in the dressing room.

When Imlach first grabbed the reins of the Leafs in 1958, he supplemented the team with inexpensive acquisitions of experienced players like Johnny Bower, Allan Stanley and Bert Olmstead. The 1960 trade that brought Red Kelly from Detroit for fringe player Marc Rheaume was another acquisition of brilliance, and Imlach made it more productive by permanently shifting the smart, versatile Kelly to forward from defence. But the Bathgate trade was not viewed as generously, largely because of what Imlach had surrendered to take a stab at a third straight Cup. Still, with Bathgate and McKenney in their lineup and Duff and Nevin on the visiting team bench, the Leafs defeated the Rangers 5–2 on the night of the spectacular swap and finished with a 7–5–2 record in their final 14 regular season games.

When the Leafs did indeed go on to win the Cup, Imlach confidently boasted that the Bathgate trade had made the difference, that the Leafs would not have prevailed without McKenney's 12 playoff points (fourth on the team behind Mahovlich, George Armstrong and Kelly) and Bathgate's five goals (tied for second behind Keon) in 14 playoff games. But many players disagreed with Imlach and shared the anger of Davidson. They saw February 22, 1964, as the beginning of the end, an end to the grooming process that had built the 1962 and '63 champs and the guts of the '64 winners. "It was the end of us developing from within. We started going for the quick fix," recalls Keon. "The system continued to deteriorate and when the draft started [in 1967] our slide continued, while the Montreal Canadiens continued to do things right."

Bathgate's Hall of Fame career included only a brief stop in Toronto as he was traded after the 1964–65 season along with Harris and Gary Jarrett to Detroit for Marcel Pronovost, Larry Jeffrey, Ed Joyal, Lowell MacDonald and Aut Erickson. Armstrong, the captain of the Leafs, said the Bathgate trade was a telling mistake even though they won the '64 Cup. "At the time, we were disappointed to see Duff and Nevin go, but in Bathgate we thought we were getting the next Gordie Howe," recalls Armstrong. "We were wrong. We discovered that both Duff and Nevin were better team guys than Bathgate. In New York, their system was set up to feed Bathgate, but the Leafs played as a team. We all liked Andy and he is a Hall of Famer, but we won in spite of that trade. He didn't fit in with the Leaf system like he had with the Ranger system." Forty years later, that insider's description of the Bathgate blockbuster still seemed to apply to the club's approach to the hockey business after sensational deals to acquire major stars Owen Nolan and Brian Leetch failed to get the club close to a Stanley Cup. In a twist of history, both Nolan and Leetch were acquired at significant cost while Dryden, the kid from Humber Valley who had eluded the grasp of the Leafs, was a senior executive with the club before leaving for federal politics in May 2004.

McKenney's stay with the 1964 champion Leafs was just as brief as Bathgate's as he was claimed on waivers by Detroit in June 1965. Duff played only 43 games with the Rangers before moving on to be a major part of Montreal's string of championship teams, winning four Stanley Cup rings as a Hab. Nevin skated another seven full seasons on Broadway, scoring 20 goals in each of them. The Rangers were so impressed with Nevin that soon after acquiring him from the Leafs, he replaced Camille Henry as team captain, holding the post until 1971. Seiling and Brown, meanwhile, were fixtures with the Rangers for the rest of the decade. The Bathgate deal had produced short-term results, but the negative effects of losing so much young talent lasted for years, as did the sense the Leafs had changed their focus in a fundamental way. "[The Bathgate trade] ripped the heart out of the club," says defenceman Bobby Baun. "We were in top form and sailing along. We would have won the Cup that season and won even more if Imlach hadn't tinkered with the lineup." Young players like Seiling, in the minds of many Leafs at the time, would have helped the Leafs survive the aging of the core of their roster and the loss of more players to the six new expansion franchises after the 1966–67 season. "We lost something as an organization," says Mahovlich.

In June 1964, a few months after the Bathgate deal, the Leafs snapped up Terry Sawchuk in the inter-league draft after Detroit had surprised everyone in hockey by leaving the brilliant but aging goalie unprotected. At the time, the Leafs were developing young Gerry Cheevers to be the successor to Bower in the nets. He was another youngster who had played at St. Mike's for Father David Bauer, with the hockey-minded priest occasionally playing the promising netminder at forward to improve his skating. Cheevers' father, Joe, had been a lacrosse star in nearby St. Catharines and had worked for the Leafs as a part-time scout. Like the Orr family of Parry Sound, Joe Cheevers dearly wanted to see his son play for the Leafs, and it appeared his dream was to become a reality when young Gerry played two regular season games for the Leafs in the 1961–62 season. By the end of the 1963–64 season, he was regarded as one of the top minor-league goalies in hockey, leading the AHL in victories while playing for Toronto's top farm club in Rochester. But in June 1965, a year after thinking they'd engineered a coup by grabbing Sawchuk, the Leafs were faced with the dilemma of being able to protect only two among Sawchuk, Bower and Cheevers for that year's inter-league draft. Sawchuk was 35, Bower was 40 and Cheevers just

24 years of age. While most expected Sawchuk to be exposed after being used in only one playoff game that spring, Imlach instead left Cheevers unprotected. The Boston Bruins, who had finished dead last with 21 wins but were building, pounced on Cheevers as eagerly they had on Orr several years earlier. "[Sawchuk] might not have reported," said Bruins president Weston Adams at the time. "Imlach solved our problem by making Cheevers available and he fit our youth movement." Cheevers went on to play 416 regular season games and 88 playoff games for the Bruins, winning two Stanley Cups and election to the Hockey Hall of Fame in 1985.

Less noticed was that the Leafs, who crowed they'd made $110,000 profit through other teams grabbing their players, also lost 25-year-old Pat Stapleton to Chicago that day. Stapleton, just 5-foot-8, was a centre, but the Blackhawks immediately switched him to defence—the opposite of the canny move the Leafs had made with Kelly—and Stapleton made the big club the following fall. Stapleton went on to play eight stellar seasons with the Hawks and was a member of Team Canada for the 1972 Summit Series. Stapleton's loss became more glaring four months later when defenceman Carl Brewer walked out on the Leafs. Brewer, as an established star rearguard, had been understandably protected instead of Stapleton for the inter-league draft that previous June, but now the Leafs had lost both. Despite their personnel losses, the Leafs were pleased with the cash they'd raked in. Imlach was inclined to spend $30,000 in the draft to bolster his lineup with forward Bill Hicke, who'd been left unprotected by the Rangers. "But I talked him out of it," said Stafford Smythe proudly.

In Orr, Seiling, Brown and Stapleton, the Leafs had lost their defence of the future, and soon after that the team had another young marvel slip through its fingers. In September 1966, a young Toronto lad named Brad Park was the last player invited to the Toronto Marlboro training camp. Park, a seemingly undersized defenceman who had been playing on the backline for only a season, sprouted from an even 5-feet at age 15 to 5-foot-8 at age 16. "I came out of nowhere," said Park. Well, not quite. Park's father, Bob, had been transferred by his company from Montreal to Toronto several years earlier, and the Leafs were aware of young Brad's potential, enough to offer Bob Park a job coaching Neil McNeil if Brad would play for the team. With the sponsorship system being phased out in favour of the still-developing universal draft system, getting Park to Neil McNeil didn't give the Leafs control of the player's rights—unless they opted to drop another player from their reserve list. By the time they grasped his potential, the lists were frozen, and Park had freedom young players couldn't have dreamed of six or seven years earlier.

When he went to try out for the Marlies, he wasn't expected to make the team and felt insulted when he was given the worst set of hockey underwear and pieces of mismatched equipment. But he made himself noticed immediately. "In my first scrimmage, the first guy I knocked out with a hit was Brent Imlach," he recalled. Kayoing the son of the Maple Leaf coach was sure to catch the eye of someone, and Park managed not only to make the team, but quickly became a well-regarded young prospect. "In my first negotiation with [then Marlies GM] Jim Gregory, he offered me $20 a week if I played Junior B and $40 if I stuck and played Junior A," said Park. "I said I wanted $30 and $50. He said what about $25 and $45. I said okay." When the 1966 NHL draft rolled around, the 16-year-old Park was eligible to be taken by any of the six NHL teams because the Leafs had earlier been unable or unwilling to lock up his rights. Boston had the first pick, and Cotton, the famous Bruins scout, recommended that the team select Park. "If they'd listened, they'd have had Orr and me right from the start," chuckles Park. Instead, the Bruins selected defenceman Barry Gibbs from the Estevan Bruins, their former junior affiliate.

The Rangers, building a strong young team, then took Park. The Leafs, picking third, never had a chance to take Park, but probably wouldn't have even if the Rangers had passed.

That previous season, an incident at a Marlie game had permanently poisoned the waters between Park, his Leaf-loving parents and the Leafs. Bob Park was very vocal with his criticisms while watching the Marlies play, and one night Dodo Imlach, wife of the Leaf coach and mother of Brent (who also played for the team), grew weary of Bob Park's constant chatter and told him so. One version of the story suggests that brought her into conflict not with Park's father, but his mother. "Sit down and shut the fuck up," said Betty Park to the wife of the Maple Leaf coach. Brad Park, on the other hand, believes it was his father who did the talking. Shortly thereafter, Punch Imlach made it well known to his underlings that the Leafs shouldn't consider taking young Park in the draft, although Davidson had him rated as the top prospect available.

Twenty-four young players became the property of NHL teams on April 25, 1966, but only one went on to a Hall of Fame career in which he was named a first-team NHL all-star five times. For the next two seasons, the Leafs had to stand back and watch in frustration as Park blossomed into a terrific defenceman right under their noses, starring on the Marlboro blueline while skating his home games at Maple Leaf Gardens. In five years, Imlach and company had seen four future Hall of Fame players in Orr, Cheevers, Dryden and Park slip from their grasp and join other organizations.

The Leafs thus went into the 1966–67 season with an ancient defence corps consisting of Stanley, 41, Tim Horton, 37, and Pronovost, 36 years of age. The "kids" of the group were Bobby Baun and Larry Hillman, who were both 30 years old. A newspaper article previewing the February 18, 1967, meeting between the Leafs and Bruins highlighted the oldest blueline in the NHL, that of the Leafs, against the youngest blueline in the league with Orr, 18, Gary Doak, 20, Gilles Marotte, 21, Joe Watson, 23, and Bob Woytowich, 25 years old. The Leaf defence, to its immense credit, proved savvy enough and good enough in front of Bower and Sawchuk to win the Cup, but the necessary buffer against the future had been lost or overlooked along the way. Winning the '67 Cup just meant nobody noticed what was really happening and allowed Leaf management to believe their short-term fixes were the best course. After all, with four Cups in six years, who was going to question the Leafs?

By the following winter, however, the Leafs no longer had the swagger of a champion. In fact, they were in deep trouble, plummeting out of playoff contention. The sharp decline of the club put increasing pressure on Imlach and not surprisingly soured his iffy relationship with team president Stafford Smythe even further. The St. Mike's pipeline was gone forever. The universal draft had ended their control over Marlie talent. The club had cut back on scouting and was in the business of selling off its minor league affiliates in Victoria, British Columbia and Rochester, New York—the teams that had fed the club talent for years and always supplied ready replacements in emergencies. In July 1966, the Leafs sold the Calder Cup champion Rochester Americans for $400,000 to a group of investors that included Imlach and Amerks coach, Joe Crozier. In June 1967, a month after winning the Cup, the Leafs then sold the Victoria Maple Leafs to a Phoenix group for $500,000. Twelve months later, Rochester was then sold to the Vancouver Canucks of the Western Hockey League. As the sales unfolded, the investor list in the Canucks was revealing to Toronto fans, for it again included Imlach, Crozier and Leaf broadcasting legend, Foster Hewitt. Imlach's financial dealings had previously attracted interest when, despite his upper management status, he sold off blocks of shares in Maple Leaf Gardens in 1967 and 1968. In December 1969, the

WHL Canucks were sold to the Minneapolis-based Medical Investment Corporation for $2.3 million as part of that group's $6-million purchase of an NHL expansion franchise. Imlach, who controlled 1,020 shares in the Canucks, reportedly profited to the tune of more than $250,000.

Over time, dumping the minor league teams and players on the rosters of those teams undermined the Leafs on the ice by costing them depth in the organization. It has long been speculated by former Leaf players and executives that some player transactions around the time of the sale of Victoria and Rochester helped those teams at the expense of the Leafs. One such curious transaction involved fiery winger Jean-Paul Parise, a 25-year-old from Smooth Rock Falls, Ontario, who had been a promising prospect in the Boston chain before being lost to the Oakland Seals in the June 1967 expansion draft. The Seals didn't see the potential, however, and shipped Parise and Bryan Hextall of the famous Hextall clan to the Leafs four months later for Gerry Ehman, a 34-year-old journeyman forward. Parise played one game for the Leafs that fall, picking up an assist, but then was shuttled off to Minnesota on Boxing Day, 1967 with Milan Marcetta, who had been on the Leaf roster in the Cup drive of the previous spring.

The deal was a curious one, for in return the Leafs received Murray Hall, Don Johns, Ted Taylor, Len Lunde, Duke Harris and the loan of goaltender Carl Wetzel. Harris played four games for the Leafs in the 1967–68 season, but most of the acquired players only played for the Leaf minor-league affiliates. Parise, meanwhile, went on to a solid 11-year career with the North Stars and New York Islanders, enjoying five 20-goal seasons and playing on Team Canada at the '72 Summit Series. It may have simply been a bad trade, and it's possible to argue that by strengthening the Americans, the Leafs aided the development of prospects they had on that team. But Imlach's financial interests, specifically the sale of the Americans to Vancouver and the subsequent sale of that team to a U.S. company that put Vancouver in the NHL, certainly created a murky picture. Keeping the Americans happy and getting them deep into the AHL playoffs every spring benefited Imlach and other investors.

Months earlier when Johnny Bower's season was ended after Game Three of the '67 final, Imlach hadn't recalled Bruce Gamble to back up Terry Sawchuk for the final games against Montreal, even though Gamble had firmly established himself as the club's third-string goalie and had extensive NHL experience. Instead, Imlach summoned the totally inexperienced Al Smith, leaving Gamble to play for Rochester as they pursued the Calder Cup and lucrative playoff gates. Earlier that season, when Imlach had been hospitalized at a time when NHL clubs didn't have assistant coaches, the Leafs nevertheless declined to summon Crozier to the big club. Instead, they turned to the unproven King Clancy. In 1968, the Leafs chose to protect Hextall, a journeyman NHLer, rather than Brian Conacher in the NHL intra-league draft, even though Conacher had played in the NHL for the previous two seasons. Hextall never made the Leafs or took Conacher's lineup spot, but he was, and continued to be, a very important player for Rochester and Vancouver, and Imlach had a financial interest in keeping those teams competitive and profitable.

The rot eating away at the Leaf infrastructure had been covered over by the stunning Cup victory of the previous spring. But in the 1967–68 season, problems were becoming clear. Even Imlach's ability to use demotion to the minors as a motivating tool was sharply circumscribed because, under post-'67 rules, he now had to ask for waivers on most veteran players before he could send them down. Winger Jim Pappin, who had led the club in scoring en route to the Cup the previous spring, refused to report to Rochester after being demoted. After being in position to joust with Montreal for first place in late January, the Leafs went into a terrible slide, dropping 13 of 17 games at one point to fall 13 points behind fourth-place Boston for the last playoff berth. With Park playing brilliantly in junior but unavailable to the Leafs, Orr wowing audiences everywhere with his dazzling skills and young Jim McKenny not yet ready for NHL competition, Stafford Smythe bemoaned the absence of an offensively talented defenceman. "How we could use a rushing defenceman," he said. "We don't have defencemen who can get the puck out of our end." At that time, Imlach sold off 800 of his Gardens shares as the possibility that the Leafs would miss the playoffs loomed—and that meant company revenues would be adversely affected. Smythe essentially wrote off the season. "There's no point in talking trade now," he told reporters, saying only sixth-place Detroit would be interested in players off the Leaf roster and that such a deal would be pointless.

Smythe's public comments made it all the more stunning two days later when Imlach, playing the quick-fix card one last time, peddled Mahovlich, Peter Stemkowski, the rights to Brewer and prospect Garry Unger to the Red Wings for Norm Ullman, Paul Henderson and Floyd Smith. It was an absurd deal and appears even more so in retrospect. Given the team president's words of surrender 48 hours earlier, the trade portrayed the Leafs as horribly dysfunctional. Mahovlich, the greatest goal scorer in team history, was only 30 years old. The Leafs were clearly worried that Mahovlich was a declining asset. He had received psychiatric treatment twice in four years while apparently on the verge of nervous breakdowns. The Leafs' assessment proved not to be accurate, of course, as Mahovlich scored 49 goals the very next season with the Wings.

Stemkowski, meanwhile, was only 24 years old, and had been the consummate playoff warrior for the team in previous springs. The very promising Unger was just 20 years old and in his first pro season. The following campaign, he scored

24 goals for the Wings. Over the course of his distinguished, gritty career, Unger scored more than 30 goals nine times and gained a reputation as the NHL's "Iron Man," at one point playing 914 consecutive games. Brewer, meanwhile, was only 29 years old but had been absent from NHL competition since walking out on Imlach and the Leafs three years earlier. After stops with the Canadian national team and a team in Finland, he returned to the NHL with the Wings and was a second team NHL all-star in his first season.

By contrast, both Ullman and Smith were 32—older than any of the four Leafs that had been sent to Detroit—while Henderson was 25 years old. "That trade was all about the arrogance of Punch Imlach," says Keon. "He traded for inferior players on another team because he was so arrogant he felt he would make them better players. That proved not to be the case. To make matters worse, the guys from Detroit were being paid at a better rate than the Leaf guys, and that caused more resentment." Despite winning eight of their final 13 games, the Leafs missed the playoffs by four points in the first year the NHL had created new balances of power by expanding to 12 teams from six. The Mahovlich deal had simply sacrificed more young talent while accomplishing nothing.

That disastrous transaction, however, just seemed to make Imlach more determined to seek blunt, immediate solutions to complicated organizational problems that had been festering for years. Two months after the Mahovlich deal, Imlach believed the Leaf defence was so ragged and weak that he made another disastrous effort to find immediate help. Pappin, another Marlboro product, was moving into his prime at age 28. But Imlach needed blueline help, and so he sent Pappin to Chicago for 36-year-old Pierre Pilote, who had won the Norris Trophy three times as the NHL's best defenceman and was an eight-time all-star, five times on the first all-star squad. He was also on his last legs. In fact, Pilote had been repeatedly victimized by the Leafs in the playoffs the year before, while Pappin had played superbly on a line with Stemkowski and Bob Pulford. It was as though all the important efforts of the '67 Cup drive had been forgotten amidst Imlach's arrogance and survival instincts. After 69 games with the Leafs and a humiliating four-game sweep at the hands of Boston, Pilote retired. "I never felt comfortable in Toronto," he said. "I felt like a rookie from day one." Pappin, meanwhile, immediately became Chicago's leading scorer with 30 goals and 40 assists, the first of seven seasons where he would notch 40 goals once, 30 goals three times and 20 goals on three occasions.

In sum, the personnel mistakes and oversights of the years immediately before and after the Leafs' 1967 Cup victory took a terrible toll on the organization while strengthening other Original Six teams. When Conn Smythe later looked back upon those years, he said Imlach was "a good coach and a lousy manager." Orr became the best and most exciting player in the game. Park, Cheevers, Stapleton, Parise and Seiling all played leading roles for their teams, and all but Cheevers skated for Team Canada '72. Stemkowski, Pappin and Unger enjoyed long, productive NHL careers.

The damage was cumulative. Even after Imlach was fired following an embarrassing playoff defeat to Boston in the 1969 playoffs, the club's destructive tendencies proved to be systemic. Prior to the entry draft that June, Toronto newspapers touted Bobby Clarke of Flin Flon as the top junior in Canada. Many NHL scouts disagreed, largely because Clarke was a diabetic, but few believed Clarke would last until the Leafs picked ninth overall. When it came time to pick, however, Clarke was still available. The Leafs instead took right winger Ernie Moser of the Estevan juniors from the Western Hockey League. "We still don't think Clarke is healthy enough to play in the NHL," Smythe told *The Globe and Mail*. Clarke went on to play 1,280 NHL regular season and playoff games, exactly

1,280 more NHL games than Moser appeared in. "Moser wasn't even a really good junior," recalls Clarke.

Eighteen months later, Pulford was traded away to Los Angeles for Gary Monahan and played very well for the Kings, picking up 17 goals and 26 assists in 59 games. That helped the Kings avoid finishing dead last in the NHL. Instead, that honour went to hapless Oakland, which had already surrendered its first round draft pick to Montreal. The Leafs, therefore, had inadvertently assisted their Original Six rival by strengthening the Kings and helping the Seals finish at the bottom. The Habs used Oakland's pick to grab future superstar Guy Lafleur first in the 1971 draft. As the 1960s ended, one form of tradition had given way to another.

GAME TWO
MAPLE LEAFS AT CHICAGO, APRIL 9, 1967

If only they'd known what they were looking at.

During the second intermission of Game Two of the 1967 opening round Stanley Cup series between the Toronto Maple Leafs and Chicago Blackhawks, Hockey Night in Canada featured an inside look at the personal lives of the Hawks, complete with still pictures of their homes and families. The theme was the domestic bliss of the Hawks, and their homogenized all-Canadian roster. The team was portrayed as being so successful partly because of the players' harmonious home lives: All the players, save recently acquired Bill Hay, had brought their families from Canada to live in the Chicago area. With Ward Cornell and Jack Dennett supplying the soothing descriptions, there was Glenn Hall and his smiling wife and children, Pat Stapleton and his growing brood, and Bobby (the Golden Jet) Hull, his smiling wife, Joanne, and his three boys—Bobby Junior, Blake and two-year-old Brett, living in a modest home in suburban Addison. Years later, we would learn that the Hull family life was not nearly as happy as it seemed, and we would learn that there was not one, but two, legendary NHL scorers in that family photo. Bobby Hull would end up with 610 career goals in the NHL, and on April 23, 2000, the fair-haired Brett—dubbed the Golden Brett—would equal that total while playing for the Dallas Stars. His father scored another 303 goals in the World Hockey Association, and in February 2003, Brett became the sixth NHLer ever to hit the 700-goal plateau. It has proved to be the greatest father–son scoring combination in NHL history and perhaps sports history—a spectacular accident of genes and bloodlines captured innocently on television on April 9, 1967. That night, to hundreds of thousands of Hockey Night in Canada viewers, it seemed just another hockey photo flashing across their television screens.

Down in the Chicago dressing room at that precise moment, however, the Golden Jet was feeling grim. His team, having flattened the seemingly overmatched Leafs in the opening game of the series three nights earlier, found itself trailing 3–0 in Game Two. On a warm, spring day in the Windy City, the two teams had wandered onto the playing surface two hours earlier to be greeted by ponds of water and slush. Two days of an ice show had all but ruined the rink at the Chicago Stadium, and the Leafs couldn't have been happier. After losing Game One, the Leafs had concluded that they could not hope to skate with the freewheeling Hawks as they had attempted to do in their disastrous Game One performance. They needed to check and slow down Hull, Stan Mikita and the rest of the Hawks, and they now found they had an unexpected ally in the dreadful ice conditions at the Hawks' home arena. A decade later, Leaf forward Bob Pulford would join the Hawks as head coach and general manager, positions he would hold off and on for years, as well as team president. He long maintained vivid memories of the dreadful skating conditions at Chicago Stadium in the spring of '67 that so favoured the Leafs. "I always tell [Hawks owner] Bill Wirtz that the brutal ice at the Stadium hurt the Hawks," he says. "They were the better skating team. But that ice show had ruined the ice."

Back at the motel in Peterborough between games, the Leafs had arrived in a foul mood, partly because of their 1–0 series deficit, and partly because flying back and forth between Ontario and Illinois seemed pointless. "Don't tell me how to coach my hockey club," snapped Imlach when asked why he had taken his team back to Peterborough. "If I want to fly 'em across the continent for a practice, I'll fly 'em." He told reporters he didn't trust his players to rest and prepare for Game Two while hanging around lively Chicago. "He always felt we were up to something no good, which was almost always not the case," recalls winger Brian Conacher. Winger Eddie Shack, however, was careless enough to miss the return flight to Chicago and ended up parked on the bench for the second game of the series. But after seeing his players play lifelessly in Game One, Imlach relaxed the boot camp regimen between games, scheduling less arduous practices and giving the players more time away from the rink. "I think Imlach might have figured like everyone else that we didn't have a chance and said to hell with it," says forward Jim Pappin.

The more relaxed atmosphere gave the team a chance to regroup and focus on the need to short-circuit the Chicago offence by paying more diligent attention to their defensive responsibilities. Captain George Armstrong told his teammates that with all their curved sticks, the Hawks needed time to shoot. By cutting down their space and time they might be induced to try backhands, difficult with those sticks, and then turn the puck over. As well, the Leafs wanted to hit Mikita at every turn, taking advantage of the fact the transformed Chicago star was no longer a mean cuss who would quickly retaliate, but a player committed to scoring and staying out of the penalty box. Hull, too, was to be a target, although his legendary strength and speed made him a more problematic quarry to track.

In the early moments of Game Two, the Leafs demonstrated their intentions, with defenceman Tim Horton engaging in a brief shoving match with Hull after a whistle. Horton was in Hull's face every time he turned around. Four minutes in, Hull's brother, Dennis, wheeled into the Leaf zone and hammered a slapshot past Terry Sawchuk, who was making his second straight start for the Leafs after delivering a mediocre effort in the opener. The younger Hull's blast, however, rang off the post, and when Bobby Hull's dangerous slapper crashed into Sawchuk's chest soon after and stayed out, it was clear the Leafs had avoided an early Chicago goal that might have buried them. With eight minutes gone in the first period, the line of Peter Stemkowski between Bob Pulford and Pappin struck, this time with Stemkowski putting Pulford's goalmouth feed past Denis Dejordy to give the Leafs a 1–0 lead. Four minutes later, Sawchuk made a spectacular save on Eric Nesterenko, and six minutes after that Dave Keon potted a gorgeous shorthanded goal to give the Leafs a 2–0 lead. Hawks captain Pierre Pilote, victimized on the first goal, stumbled and fell at the Leaf blueline after Chicago had won the draw in the Leaf end. The puck skittered towards Bobby Hull at the left point but was moving slowly enough that Armstrong was able to chip it down the ice to a streaking Keon, who went in alone and beat Dejordy with a forehand move.

Armstrong also scored in the second to make it 3–0 before being knocked out of the game by a low hit from Bobby Hull. First Shack, then Conacher, replaced the fallen Leaf captain on the line with Keon and Frank Mahovlich, and the Leafs checked the Hawks to a standstill in a sluggish game filled with offside calls, poor passing and messed up rushes. Only Mikita beat Sawchuk with a meaningless third period tally as the Leafs tied the series. The victory ended a seven-game playoff losing streak for the Leafs dating back to 1965 and, for the moment, saved their season. King Clancy passed out cigars on a jubilant flight back to Canada. A loss would have meant certain early dismissal by the Hawks and the reverberations might have ended the Imlach era there and then.

In Augusta, Georgia, golf's most traditional event, The Masters, had concluded with an upset winner in Gay Brewer, creating a scent of possibility in the sporting airs. The Leafs had collected their surprise win using mostly three lines and two pairs of defencemen. The Stemkowski line stayed intact, while Keon and Mahovlich were joined at times by Shack and Conacher. Conacher had actually replaced Larry Jeffrey on a unit with Red Kelly and Ron Ellis before moving to the Keon group, forcing Jeffrey back into duty. Clever young forward Mike Walton played only a couple of shifts, including one on the left point during a second-period power play. Imlach went almost exclusively with the defence pairings of Horton beside Allan Stanley and Marcel Pronovost with Larry Hillman.

The boos rained down on the hometown Hawks as they left the ice It had become clear the Leafs were going to rely on a shrinking cast of players to chase the Cup, and some of those players, like Stemkowski, Conacher and Hillman, were not the big names that had been associated with previous Leaf Cup winners. To be sure, while the modern Stanley Cup tournament is a four-round marathon, it was more sprint-like in the dying days of the Original Six, with only eight victories required to win it all. Still, Imlach was plainly intent on covering the distance with the bare minimum of available bodies, giving surprising prominence to some who were not then regarded as prime-time athletes. After only two games, it seemed clear the margin of error was going to be very small.

2 The Tribe

It emerged like a dusty relic from a lost civilization, a reminder of glorious victories from the misty past. Gold and thick, with "Toronto Maple Leafs" and "1967" surrounding an enormous diamond, the last championship ring of the late Tim Horton appeared before the eyes of the public in August 2002, placed up for public sale at an established Toronto auction house for the starting price of $25,000. Horton had played on the Leaf championship teams in 1962, 1963, 1964 and 1967, and the diamond had started as a one-quarter carat in 1962 and been replaced with a larger stone with each succeeding championship. Many pieces of Horton's memorabilia had disappeared after his death in 1974, and the ring had been lost to the family in 1999. Suddenly, here it was, advertised on the website of Waddington's Auctioneers and Appraisers to the surprise and shock of Horton's children.

With the appearance of the ring came controversy and a flood of memories. Who owned the ring? How had it been lost to the family? Who were its rightful owners? One of the greatest Leafs ever, an important link between the post-war years and the organization's 1967 Stanley Cup victory, had produced a new mystery almost two decades after his death.

———————— ✤ ————————

The day was sunny and the air was warm, not warm enough yet to go swimming in chilly Gillies Lake, but a day on which the ladies could wear short-sleeved dresses that waved in the northern Ontario breeze while the men in suits could go without overcoats. It was a day for memories and the end to a long, exhausting emotional journey for Faye Barilko. She wore a smart-looking hat and a black dress as she finally got to say a fond farewell to her long-lost son Bill. His death was the first indelible link in a sombre Maple Leaf chain that would be formed by time and tragedy.

He had been a joyous lad, a heroic one, too. The day Donald Beauseigle made the mistake of trying to ride his bike across a mostly frozen Gillies Lake, it had been Bill who, thinking it was his older brother Alex shrieking for help, had hustled over and pulled young Donald out of the drink. "Bill got such a spanking that day when he got home because he was all wet," recalls his kid sister Anne. He later became famous for his heroism on skates as well, of course. Five years after leaving the mining town of Timmins, Ontario, he'd scored the winning goal in overtime to bring the 1951 Stanley Cup to the Maple Leafs. The year before, a youngster he'd played with on the juvenile Holman Pluggers, Pete Babando, had done exactly the same thing for the Detroit Red Wings. Two Timmins kids, back to back. Allan Stanley, the son of the fire chief, had played with the Pluggers, as well, and he'd also gone on to the NHL. Bill, who started out as a goalie until his brother got tired of listening to him complain about cold feet and suggested that if he learned to skate he could play defence, had been a stick boy with the Pluggers, but then he'd later played alongside his brother, Stanley and Babando.

Such was the magical story of Bill Barilko, the son of Russian immigrants who had come to Canada seeking a new life after fleeing their homeland in the wake of revolution. Steve Barilko, father of Alex, Bill and Anne, worked as a cook in the bush camps near the mines of South Porcupine, Schumacher and Timmins, Ontario. He died early in 1946 after spending his last days in a local sanatorium. That was the year before Bill had gone to California and the Pacific Coast Hockey League to play for the Hollywood Wolves, while Alex played against him with the Oakland Oaks. Indeed a bunch of local lads had headed to California to play hockey, a way to escape the mines and keep playing the game they loved. It was a long way from home, but that was where hockey opportunities existed in those days for players not deemed good enough to play in the NHL or in the highest levels of the minor leagues. The boys always came home in the summers to fish and play baseball, and Bill and Alex often sent clothes home for their little sister, making sure she was the best dressed girl at school. "We really didn't know what the NHL was," recalls Anne. "All we knew was Foster Hewitt and Saturday night hockey on the radio. There was no TV, of course, in those days."

The call came from Bill in the winter of '47, asking if his mother could please send his winter clothes down to Toronto. "Why?" came the response. "I'm going to play hockey in Toronto," said Bill. He arrived breathless, blond and blue-eyed with perfect white teeth, dropped off at Varsity Arena on the campus of the University of Toronto in time to jump on the ice and practise with his new defence partner, Wally Stanowski. The Leafs had injuries, Bob Goldham foremost among them, and Barilko had skipped the Leafs' top farm club in Pittsburgh and come straight to the big leagues from Hollywood. He never played another game for any team but the Leafs, winning four Stanley Cups in his whirlwind of a professional career. He was humble, but he also had colour and panache and was a hit with the fans and the writers. He was canny enough to open Barilko Brothers on Danforth Avenue, where he used his fame to peddle appliances, radios and sportswear. "When he entered a room, you'd know it by his presence," says his sister Anne. "The room would light up." He still went home in the summers, skating at the McIntyre Arena in Timmins to get ready for the next NHL season. One local lad from nearby Schumacher stood in awe watching Barilko and pal Les Costello practise so hard in the summer of 1950 in the McIntyre that Barilko ran Costello right over the boards. That boy, Frank Mahovlich, might well have played with Barilko one day had fate not intervened.

In the spring of 1951, Barilko scored his timeless overtime winner of the fifth game of an unusual final in which all five games went to overtime between the Leafs and Montreal Canadiens. He'd taken a charging penalty in the first period and a roughing penalty in the third, evidence of his rambunctious style, which was complemented by his fearless shotblocking. His Cup winner was his only point of the series, and the sight of his skates lifted off the ice as the puck entered the Montreal net was the last dazzling moment of his career. Barilko had just turned 24.

Eleven years later, the sun flashed off the fuselage of a long-hidden yellow floatplane as it lay in the deep forest 30 miles north of Timmins. In the plane were the bones of Bill Barilko and dentist Henry Hudson, two fishing pals who had gone north to the remote Seal River, in search of prime fishing grounds. The years of rumour and speculation since their disapperance had been hard on Faye Barilko, who tended to react with newfound hope whenever a soothsayer, newsperson or crackpot suggested they knew where her long-lost Billy was and how she could find him. The searchers had years earlier called off their hunt for the plane, but suddenly, there it was, as though Barilko and Hudson had been patiently waiting to be found. "It was a relief," says Anne.

The Leafs had offered a reward for finding Barilko immediately after his disappearance, but claimed when he was found that the reward had long since expired. Back in 1951, the family had urged Bill not to go, but there were these wondrous fish, you see, dancing in his imagination. Stanley, who by then had found his way to the NHL and the New York Rangers, had been scheduled to go on the trip but had been late getting to town, and when he showed up Hudson told him the plane was full.

"You come on the next trip," he told a disappointed Stanley. Eleven years later, on that warm northern Ontario day in June, Stanley was one of the pallbearers as a coffin containing the remains of long-lost Bill were buried at the Timmins Cemetery underneath a large, granite tombstone with a hockey stick engraved on either side. Harry Watson, who had assisted on Barilko's famous goal, was there to serve with Stanley, as were childhood friends Leo Curik, Mel Richards, Steve Denisavitch and Gaston Garant. Bill Barilko's journey was finally over.

The Maple Leafs, by necessity, soldiered on without Bashin' Bill, but the 1950s were unkind, a fruitless search for another championship season, and the loss of a defenceman just hitting his prime left a huge hole. They needed a right-handed shooting defenceman to replace Barilko, and they found such a player in another northern Ontario boy, Myles Gilbert (Tim) Horton from Cochrane, Ontario. The Leafs tried Horton for four games in Barilko's spot the season after the plane had disappeared, and by the 1952–53 season Horton, shortsighted but strong of frame, had completed his apprenticeship with the Pittsburgh Hornets and had graduated full time to the Leafs.

The team, however, had fallen on difficult times, sometimes finishing as high as third, sometimes as low as fifth. In the 1957–58 season, they'd finished dead last, prompting owner Conn Smythe, with the urging of his eager son Stafford, to give GM Hap Day the boot, put coach Bill Reay on notice and hire pushy George (Punch) Imlach as the team's new assistant GM. Imlach figured finding help on defence was a priority, and the following October he struck a deal with Boston to send Jim Morrison to the Bruins for Stanley, by then a crusty veteran of 32 years of age who had enough of the losing with the Rangers and then the Bruins. "It was a dream come true," recalls Stanley. He'd found out about the deal before practice after first reading an incorrect news report that suggested teammate Red Armstrong was the one headed to the Leafs. Then he went out and practised with the Bruins anyway. When he decked a teammate coming down on a rush and others shouted at him to take it easy, he shouted back, "Not anymore, I'm a Toronto Maple Leaf now!"

Had Barilko not disappeared, he probably would have been waiting at the train station for Stanley, who had actually been closer with Alex Barilko but came to love the younger brother just as much. Instead, Stanley joined forces with Horton, Barilko's successor, whose career had come to a halt. Two and a half years earlier, Horton had been laid out with a heavy bodycheck delivered by Ranger defenceman Bill Gadsby, a hit that left Horton with a broken jaw and leg. He recovered slowly and couldn't play effectively when he returned, and the Leafs had considered sending him to Boston rather than Morrison. Reay only lasted 20 games that season, but before he was fired and replaced by Imlach, he constructed a new defence pairing of Horton with the newly acquired Stanley, hoping the tandem would gel. It did, so much so that for the next decade, as the Leafs improved and Horton became the league's iron man by playing in 486 consecutive games, the two men rarely skated apart. "We fit perfectly together," recalls Stanley. "I liked to play up outside the blueline to break up the play. I talked to Horton about my style. I told him that if the forward cut to left towards the boards, that wasn't a problem, but if he cut right and into the middle, I would need backup. He said, 'Allan, if he cuts into the middle, I've got him.' It's the only discussion we ever needed to have." When the Leafs won Stanley Cups in 1962—the year Barilko's body was finally found—1963 and 1964, it was with the Stanley–Horton pairing as a key element. Two younger rearguards, Carl Brewer and Bobby Baun, made up the second pair.

When the charge to the '67 Cup came, however, things had changed on the Leaf blueline. The regular season had been trying, and both Stanley, now 41, and Horton, 37 years old, had been injured, although they were reunited for the first round of the playoffs against Chicago. Given the way in which the Leafs treasured older players throughout the 1960s, it's reasonable to speculate that Barilko, had he not died, would have likely been on that 1966–67 roster, turning 40 in March of that season. The team was filled with players who had been his contemporaries, including George Armstrong, Marcel Pronovost, Terry Sawchuk and Red Kelly. Baun, meanwhile, had lost Brewer, his regular partner, two years earlier after Brewer had chosen to retire in a rather mysterious fashion, ostensibly because he was sick of pro hockey and life under Imlach. Without Brewer, Baun was a lost soul. He slowly lost his spot in the defence rotation, with his heroics of scoring a dramatic overtime goal while playing on a broken ankle in the 1964 Cup final all but forgotten. Still, he remembers that time as "the last of a golden era," the "best time to play any sport."

Born in Lanigan, Saskatchewan, Baun had been recruited to play for the Leaf-affiliated Toronto Marlboros in 1952 at the same time Horton was struggling to make it to the big leagues for keeps in the wake of Barilko's disappearance. His childhood pal, Mike Nykoluk, had caught the eye of the Leafs, who had invited him to a tryout. Nykoluk accepted, provided he could bring his younger friend Baun along, mostly because he wanted company on the streetcar ride along Kingston Road to Weston Arena. The two had played football together at Scarborough Collegiate, with Baun sometimes the quarterback crouching behind Nykoluk, the centre. The Leafs agreed to the condition and were pleasantly surprised by Baun. Nykoluk made the Weston Dukes, another affiliated team, while Baun agreed to play for a midget team connected with the Marlboros. That December, injuries gave him a chance to play for the Marlie Juniors, and the Leafs were so impressed they offered to sign him to a junior card. When Baun told his parents, they were surprised. "I didn't even know you played hockey," said his father. Baun, a fearless hitter and rugged competitor in the same image as Barilko and Horton, haggled over terms with the Leafs, finally agreeing to sign for $200 plus $75 per week and $35 to cover room and board costs. Nykoluk also played with the Marlies but never made it big as a player in the NHL, managing only 32 games with the Leafs in the 1956–57 season. Two decades later, however, he emerged to take on the head coaching duties with the Leafs.

In September 1953, having just turned 17, Baun arrived at his first Leaf camp like rolling thunder, devastating a player named Bill Briga with a spectacular hit in his first practice. That made him the talk of camp, and when he returned to the Marlies, it was with a new sense of confidence. By the 1958-59 season, Baun and Brewer had both cracked the Leaf lineup for good, and the two went on to make an extraordinarily success-ful partnership for the next seven seasons. By the fall of 1965, however, Baun's relationship with Imlach had started to dete-riorate. He had finished the previous season with a $16,000 salary and was looking for more, finally deciding to go over Imlach's head to Gardens director George Mara. Mara assured Baun that he would get the pay hike he wanted to $22,500 a season, but the final details had to be worked out with Imlach. On the day before the regular season began, Imlach told Baun to be in his office by 2 p.m. to finalize the deal. Baun arrived on time, but the Leaf boss didn't show up until four hours later, telling Baun he could only offer $16,000 a season. The two men argued back and forth for eight hours, finally agree-ing to a $22,000 salary.

It was Baun's awakening to the business side of the game, and over time he became one of the few players who developed a detailed understanding of the economics of the game at a time when salaries weren't published or even widely known. Years later, while playing for the Red Wings, Baun was approached by Mr. Hockey, Gordie Howe, who asked him for advice on a new contract. "What do you think I make?" asked Howe. "I think you make $50,000," said Baun. A surprised Howe confirmed his salary was $49,500, but wondered how Baun had come up with a figure so close. "I know because you are at the top level and guys like you and the Rocket [Richard] and [Jean] Beliveau have been killing us because you've never fought for what you're worth. So when we talk contract, the owners have always used your contracts against us." Howe was then 40 years old, with 22 years of NHL play with the Red Wings under his belt. "I knew that [Detroit owner] Bruce Norris had always given Howe a blank contract and told him to fill in the amount," recalled Baun. "I told him to fill in $250,000 this time around. But Howe chickened out at the last second and filled in $125,000. Norris promptly signed the contract and that was Howe's salary. Then Howe was mad he hadn't got the other $125,000. I told him not to be mad at Norris, but to be mad at himself for not going after it. That was the beginning of a period of bitterness for Gordie because he realized how he had undercut himself for so many years."

Baun's business savvy was well known to his teammates. At training camp prior to the 1966–67 season, Imlach saw a line of younger players waiting outside Baun's room at the club's camp in Peterborough. When Imlach asked what they were doing, they told him they were waiting to get advice on their contracts from Baun. Imlach, already hearing whispers of the beginnings of a players union being organized by Toronto lawyer Alan Eagleson, was enraged.

Baun was only 30 years old, but years of playing recklessly had taken their toll, and the 1966–67 season was a health nightmare. He broke his left thumb in training camp, and then suffered a fractured right toe early in the season blocking a shot. Later, his nose was broken by the stick of his own goaltender, Johnny Bower. On the day before Christmas, he strained ligaments in his elbow, again forcing him to the side-lines. He managed just 54 regular season games, and when the first round against the Blackhawks began, he was out of the mix entirely. Stanley and Horton were still together, but Pronovost and Larry Hillman now made up the second pair, with Baun reduced to sporadic shifts.

Before the Stanley Cup final against Montreal, Baun came off the ice after practice to hear Imlach say sarcastically, and in full range of the assembled media, "You don't need to do all those extra drills, you're not going to be playing anyway." Baun, the erstwhile hero, was crushed, and when the series was over and the Leafs had won the Cup, he went home rather than joining his teammates at Jim Pappin's house for a celebra-tory party. After the previous Cup win in 1964, Baun had organized the team party at the Westbury Hotel in downtown Toronto, a bash that nearly got out of hand when more than 1,000 people crowded in to the top floor of the hotel. This time, Baun wasn't going to attend, let alone organize it. At Pappin's, Armstrong realized Baun hadn't arrived and drove to his home in Don Mills in an unsuccessful attempt to get him to come to the party. It was the first time Armstrong realized how left out from the exciting playoff run Baun had felt, for Baun had hidden it well—like a consummate pro.

The next day, he attended the formal victory celebration at Stafford Smythe's house but then skipped the May 5th parade to city hall. On a cold, blustery Friday, with schoolchildren let out early from their classes to attend, the 48th Highlanders led a parade of convertibles south on Church Street, west on Wellington and then north on Bay Street to Nathan Phillips Square. While members of the team signed Toronto's Centennial Register and Armstrong accepted a gold watch on behalf of his teammates, Baun was fishing on Lake Charleston, just north of Brockville, Ontario, with his sons Jeff, Greg and Brian. "Being a team player, it probably wasn't the right thing to do," says Baun, looking back. "But I couldn't keep my emotions in check anymore. It was difficult keeping them in while I got dressed after that final game. I couldn't have held up for the parade given the way I felt and all the other things that had been going on with Imlach."

Baun's absence and the headlines it generated gave a sombre note to the parade, and it was equally newsworthy the following month when he was left unprotected for the 1967 expansion draft and was snapped up by Oakland. A decade later, Baun and Imlach finally spoke and patched up their differences. "Punch and I, I guess we kissed and made up," recalls Baun. "I don't like holding a grudge. Punch claimed it was Stafford Smythe's fault about what happened that year and with me being left open in the expansion draft. Others close to the scene disputed that, but Stafford was dead and I just took it as a form of an apology from Punch." After a season in California, Baun was traded to Detroit and then rejoined the Leafs in a 1970 trade for the forgotten Calder Trophy winner of 1966, winger Brit Selby. Baun skated another 137 games for the Leafs before suffering a serious neck injury in the fall of 1972. He was already grieving the death of his father, who had told him for the first and only time the night before he died that he thought he was a great hockey player. Two months later, with his NHL career over at age 36, Baun's mother died.

Horton and Stanley, meanwhile, had enjoyed their last hurrah with the '67 Leaf champs. Stanley played one more season in Toronto, then one more in Philadelphia before retiring after the 1968–69 season. Horton, whose Tim Horton doughnut franchises were beginning to gain popularity throughout southern Ontario, had nearly packed it in at the end of that season as well after Imlach had been fired seconds after an embarrassing season-ending playoff loss to Boston. "If they don't want Imlach, I guess they don't want me," he said.

Instead, the Leafs doubled his $45,000 salary to return for one more season. Then when that campaign appeared hopeless, they dealt him to the Rangers. From New York he bounced to Pittsburgh, and then, in June 1972, he was plucked by Buffalo in the expansion draft and reunited with Imlach, the new general manager and coach of the fledgling Sabres.

Horton, by then age 42, played hard and surprisingly well for the Sabres, skating effectively well into the winter of 1974 at age 44. By that point in his life, he was drinking heavily, and was often difficult and sometimes abusive to his family and friends. On February 20, he played in pain for the Sabres in a 4–2 loss to the Leafs, having suffered a badly swollen jaw that morning in a workout. While his teammates loaded themselves on a bus back to Buffalo, Horton hopped into his $17,000 Ford Pantera sports car and headed down the Queen Elizabeth Way to Niagara Falls. Just after 4:30 a.m., his judgement distorted by painkillers and booze, Horton's car flipped several times, rolling from the westbound lanes to the eastbound, throwing Horton 100 feet clear of the demolished vehicle. The father of four daughters was pronounced dead at hospital. "My biggest regret in hockey was giving Horton permission to skip going home on the team bus," lamented Imlach for years afterwards. Stanley, his longtime partner, found out hours later as morning dawned. "You're kidding," he said. "He's indestructible."

Five days later, Horton was buried at York Cemetery in Toronto. On a sunny day with the temperatures above freezing, his former teammates from the Leaf championship teams carried his coffin, including Armstrong, Keon, Dick Duff and Billy Harris. Meanwhile, just as he'd been a pallbearer 12 years earlier on a June day for a fellow lad from Timmins, Stanley was once again asked to serve for Horton, asked to once more mourn a fallen colleague in utterly tragic circumstances. Stanley was the link between Barilko and Horton, the connection between the brilliant memories of the 1951 championship and the final gasp of the old, Smythe-directed empire in 1967. Members of the tribe had fallen, but the tribe remained.

Baun was also a pallbearer for Horton that day. His career was over, and four years later he was broke as well, with his cattle business having failed, destroying a nest egg he had carefully built over his hockey career. He subsequently rebuilt his finances, successfully working in insurance, and in 1984 an acquaintance mentioned he was developing a retail area near Baun's home in Pickering, east of Toronto. Baun immediately had an idea. On December 21, 1984—more than 10 years after he, Stanley and four other outstanding Maple Leafs had carried the coffin of their dead teammate—he opened a Tim Horton's doughnut outlet, store No. 205 in Pickering, Ontario. It may not have been intended as a memorial to his long-dead teammate, but over time, it became the top Tim Horton's franchise in Canada with gross sales of $1.7 million. Horton's legacy had made Baun a winner again.

On August 25, 2001, one more member of the tribe fell. Brewer, the sensitive and eccentric soul who had successfully led the fights through the courts to have more than $23 million in additional payments made to retired NHL players after the funds had been illegally directed elsewhere by the league and the players union, died of heart problems. Another old Marlie star who had graduated to play for the Leafs, another fallen. When Brewer was buried four days later, after services at the Holy Rosary Church in downtown Toronto, Baun was there to say goodbye to his old defence partner. The summer of Brewer's funeral marked the 50th anniversary of Barilko's disappearance into the thick forests of northern Ontario.

From 1951 to 2001, there had been so many triumphs for the Leafs but, inevitably, also sadness, regret and tragedy. From failing hands, the torch had always been passed, from one defender of the faith to another.

In October 2002, the day before Tim Horton's lost championship ring was to go up for auction at Waddington's on Bathurst Street in downtown Toronto, police detectives interrupted the sale, swooping in to announce that the ring had been stolen from Horton's heirs and would be returned to his family. His daughter, Tracy, had been 13 years old at the time of her father's death, and was thrilled to have the family heirloom returned. She immediately placed the ring in a safety deposit box, one day to be passed on to her eldest son, Tim. "Since he was born, he was told one day it would be handed to him," she said.

Of all the Stanley Cup rings that represented the '67 victory, two were lost and never recovered. Mike Walton gave his to his agent, Alan Eagleson, and it was stolen while Eagleson was on a trip to Europe. Walton didn't learn that his ring had been lost until he ran into Eagleson in the late 1990s. "I noticed he didn't have the ring and I asked him where it was. He told me the story of how it was stolen," says Walton. "You think he would have told me that before. But that's fuckin' Eagleson for you." Goalie Terry Sawchuk gave his to his son, Gerry; the ring was stolen from his home in the 1970s.

Baun, despite his disappointments, was still wearing his on a daily basis more than 35 years after the triumph. Like Johnny Bower, Bob Pulford, Red Kelly, Tim Horton, Eddie Shack, Dave Keon, Allan Stanley, Frank Mahovlich, Larry Hillman and George Armstrong, Baun had first received a ring after the 1962 Cup win, and with every succeeding championship the original one-quarter-carat diamond was increased in size. As the 37th anniversary of the previous Leaf Cup win passed in 2004, others, like Baun, continued to wear the '67 ring every day. They included Hillman, Pappin, Stanley, Ellis, Shack, Jeffrey and Stemkowski, who moved the ring to his pinky finger as he aged and never had it re-sized. Red Kelly battled through serious illness in the winter of 2004, but the ring stayed stuck to his finger. All of Frank Mahovlich's Montreal championship memorabilia was stolen from his home by thieves who even used one of his hockey bags to cart away the loot. His Leaf ring, however, wasn't taken, and he wore it every day before and after being named to the Canadian Senate. Bob Pulford, Brian Conacher, Keon and Marcel Pronovost kept theirs hidden away, usually in safety deposit boxes. Both Armstrong and Bower, meanwhile, gave their rings to their wives, who wore them every day.

Over the decades, the rings have become heirlooms, gold touchstones to more successful times in the franchise's history. By 1993, the Leaf organization had become so starved for an important achievement that when the Leafs beat divisional rivals Detroit and St. Louis in the first two rounds of the play-offs, the players and team management were awarded rings for capturing the Norris Division "championship," a distinction entirely invented by the club. Those rings were seen as pale, pathetic imitations. The rings from '67 still stood as the real deal. When Horton's ring was gratefully reclaimed by his family, it emerged as a faded symbol of true membership in the Leaf tribe.

GAME THREE
CHICAGO AT MAPLE LEAFS, APRIL 11, 1967

One can only imagine how hockey history might have changed had Bobby Hull's shot managed to knock a little common sense into Harold Ballard. Or a lot.

Instead, one of the stranger incidents of the 1967 Stanley Cup playoffs only served to give Maple Leaf fans a hint of the bombast and silliness that was to come their way. Ballard, the executive vice-president of the club, was sitting in the north end of Maple Leaf Gardens watching the warm-up prior to Game Three of the Leafs' suddenly intriguing first-round collision with the Chicago Blackhawks. Here, the story grows a little hazy. It seems clear that a shot from Hull did skim the glass and strike Ballard in the face, breaking a pair of gold-rimmed glasses he was wearing. Ballard later claimed his nose was broken in four places and was saved from serious eye damage by his glasses. The injuries may not have been quite that dramatic, although *Toronto Star* sports editor Milt Dunnell did write that "there hasn't been such devastation to one snout since the night Ezzard Charles wrecked Rocky Marciano's bugle in the second fight."

Suffice it to say, Ballard was the centre of attention, and for decidedly non-hockey reasons. Later in the series, he approached Hull outside the Chicago dressing room and tried to get the always accommodating Hawks star to pose for a picture with him. "C'mon Bobby, it'll make a helluva picture," brayed Ballard, holding up the alleged puck that had done the damage. When Hawks coach Billy Reay happened upon the scene, he ushered Hull towards the ice and told Ballard to get lost. A week later, a laughing King Clancy officially presented Ballard with the puck for the benefit of news photographers. The sideshow was indeed a sign of things to come.

Meanwhile, by stealing a victory in Game Two at slushy Chicago Stadium, the Leafs had received a significant injection of confidence. At the same time, however, captain George Armstrong was missing from the Toronto lineup after being injured by Hull's devastating bodycheck in the second game of the series. Leaderless, the Leafs hit the ice determined to continue the tight-checking approach that had carried them to that surprise win after being demolished in the opener, and determined to increase the pressure on Hull and NHL-scoring champ Stan Mikita. Hull, who had been enraged the previous spring by the shadowing tactics of Detroit pest Bugsy Watson, offered no complaint about Toronto's defensive schemes. Mikita, on the other hand, was becoming increasingly annoyed. "Holding is a Leaf specialty," he fumed. "Nobody does it as well as they do." The Hawks had eliminated Armstrong, but they really didn't have Leaf targets to single out and attack in a series that was becoming increasingly hard-hitting and violent. So they went after the nearly skeletal Terry Sawchuk in the Toronto net, a man who had seen his weight fall to a mere 165 pounds from a season-high of 180 pounds in December.

The Chicago offensive was furious in the first five minutes of the third game, with Sawchuk turning away excellent chances from Mikita, Lou Angotti and Ed Van Impe, plus two off the stick of Hull. For Marcel Pronovost, thrust into a pivotal blueline role with the Leafs at age 36, Sawchuk's brilliance was neither surprising nor unprecedented. He'd seen it before, way back in 1952 when he was a youngster out of Shawinigan Falls playing in his first full NHL season with the Detroit Red Wings. That spring, Sawchuk delivered one of the most extraordinary post-season efforts by a goaltender in NHL history. The Wings swept both the Leafs and Canadiens en route to the Cup, with the 22-year-old Sawchuk posting four shutouts and allowing only five goals along the way. Both veterans had seen long stays with the Red Wing organization ended with surprising moves to the Leafs. Sawchuk had been picked up by Toronto in the intra-league draft from the Wings in 1964, while Pronovost had arrived a year later after the Leafs' association with Andy Bathgate was concluded after only 15 months and he was peddled to Detroit. Pronovost had been a first team all-star as recently as 1961 with the Wings, and he was one of five Detroit players the Leafs received for Bathgate, Billy Harris and Gary Jarrett. Imlach correctly guessed Pronovost had something left to give.

With the two Red Wing lifers, Pronovost and Sawchuk, attempting to repel the furious Blackhawk onslaught early in Game Three of the '67 semifinals, it was easy for Pronovost to recall the sensational goaltending from Sawchuk he'd witnessed 15 years earlier. "It was the absolutely greatest playoff performance ever by an NHL goaltender," said Pronovost. But the Leafs didn't need memories against Hull and the Hawks. They needed an aging, and perpetually disgruntled Sawchuk to stand tall.

He did. After that furious five minutes, it was the Leafs who took over Game Three, building a 3–0 lead on goals by Ron Ellis, Frank Mahovlich and Jim Pappin. Hull, probably not realizing he had bopped Ballard in the pre-game warm-up, ultimately wrecked Sawchuk's shutout bid with a late goal and attracted the wrath of the Leafs for a late, questionable hit on scrappy Toronto winger Brian Conacher, who himself was gradually becoming an irritant in the Hawks' side. Stunningly, a Leaf team that had suffered through a 10-game losing streak two months earlier was now leading the feared Chicagoans in the first round of the Stanley Cup play-offs, two games to one. Sawchuk, his body black and blue with bruises, drew raves for his performance in the 3–1 victory. Pronovost and defence partner Larry Hillman, meanwhile, were proving to be a surprisingly stub-born defensive obstacle for the explosive Hawks. Best of all, there would not be a return for the Leafs to the Rock Haven Motel in Peterborough for more training. This Leaf team wasn't going anywhere.

3 *Five to a Crease*

Under most circumstances, using five goalies in an NHL season would spell doom for the team in question. If the cliché that having two goalies really just means you don't have a true Number 1 has a ring of truth, then having to use five suggests a rather spectacular problem. The 1966–67 Maple Leafs, however, were a team in a unique situation. No team with championship aspirations had ever tried to go forward with a 1–2 netminding punch as aged as that of the Leafs that season.

In 42-year-old Johnny Bower and 37-year-old Terry Sawchuk, the Leafs had tremendous experience and pedigree, but also two well-worn netminders who had great difficulty staying healthy for any extended period of time. They were very different in almost every way, but they shared, by that point in their respective careers, a propensity to be injured. They had been among the NHL's finest for years, but both had paid an enormous physical price. That meant reserves and replacements were frequently necessary, and by the end of the 1966–67 regular season three other goalies had played for the club including Bruce Gamble, Al Smith and Gary Smith. The saga of the Leaf goaltenders in that season really became a story within a story, and the lives of those five men beyond that magical Stanley Cup season is a compelling part of the legacy of that unique team.

Of that quintet of padded heroes, three died young, two of them before they turned 45. Another had an intimate connection to a tragic and senseless murder that made headlines across Canada. During that season, the paths of those five men intersected and criss-crossed multiple times, yet they barely knew each other. They were as diverse a group of characters as one could imagine, with little in common as they tried to maintain their place or work their way up the Leaf goaltending food chain during a season that contained an extraordinary number of twists and turns. At that point in hockey history, the game was changing drastically for all men in the nets, most of whom weren't yet masked.

They were just out of the era in which teams carried only one goalie because, for the most part, they needed only one, and one man could do the job on a regular basis. The schedule before World War II and in the immediate post-war years was shorter and the style of game was different: goaltenders weren't yet the punching bags they later became. But then came the 1950s and 1960s with longer schedules and new styles of play and the curved stick, and gradually the toll on goalies rose exponentially. No longer could one man play all the games. He needed relief on certain nights and entire evenings off just to survive.

In '67, the Leafs had Sawchuk and Bower, two relics from earlier NHL times, and the combination of their ages and the heavy new demands of the game meant neither could play half the games, let alone all of them. By the end of that memorable championship season, the contributions of Bower and Sawchuk were easy to measure. Less obvious were those of the other three men, who weren't stars then, and who never became stars, but were very much needed that season. On a team of unique individuals, the fraternity of goalies was a breed apart.

———— ✿ ————

It is possible to make the argument that Johnny Bower is the most popular Maple Leaf player ever to wear the team's colours. By 2004, more than three decades after he retired,

Bower could appear to the multitudes at the Air Canada Centre, a building in which he never played, and receive thunderous applause and often standing ovations. He had been utterly lovable for decades, never sullied by controversy or public misstep. His name was synonymous with the sport in the same way as the names of Bobby Orr, Gordie Howe and Bobby Hull, and in the way Wayne Gretzky's has become to a wider North American audience. There are those who might trumpet other Leafs over the decades as the most popular, players from Ted Kennedy to Dave Keon to Darryl Sittler to Wendel Clark. But Bower's fame and appeal have stood the test of time, enduring still at a time when younger fans seem less likely to be knowledgeable of the team's glorious past. Through his unusual career, Bower forged a unique connection with the city of Toronto and the world of hockey. "If you don't like Johnny Bower," hockey executive Lynn Patrick once said, "there's not much hope for you."

Looking back, the run to the Cup in '67 was not Bower's finest season, nor were those playoffs the best of his career. In reality, he was just about finished, understandably, at age 42. Before Christmas alone, he was injured five different times: a groin problem, a busted finger, a sore back, a bum shoulder and a broken hand. When it came time to prepare for the playoffs, he injured a finger on his blocker hand and couldn't start the playoffs against Chicago. When he did make his initial appearance in the fifth game of the opening round, he was pulled after one period. In the warm-up before Game Four of the final against Montreal, he pulled a groin muscle and wasn't available to play again. But in the second and third games of that series, he arrived to play two outstanding games, winning both and setting the stage for his teammates to conquer the Habs down the home stretch.

Part of the Bower allure lay in the strange path he took to the upper echelons of pro hockey, and part lay in the mystery that surrounded his age during his playing days. With respect to the latter, it wasn't until 1978, a time when Bower had been retired for eight years but was still willing to put on the pads for a Leaf practice, that he finally admitted he was at least two years older than most had believed. During the 1960s, the uncertainty over Bower's age had become a running gag, and he had invented a variety of stories to explain why no documentation existed to give his precise age.

Notoriously tight with a dollar, it made sense that Bower only bothered to trace his age records when he learned he needed them in order to collect U.S. social security benefits. This stemmed from the 13 years he had played in the United States earlier in his career. It was only then that he could say with certainty that he had been born on November 8, 1924, in Prince Albert, Saskatchewan. "I changed the story so much over the years I got all mixed up," he told veteran sportswriter Jim Proudfoot. "But people seemed to get a kick out of it and so did I. The only time I regretted it was when I'd sit down to negotiate and Punch Imlach would say he'd be crazy to give a long-term contract to an old codger who might fall apart on him at any time. Then I'd try to convince him I was really younger than I'd been letting on."

Bower figured the process had started when he'd lied about his age in 1940 to get into the Canadian army, joining the Queen's Own Cameron Highlanders when he was really only 15. He made it overseas but didn't see action and was discharged in 1944. By the next season, he had turned pro with Cleveland of the American Hockey League, and by 1953 he was in the NHL with the New York Rangers and earning the princely sum of $9,500 per season. Five years later, however, he was back in the minors again, and when the Leafs acquired the rights to the then 34-year-old netminder on June 3, 1958, Bower initially declined to report. "I couldn't see the point of pulling up stakes again," he said. Cleveland manager

Jim Hendy convinced him to give the Leafs a try on the condition he could return to the minors if he wished, so Bower agreed to join the Leafs.

It turned out to be a perfect marriage. Bower was obviously more than good enough, and the Leaf junior system, built on St. Mike's and the Marlboros, was producing outstanding players who would turn the Leafs into a winner again. The Cup came back to Toronto in 1962, 1963 and 1964 with Bower in net, which made it all the more difficult to understand why he had such a difficult time getting a fair paycheque out of Imlach and the Leafs. Players like Frank Mahovlich, Bob Pulford and Bobby Baun weren't afraid to lock horns with Imlach over money, but the Leaf GM preyed on weakness; he decided that Bower was a player with whom he could save a few dollars, simply by being a bully.

After the Leafs won the '62 Cup, Bower figured he was up for a raise on the $11,000 salary he had earned that season. Most of the team was making around $18,000 or $19,000, so Bower believed his request of $21,000, given his crucial role in helping the team win, was reasonable. In his first meeting with Imlach at training camp in Peterborough in September, the Leaf GM whined about the financial woes of his budget, although Conn Smythe had sold 60 per cent interest in the company a year earlier for $2 million and the entire Leaf payroll didn't exceed $300,000. He told his star goalie that, given the difficult circumstances, he felt he could squeeze a little more out of the new ownership team of Stafford Smythe, John Bassett and Harold Ballard and maybe get Bower a raise to $15,000. Bower had rehearsed for this scenario, concocting his own woe of poverty and had even decided to lie and say that his wife, Nancy, was pregnant when, in fact, she wasn't. Bower told Imlach he really needed a $10,000 raise, not less than half that. "Get the fuck out of my room and you better be on the ice on time or it's a $25 fine," stormed the always profane Imlach.

The two sides met on a couple of other occasions, and Bower's teammates urged him to hold firm. They knew his value, and they also knew that a better salary for him might mean improved paydays for them. Imlach upped his offer to $16,000 per season on a take-it-or-leave-it basis. During the meeting, assistant GM King Clancy suddenly joined and innocently asked Bower the nature of the dispute. Bower told him, and Clancy, taking the "good cop" role, first reiterated Imlach's budget constraints and then offered a compromise. "What if I got Punch to throw in another $1,000?" he said. Bower leapt at the offer, only realizing years later that Clancy and Imlach had certainly rehearsed their negotiating routine and that he'd been pressured into signing a less lucrative contract than he wanted. When Jim Gregory succeeded Imlach in 1969, he was embarrassed to find how little Bower was making and made a two-year offer with a $25,000 salary. Bower, however, misunderstood the offer and became upset and angry, thinking the dollar figure was to be split over two seasons. When Gregory told him it was $25,000 for each of two years, Bower calmed down and was forever grateful.

Winning the Cup in '67 gave Bower four championships in six years, a mini-dynasty built largely on his goaltending. He was near the end, but he couldn't imagine the Leafs were going to do anything but continue to dominate the league. After the celebration at Stafford Smythe's house following the '67 Cup win, he took two full bottles of champagne home with him, planning to open them when the Leafs won their next Stanley Cup. After a few years, the still hopeful Bower planned to pull the corks when the Leafs won the Cup or when he and his wife marked their 50th wedding anniversary.

On November 3, 1998, Johnny and Nancy Bower celebrated a half-century of marriage. One of those 31-year-old champagne bottles was finally opened. Inside, the bottle contained only two-thirds of its original volume and a taste that

more closely approximated vinegar. Bower put the other bottle aside, still waiting.

———————— ❧ ————————

By the time he was 32, Bruce Gamble figured he had finally
landed where he wanted to be. He was the starting goaltender
in the 1971–72 season for a promising team, the Philadelphia
Flyers, making $36,000 a season, the best coin of his career.
Just five years earlier as the Number 3 man on the goalie chart
of the Maple Leafs, Gamble had watched the legendary Terry
Sawchuk help the Leafs win the Stanley Cup while playing for
half the salary he was making with the Flyers. "I figured over
the next four, five years I'd be making forty thousand easy,
maybe fifty thousand," he later told acclaimed Toronto sportswriter Trent Frayne. "That'd do things for my pension." By
that point in his career, it wasn't about greatness or championships for Gamble, a native of Port Arthur, Ontario, who had
played for 14 teams in the previous 11 years and was now
strictly in the business of being a mercenary in pads. It had
gone beyond sport. It was his living, wherever it took him. But
on February 9, 1972, it all changed for Gamble. His life was
altered in the blink of an eye and was never the same. And
when the announcement came 10 years later that he'd died
quietly, barely into middle age and far from the limelight he'd
never wanted anyway, everybody had long stopped wondering
what had ever happened to him.

His journey to being part of Maple Leaf history began, really, in the winter of 1966 when he was recalled from the Tulsa
Oilers with Bower and Sawchuk both out with injuries. The Leaf
system was otherwise filled with creaking veteran goalies or
young netminders not ready for prime time. He was 28 years old
then, sort of in the middle between the old men and the promising kids, and had played 82 games in the NHL with the Bruins
and Rangers earlier in his career, winning only 18 of them. He
came with the adjective "journeyman" figuratively tattooed to his

forehead, and there were certainly no lofty expectations that he'd be much of anything for the Leafs. Instead, he stunned the hockey world and took Toronto by storm, going unbeaten in six starts with an extraordinary four shutouts.

Eventually, Bower and Sawchuk got healthy again, and Gamble resumed the nomadic life of a spare goalie, bouncing around between Tulsa, Victoria and Rochester, bolting to the bigs whenever he got the call. With six teams, you went where you were told unless you wanted to live without a paycheque. An NHL club could move you around multiple times without the courtesy of waivers or anything very official at all, but Gamble didn't seem to mind the life. He was quiet and reserved, almost introverted, but he loved country and western music with a passion, particularly Stompin' Tom Connors. He was such a big fan of a country star named Smiley Bates that teammates called him "Batesy," although sportswriters called him "Paladin" for his majestic, thick, black sideburns. He drank, certainly enough for others to think he was an alcoholic, but eschewed the regular hangouts of the Leafs for the dim environs of the Cameo Room at the Isabella Hotel on Sherbourne Street, about 20 blocks from Maple Leaf Gardens. He didn't want the fanfare or the applause—just a cold beer and the right music and a teammate who knew not to talk too much.

Bower and Sawchuk were hurt so often during that 1966–67 season that it seemed Gamble was around most of the time, more than either of the unrelated Smiths, Al and Gary, and certainly more than aged retreads Al Millar and Bob Perreault, who were forever exiled to the minors. He played 23 games, won only five and, like a gutsy middle reliever in baseball, ate up minutes while the more important Leaf goalies convalesced and healed. When the playoffs rolled around, he was back in the minors, and nowhere near the celebrations when the Cup was won. By the following season, Sawchuk was gone, Bower was past it and Gamble was the Leaf starter for three seasons until he was traded to Philadelphia in a complicated deal that brought Bernie Parent to the Leafs, moved Mike (Shakey) Walton to Boston and also landed future 50-goal shooter Rick McLeish for the Flyers.

Those events led him to February 9, 1972. Standing in his crease at the Pacific Coliseum in Vancouver, he was suddenly down—face down—and didn't know how he'd got there. He asked teammate Barry Ashbee who had hit him, and Ashbee told him nobody had. Gamble collected himself and finished the game, and it wasn't until he was examined by doctors afterwards that he learned he had suffered a heart attack—right there in the crease in the middle of an NHL game. Just as quickly as he'd fallen to the ice, his career was over, his body too fragile to continue as a pro goalie. The expectation of those good breadwinning years ahead suddenly vanished.

He scouted for a while, and then just sort of faded away. By the late 1970s, newsletters from the NHL Players Association were asking for any information on the whereabouts of Gamble, and there was a story in *The Windsor Star* that reported he'd gone missing. That wasn't quite true, or at least not according to his estranged wife, who let everybody know he'd been living in Niagara Falls, Ontario, on the margins and leading the life of a recluse. He had three sons, but didn't see them much, and there were odd jobs, including one driving a catering truck. Even to those who knew him, or thought they did, he was more ghostly than real, and then he suddenly emerged again in 1981 with a heavy black beard and a lot more weight than he had carried in his NHL days. He started playing for a local old-timers team, the Niagara Falls Flames, and began slimming down again. Five days after Christmas, 1982, with friends and former NHL teammates suggesting he seemed happy again, Gamble practised with the Flames and then skipped the post-workout beers to head home to bed. He woke in the middle of the night complaining of chest pains and by 3 a.m. was declared dead at a local hospital. He was only 43.

—————— ⚜ ——————

Gary Smith was loud and colourful and fun, and just about as different from Bruce Gamble as one could imagine. Still, the two goalies had a connection, and that connection was the legendary defenceman and curmudgeon Eddie Shore.

After his brilliant playing career, Shore owned and operated the independent Springfield Indians of the AHL, conducting business in such a way that, by 1966, his players mutinied. Before all that, in June 1963, he'd traded for Gamble and a few other bit pieces in a deal with the NHL's Boston Bruins, a time when players could be traded to teams in different leagues. Gamble played 21 games for Shore the next season, but by then had seen more than enough. Shore had peculiar ideas on just about every position—how players should skate and move and practise and prepare—and Gamble didn't like any of them. So he walked out. Well, more accurately, he just refused to play and missed an entire season, the 1964–65 campaign, at a time when he really needed to get his pro career on track.

Shore let him sit, but by September of the following season he had decided he really needed to get his hands on a goalie. His buddy Punch Imlach was running the Leafs, and Imlach had lots of puckstoppers at his disposal. So Shore figured he'd trade the rights to Gamble to the Leafs. He was pretty happy about the deal until forwards Billy Smith and Larry Johnston arrived on his doorstep. He took one look at the diminutive Smith and knew he had a problem. "I thought you were blond and much taller," he told Smith. "And where are your goal pads?" Shore, it seemed, believed he'd traded for 6-foot-5 goalie Gary Smith, the son of a former Boston teammate, Des Smith. He got right on the phone again to Imlach to complain. Imlach, probably chuckling in glee, said he'd be happy to take the two players back if Shore didn't want them. Shore declined, and in one transaction Gamble was out of Shore's clutches and Gary Smith had avoided the pleasure altogether.

Other than Gerry Cheevers, Smith was probably the best goalie the Leafs developed during the 1960s. In five, well-spread-out career appearances as a Leaf, he never won a game. But five years after leaving the club, Smith shared in the Vezina Trophy as a Chicago Blackhawk with the great Tony Esposito, although he doesn't remember that as a particularly collegial experience. "[Esposito] was the type of guy who wouldn't let his backup play," he recalls.

Culled from the Ottawa Cardinals peewee team after being recommended to Leaf chief scout Bob Davidson by bird dog Brian Lynch, a man who just lived up the street, Smith was recruited to the St. Mike's hockey factory at age 14. His dad was by then calling races at the Ottawa–Rideau race track, and his older brother Brian was a forward beginning his trek through the Montreal organization. After St. Mike's stopped entering teams in Junior A competition following the 1961–62 season, Smith moved on to Neil McNeil, but school wasn't really his thing. Instead, his regular gig became being the spare goaltender for the visiting NHL team at Maple Leaf Gardens. He held the job between 1961 and 1964. It paid him $10 a night and a seat to watch the game, plus $100 if he actually had to play. However, he was never called into action. The Leafs frequently used a rink rat named Sockeye Wasserman as their practice goalie, a much more painful and lower-paying chore than the lofty position of spare goalie for the Leafs' opposition. Smith remembers Wasserman being perpetually sore at him for getting the extra cash instead. "Hey, they needed someone who wasn't totally crazy," says Smith.

It was, in fact, around that time that Smith picked up the nickname "Axe," although most remember him as "Suitcase" for the frequency with which he changed teams later in his career. Smith's version was that he picked up the nickname Axe from a deranged street person named Wilbur who hung around near the Gardens and had a prominent dent in his head from some previous misadventure. The players called him "Axe in the Head" while flipping him the odd dollar here and there, and Smith and junior teammate Mike Corbett got to calling each other by that same name. "After a while, it just sort of fell to me, and was shortened to just 'Axe,'" says Smith. The story has been retold in various forms, some suggesting Smith got the name by intercepting Wilbur as he chased a woman down Bloor Street with an axe, but Smith says that's all just urban myth.

After being part of the Toronto Marlboros junior team that captured the 1964 Memorial Cup, Smith faced the prodigious task of finding a way to be noticed in an organization that had Bower coming off three Stanley Cups, had just picked up Sawchuk from the Red Wings and also owned goalies like Gerry Cheevers, Al Millar, Bob Perreault and Don Simmons. Gamble was added to the pile a year later, and Smith remembers having a few beers at training camp with the journeyman goalie and being surprised when Gamble said he had the next day off. "Why?" wondered Smith. "I have to go get my teeth pulled," replied Gamble. The next day, Gamble went to the dentist and had all of his teeth pulled, a relatively common practice in those days, since it was considered a realistic possibility a hockey player would lose them all anyway.

Smith was a good enough goalie, but the competition was stacked too high all around him. After a full season in the minors, he got his first chance to play for the Leafs in February 1966 after Bower was cut in the face and required 26 stitches. Sawchuk was already on the sidelines with an injury, so the 22-year-old Smith was summoned to be the starter for a pair of weekend games against the Rangers and Red Wings. Al Smith, a goalie with the Marlies, was his backup. Against the New Yorkers on Saturday, February 20, a game played before a national TV audience on *Hockey Night in Canada*, Smith came up with a way to get noticed. He stopped a shot with his glove, dropped it and began skating up ice to his own blueline, stickhandling like a defenceman, all the while looking for a teammate to hit with an outlet feed.

The Leafs lost the game 3–1, but the pictures and headlines were all about this "wandering boy" who had played his position in a previously undiscovered style. It was strange but fun, and even Imlach didn't seem to mind. "No, I didn't blast him," said the Leaf coach. "Anything that adds colour is good as long as you don't get hurt by it. And besides, he beat two of our guys to the blueline." Smith played again the next night in Detroit, losing 4–1. But a star, at least in his own mind, had been born. "When I went back to the minors, I started doing it all the time," he recalls. Jim McKenny, then a young Leaf prospect who had on occasion been intercepted by Smith on his way to school and been re-routed to Greenwood Race Track, says that became a focal point of the oddball goaltender's game plan. "Axe's dream was to skate the puck to centre ice at Maple Leaf Gardens, pick it up and kick it high enough so it would hit the scoreclock," he laughs.

Smith played a third game as a Leaf against Chicago two days after the Detroit game, facing the feared Bobby Hull. "I guess I'll try to get a piece of his shot with some part of my anatomy," he told reporters. "And I'll probably pray a little." Less than three minutes into the game, he suffered a groin injury that knocked him out of action for nine weeks and ended that NHL stint. As luck would have it, the Leafs beat the Hawks that night, but with Al Smith in goal.

The following summer, Gary Smith was included in the Leafs' sale of their Rochester farm club to a group of investors. Nineteen player contracts went in the deal, including those of Smith, Al Arbour, Don Cherry, Duane Rupp, Darryl Edestrand,

Brian Conacher, Peter Stemkowski, Eddie Litzenberger and Larry Jeffrey. A condition of the deal was that the Leafs could buy any two of those players back during the regular season, or they could invite any to training camp the following fall and send Rochester another contracted player. So even though he had been sold, Smith remained in the Leaf chain. He started the next season in Rochester, left for several weeks in a salary dispute, then returned and promptly was put on the injury list for five weeks with a groin problem. "When I look back, I probably would have been better if I'd had a little more dedication," he says. Most of the season, he split his time between Rochester and Victoria and kept a light perspective on the game. "The guys wanted to be where Axe was," recalls McKenny. "It was better than playing on a Stanley Cup team."

Smith's reputation as a crowd pleaser kept the Leafs interested, and in December 1966 he was again called up when Bower and Sawchuk went down with injuries. He lost again in Chicago on December 18, but saved his best and last appearance as a Leaf for three nights later against the Stanley Cup champion Montreal Canadiens. It was a tough night for the Leafs, who fell behind early, and another game in which Leaf winger Eddie Shack and Montreal forward John Ferguson dropped the gloves early. Smith was to back up Gamble that night, but Imlach pulled Gamble just 5:23 into the match after the Habs had scored to go up 2–1. "I was sitting at the end of the bench, yelling and swearing at Ferguson, when Punch walked down, pulled the towel off and said, 'Go get 'em,'" recalls Smith. The Canadiens put another three past Smith, who decided it was time to try something a little different. "I thought, well, maybe I should try to score," he says. He grabbed the puck, and this time, instead of stopping at his own blueline, he stickhandled all the way past the red line before he encountered Montreal defenceman J.C. Tremblay. "Tremblay never hit anybody, but he just decked me," he said. "As I was spinning around the ice, all I saw was Punch pulling his hat down over his eyes and Claude Provost going in alone on Marcel Pronovost, who then made the best save I ever saw."

The Leafs lost 6–2, and the headlines about Smith's antics were big. Still, he went back to Victoria the next day, never to play for the Leafs again. The NHL ultimately changed its rules to prevent goalies from skating across the red line with the puck. The following June in the NHL expansion draft, Smith was claimed by the California Golden Seals. Over the course of a long career that included stops in Chicago, Vancouver, Minnesota, Washington, Hershey, Fort Worth, Indianapolis (he was briefly a WHA teammate of Wayne Gretzky's), Winnipeg and Tulsa, Smith never did score a goal. "My life is unfulfilled," he jokes.

He did have one last memorable escapade as a Leaf before he left, however. When the Leafs gathered two nights after winning the Cup in 1967 for a dignified party at the home of team president Stafford Smythe, Smith was accompanied by a buxom young woman, or at least that's how he remembers it. Stemkowski, one of his running mates at the time, insists it was he who accompanied the young lady. The presence of a female more than happy to reveal her assets ticked off the Leaf wives in attendance, and inspired famed columnist Jim Coleman to write, "Gary Smith showed what most goaltenders need the most—great vision—as he arrived with a handsomely filled décolletage on his arm. My own glasses fogged up as I stared across the room from the 30-foot range." It remains unclear who precisely was the woman's date that night. "Stemmer might be claiming her 30 years later, but that night, he wasn't," laughs Smith.

Smith's beloved father, Des, died in 1981. In August 1995, his 54-year-old brother, Brian, an Ottawa sportscaster, was gunned down with a .22 calibre bullet in a bizarre, senseless act of violence while leaving work. Brian Smith played in the

NHL for both Minnesota and Los Angeles in the late 1960s, and over the course of his broadcasting career became a beloved public figure and member of the Ottawa sports community. His funeral at Ottawa's St. Patrick's Basilica was an enormous event, attracting hockey and television celebrities from both sides of the border. On the day he was buried, it was announced his transplanted heart had saved the life of a 61-year-old local man. A paranoid schizophrenic was charged with first-degree murder in the wake of the shooting, and later testified that he believed the media was rebroadcasting his thoughts and had compiled a list of local reporters as potential targets. In May 1997, the 40-year-old man, who had refused treatment for his illness, was ruled not criminally responsible for the murder and confined to a mental hospital. National outrage over the killing spawned a major legislative change dubbed "Brian's Law," which compelled mentally ill patients to take medication if they posed a risk to themselves or others. The press box at the Corel Centre in Ottawa, home to the Senators, was named in honour of the fallen broadcaster. "It was hardest on my mom," says Gary Smith of his brother's murder. "She was so strong about it for years, but finally it got to her. My brother was loved by so many people."

Smith's post-hockey life was as varied and unusual as his hockey career, and eventually landed him in Vancouver working as a "skip tracer," chasing credit debtors south of the border. He was married and divorced, and his marriage produced two daughters, who eventually went to live with their mother in California, and a son, Marshall, who was born with spina bifida. After years of careful treatment, Marshall fell and broke his leg, and by his 30th birthday was confined to a wheelchair for life. Living together in the Vancouver area, Marshall and his father whiled away hours at the local racetrack, just as Gary and his father had done. Sometimes Gary and Marshall would watch thoroughbreds that were partially owned by the former NHL goalie. He had bought a share in them with an $80,000 NHL pension upgrade in the mid-1990s. They never became champions, but that didn't spoil the activity for father and son. "Marshall gives me a lot of pleasure," Smith says. "He's my best friend."

———— ❧ ————

The play was called *Confessions to Anne Sexton*, an artistic effort few remember because very few saw it. On opening night, 17 people showed up at the Alumnae Theatre on Berkeley Street in downtown Toronto to see the performance. It was a story about a former World Hockey Association goaltender named Billy Henry who, in the middle of a Buffalo blizzard in 1977, came to understand the "absolute truth for life." Thirteen years later, he crosses the border into Canada to visit an old friend, a corporate hotshot, and tries to give him his secret. There were 21 shows in all, and on six occasions, nobody showed up. After a while, the operators didn't even bother unlocking the theatre unless a potential customer came and pounded on the front door. Al Smith poured his heart into writing that show, plus $34,000 of pension benefits he'd received as part of the NHL's settlement with its former players around that time. If *Confessions to Anne Sexton* was good, the public didn't think so, and it closed a few weeks after it opened. Still, perhaps Smith deserves some credit for his literary efforts. If you sift through the stockpile of NHL trivia, Smith is the only former player to have ever written a play and brought it to stage.

That was in 1998. Thirty-one years earlier, Smith had sat perched on the end of the Toronto Maple Leafs bench for two of the final three games as they wrapped up the 1967 Stanley Cup final over the Montreal Canadiens. Bower had been hurt in the warm-up before Game Four, forcing a reportedly hung-over Sawchuk to take the net. Smith had been rushed to the rink as a backup and didn't arrive until the second period.

Even though Smith wasn't the third goalie on the club's depth chart, he nonetheless was also the backup to Sawchuk for the fifth and sixth games of the final. Prior to that, he'd only played 122 minutes in the NHL. Before Game Six, he was asked if he was hopeful of getting a chance to play. "Everyone likes to feel he's part of the team," he said. "But I think I can get that feeling while sitting on the end of the bench."

It would be hard to imagine today that an NHL coach would take the risk that Imlach did in using the untested Smith as a backup in the Stanley Cup final, particularly since Sawchuk had been injured off and on all season and Smith, a quirky, unpredictable sort, had quit hockey 18 months earlier while playing for the Marlboro Juniors to go to work for a hospital supply firm. If Sawchuk had been hurt, the gates would surely have been opened for Montreal to win the Cup by victimizing a young player like Smith. But Imlach, always anxious to protect Rochester's roster at playoff time and his investment in that team, preferred to keep Gamble playing in the AHL playoffs and took the gigantic risk of letting Smith back up Sawchuk.

Smith didn't play in the final, much to his relief. Smith, Sawchuk and Bower all participated in the warm-up to Game Six, but Smith, dressed in full uniform, ended up watching the game on television in the bowels of the Gardens. As it turned out, Smith's most significant moments as a Leaf came before that final and after. Fifteen months earlier as a call-up from the Marlboro Juniors, he'd relieved Gary Smith after 2:15 of play at a game in Chicago. He played wonderfully, eventually back-stopping the Leafs to a 3–2 victory and stalling Bobby Hull at 47 goals. "It seems like a dream," he said after that game. "I never thought this would happen to me." He played one more game for the Leafs in the 1965-66 season, losing 5–1 to the Blackhawks on New Year's Eve.

His other moment of glory with the Leafs came at the 1968 all-star game when, as defending champs, Imlach's club hosted the NHL all-stars in what was at the time a rather more serious affair than it is today. Gamble started and played well, and then Smith was sizzling in relief, stopping 13 of 14 shots and preserving the win with a sensational save on Hull in the dying moments. "It's like getting a minute and a half on prime time on NBC," gushed Smith afterwards. Opportunity with the Leafs knocked for Smith that year after both Sawchuk and Gary Smith had been lost to expansion the previous June, but he played in the minors the entire season. The next season he again played mostly in the minors, getting into seven games with the Leafs, before being claimed by Pittsburgh in the following summer's intra-league draft when the Leafs decided that 34-year-old retread Marv Edwards was more to their liking. It was a mistake by the Leafs, but not as enormous as one the Montreal Canadiens made the same day when they left goalie Tony Esposito unprotected and available to the Chicago Blackhawks.

Al Smith went on to a solid pro career after leaving the Leafs, including being named the WHA's top goaltender in 1978. He'd gone on to play for the New England Whalers, a team in that dying league, after bolting the Buffalo Sabres the previous winter in a most memorable exit. Imlach, who had never given Smith much of a shot in Toronto, had resurfaced in Buffalo as GM. Sabre starter Gerry Desjardins had suffered an eye injury on February 10, and three nights later Smith was told he'd get the start for a home game against Minnesota. The Sabres, however, had also recalled promising minor league goalie Don Edwards, and less than an hour before game time Imlach ordered coach Floyd Smith to play Edwards. The conclusion to the story has been told in many different ways, but the facts seem to be that a disappointed Smith waited until the national anthem was over, stepped off the bench, saluted Buffalo owners Seymour and Northrup Knox in the stands and headed for the dressing room, never to wear a Sabre uniform again.

"Does this happen a lot?" asked young Buffalo forward Derrick Smith, who was playing his first NHL game that night. Years later, at Imlach's funeral, Al Smith and Edwards ran into each other again. "I know I'm a raving fool for what I did," said Smith. "But if the game doesn't make sense to you, get out."

By 1981, after playing 37 games for the NHL Colorado Rockies, Al Smith's career was over. He began to look for fulfillment in new areas, but the search wasn't fruitful. He jumped on a train to Vancouver, leaving his wife and children behind, and began selling cars. Shortly after, he headed into the B.C. interior to pick fruit, emerging with stories about the trouble a 250-pound man can get himself into while perched on a ladder in an orchard. There was another brief stint in sales in which he attempted to sell the Reuters news service to new clients. He returned to Toronto, and began putting his diverse ideas on life and sport down on paper, writing bits of books, short stories and plays, ultimately creating the disjointed and vaguely autobiographical play *Confessions to Anne Sexton* and the beginnings of a book called *The Tragedy of Lake Tuscarora*.

To survive, he began driving a cab in Toronto, and for 17 years he could be found at the wheel of an orange and green Beck taxi, often picking up old pals, former teammates and sportswriters. "He put up with a lot of crap to do what he thought was important," Smith's son, Adam, told *The Hockey News* in 2002. "I think he had a lot more in common with failed writers than failed goalies. Most of what my dad wrote was terrible. And he knew it." Mark Brender, a writer with *The Hockey News*, tracked Smith down to ask him about his post-hockey career. "You're shy about it because you're supposed to be dead, you're supposed to be gone," he told Brender. "You can feel for me, and you can be empathetic, but you can't save me and you can't save the rest of us."

He'd been friends with Jimmy Keon, brother of Dave Keon, since the two were Marlie teammates, and Keon would visit him in his dumpy apartment on Isabella Street, a flat strewn with boxes and garbage. "He had this image of the writer's life," says Keon. "He didn't think he could do it as a family man. He felt you had to live the life. He was pretty philosophical about it. All he wanted to be was a published author, to be able to have lunch on Queen Street and have credibility in the writing community."

Smith did manage one dramatic accomplishment, and that was getting his name attached to the credits of the acclaimed 1982 film *Quest for Fire* as RBM Al Smith. The "RBM" stood for Row Boat Manager. Smith's brother had been involved in the production and had rented his sibling's row boat for a day of shooting. People from his former hockey career may not have understood him, but they loved him. Pat Quinn, who eventually became coach of the Maple Leafs, was the godfather to one of Smith's children. "What a fabulous way to live life, to do what you always wanted to do," says former teammate Jim McKenny. "For years he had regular customers who would insist on Smitty as their cab driver when they called for a cab. I would run into him on the streets every now and then. I called him a few times, but he was never interested in going out. He became a recluse. But he left the game on his own terms and did what he wanted to do. What a great way to live life."

In the summer of 2002, Al Smith died of pancreatic cancer at the age of 56. If you look in the official NHL record book and guide at the Stanley Cup-winning roster of the 1967 Toronto Maple Leafs, his name isn't there.

———— ❧ ————

Of all the people Terry Sawchuk could have formed a tight bond with on the '67 Leafs, the least likely would have to have been Peter Stemkowski.

Sawchuk was 37, viewed as a difficult man to know and like, often sullen and, when drinking, quarrelsome and vicious. Stemkowski was 23, just three years out of junior hockey, not certain whether he was going to be able to stick in the NHL. "Even though he was 14 years older than me and kept to himself, we formed a friendship," Stemkowski recalls. "I think he liked me because we were both from Winnipeg and both Ukrainian. I always had some hair sticking up on the back of my head and he would tell me to just cut it all off and start over. He had an odd-shaped body and would walk like an old man, so I would walk behind him in the dressing room and impersonate him. He would turn around and pretend he was mad, but he got a kick out of it.

"A few times during the two seasons we were together he told me to bring my shaving kit and a change of clothes and stay at his place. He had a motel-type apartment on Jarvis Street near the Gardens. So we'd go out for a few beers after practice, have dinner later and I'd stay over at his place. But the weird thing was we'd be sitting having dinner in complete silence and I'd think, what the hell am I doing here, this is weird. But he seemed to like my company."

That made Stemkowski the exception, not the rule, but it gave him a glimpse into the strange world inhabited by Sawchuk, a riddle from the day he joined the Leafs on waivers from Detroit in June 1964 to the day he left in the expansion draft to Los Angeles in June 1967. It didn't cost the Leafs anything to get him other than the standard $20,000 waiver fee, and they didn't get anything for him when he left. In between there were 91 regular season appearances and 13 playoff starts and one magical spring in which he came up with six performances that helped the Leafs win the '67 Cup. Even that spring, he was supposed to back up Bower once again, but Bower suffered a finger injury on the eve of the playoffs and had to give way to Sawchuk. In the final, it looked like Bower would once more take over after winning the second and third games against Montreal, but again he was hurt, and Sawchuk took the Leafs the rest of the way.

Those years were but a sliver of Sawchuk's NHL career, which began in 1949 and ended, as did his life, in May 1970, at age 40. For 21 years, Sawchuk was in the public eye, the centre of attention while playing goal for the Red Wings, Bruins, the Red Wings again, the Maple Leafs, the Los Angeles Kings, the Red Wings one last time and, for eight games, the New York Rangers. Yet few have really explained who he was or why he was the way he was—for the most part a foreboding, brooding presence with occasional lapses into civility.

He was known to be a terrible worrier, and with good reason, perhaps. He'd started his NHL career in an age when there was no slapshot and by '67 was participating in a sport where unchecked curves on sticks meant the puck could approach speeds of 100 miles per hour while dipping and moving like a knuckleball. No wonder he wasn't cheerful about his work. No wonder he spent more time in practice avoiding getting hit than trying to make his teammates work to score. One time, Bower was struggling, and he asked Sawchuk for a little help in playing the angles. "Just watch me in practice," said Sawchuk. Bower suggested that might not be so helpful, particularly since his teammate didn't exactly exert himself during workouts. "Just watch me in practice," said Sawchuk again, and that was that.

Bobby Haggert, who as Leaf trainer was often in charge of keeping the two aged goalies healthy, laughs at the contrast between the two men. "Just one high shot and Sawchuk would leave practice and not come back even if Imlach went into the dressing room to ask him," recalls Haggert. "Bower would stay after practice if some rookie wanted to take 500 extra shots. He would stay out there until the lights went out. But at 7 p.m. on game nights, they both came ready to play."

Still, the two men respected one another enormously. In the 1964–65 season, the Leafs posted the best defensive record in the NHL at a time when the top goalie on such a club was awarded the Vezina Trophy. Sawchuk had played 36 games, while Bower had played 34, so Sawchuk was to receive the Vezina. But he refused to accept the trophy unless it was awarded to both him and Bower, and the league acceded to his request.

Sawchuk's kindred spirits were nervous men like Glenn Hall and Jacques Plante, athletes who endured the competition rather than reveled in it. He had taken hundreds of stitches in his face, before and after adopting a mask as part of his equipment in 1962. He ballooned and shrank repeatedly over the course of his career, at one time weighing close to 230 pounds and at other times weighing under 160 pounds. His body was often black and blue with sickly bruises and welts. He could be kind and friendly, and in the next moment rude and angry. Longtime sportswriter Trent Frayne had spent time with him one summer, writing a magazine piece on Sawchuk. After failing to cross paths for several years, he saw the goaltender one day in Boston and went over to say hello, mentioning his name, in case Sawchuk didn't remember. Sawchuk returned the greeting with a snarl. "Won't you sons of bitches ever leave me alone?" he shouted. "Fuck off!" Teammates learned to steer clear when Sawchuk was in a mood or at the bar. "When he was sober, he wouldn't fight anyone," says George Armstrong. "When he was drunk, he wanted to fight everyone all the time."

The years he spent as a Leaf were probably not his happiest. His relationship with his family was an unusual one, and while he lived in an apartment near Maple Leaf Gardens during the season, they stayed far away in Detroit. His teammates understood it was a subject not to be broached. "I always found that sad," says Brian Conacher. As well as Stemkowski, Sawchuk liked his old Detroit teammate Marcel Pronovost, and he liked the drinking company of younger Leafs, even younger goalies like Gary Smith. Pronovost was one of the first

Leafs to live in the suburbs in Mississauga, and he and his wife would often have Sawchuk over for dinner. The two ex-Wings liked to drink at the Toronto Radio Artists Club, a joint known by the acronym TRAC and a place where a Leaf could run up a tab in the days before credit cards. Pronovost believes Sawchuk, who was making less than most of the veteran Leafs, lived under the constant fear of not being able to provide for his large family. Indeed, in the summer that followed the '67 Cup victory, the Sawchuks gave birth to their seventh child. It was for that reason, and the possibility that expansion would give him new financial opportunities, that Sawchuk continued playing past his time in Toronto. "He struggled with the fact he missed his kids in Detroit," says Stemkowski. "As far as his marriage went, let's just say they were having marital problems and leave it at that."

To be sure, Sawchuk enjoyed winning the Cup, the first championship team he'd been on since the last Cup in Detroit 12 years earlier. "This is the biggest thrill of my life in hockey," he told Frank Selke Jr. on *Hockey Night in Canada* moments after the final game at Maple Leaf Gardens. Sawchuk cherished his NHL record 100th shutout set on March 4, 1967, in a 3–0 win over Chicago. But his stay in Toronto constituted less than one-tenth of his complete NHL playing experience, and for much of it, he didn't play well. After a very mediocre 1965–66 season, for example, he had to be coaxed back for one more season, and constantly talked about retiring during that year.

In September 1966, Sawchuk reported to Leaf camp in high spirits after off-season back surgery to repair two degenerative discs had gone well and left him standing straight for the first time in years—a full inch and a half taller than when he'd left for home the previous spring. "This is living," he told reporters. "No more headaches or backaches, and it is a pleasure to go for a walk. It's wonderful to have my health again."

That lasted until December when Sawchuk's back went out again while showering after a game in Montreal, and for the rest of his final season in Toronto his physical woes were a daily issue. After the '67 Cup, the Leafs made the rather extraordinary decision to protect the 42-year-old Bower ahead of Sawchuk and youngsters Gary Smith and Al Smith. Sawchuk had been let go in Detroit three years earlier to make room for a younger man, Roger Crozier, and now he was moving on so that a much older player, Bower, could stay in a Leaf uniform. Five days after being claimed by Los Angeles in the expansion draft, Sawchuk was named the winner of the J.P. Bickell Trophy for outstanding performance by a Leaf player in the previous season. "I was never big on Sawchuk as a great goaltender, either as an opponent or a teammate," says Bob Pulford. "But after that playoff in 1967, I believed I had never seen better goaltending. If people ask me today who I think was the greatest of all time, I still say Sawchuk because of what he did that spring."

Sawchuk had survived back surgery the previous year as well as on-again, off-again retirement plans to deliver one last meaningful playoff. He even bounced back between games in the '67 final after playing poorly in the fourth game to win the next two and clinch the Cup. "I don't like to complain," he said. "I fought hard all my life and I had to fight back again." His eldest son, Gerry, says the year Sawchuk spent in L.A. after leaving the Leafs was one of the happiest for his family. "It's actually my favourite family memory," he says. "We all went to Los Angeles and lived in a house on the ocean. It was a fabulous experience."

Gerry Sawchuk was enjoying a day surfing at the beach in 1970 when he heard the news that his father had died in hospital. Just the day before, father and son had talked about Terry possibly getting Gerry a tryout for a Junior B team in Kitchener, Ontario. Sawchuk, who had moved on to play for the Rangers, had landed in hospital after being injured in an over-aggressive wrestling match with teammate Ron Stewart. Ultimately, his body, ravaged by years of hard-living and thousands of shots on the hockey rink, didn't survive the surgery to remove blood from his liver. The true mystery man of the '67 Leafs, Sawchuk remains in death a man who couldn't, or wouldn't, be understood.

———— ❦ ————

As with most hockey champions, the '67 Leafs won with excellence in goal. Sawchuk and Bower are the ones we remember—the goalies glorified as part of Leaf mythology. But three others also played a role and made contributions. It can't be said the Cup wouldn't have been won without Gary Smith, Al Smith and Bruce Gamble, a trio that combined to play 31 regular games that season. But to exclude them from the memories would be misleading. These players didn't get the glory, but they too helped stop the pucks.

GAME FOUR
CHICAGO AT MAPLE LEAFS, APRIL 13, 1967

At a time when Canada was grappling with a new sense of nationalism, the Maple Leafs were far more concerned with superstition.

Sure, Canada was becoming a modern country, using Expo '67 to graduate from being "little Canada" to something else. Part of that was also being expressed in the House of Commons on April 12, 1967, when Canada's politicians gave unanimous approval to "O Canada" as the country's new national anthem, displacing "God Save the Queen." Only the music, composed 87 years earlier by Quebec musician Calixa Lavallee, was approved, with the words to come later. "With dignity, not too slowly," came the suggestion from the Commons as to how the new anthem should be played.

To the Leafs, however, an organization that was happy to enrage the local populace by bringing the Beatles to town and offering to let U.S. draft dodger Muhammad Ali fight at Maple Leaf Gardens, this was no time to move forward. For Game Four of their series with the Chicago Blackhawks the next night, the team refused to play "O Canada" and instead stuck with "God Save the Queen." "Senate approval of the Commons endorsement hasn't been given, and naturally we shouldn't jump the gun," harrumphed Leaf vice- president Harold Ballard, usually not one held hostage by official protocol. "Besides, we haven't had time to think about it. We're too busy trying to win the Stanley Cup."

The truth of the matter, however, was that the Leafs quite deliberately didn't play the new anthem for reasons of superstition. After all, the club's devotion to the Queen hadn't stopped a work order to rip down an enormous portrait of Her Majesty the previous summer to make room for extra seats. A year earlier, the team had changed to the new Maple Leaf flag from the Red Ensign, and gone on to lose in the playoffs to Montreal in four straight games. Ahead of the Hawks two games to one, English Canada's team wasn't about to make the same mistake again. Superstition, the staple of athletes and coaches alike, demanded no change in anthem just to please the national interest.

The Leafs scored just 3:42 into the first period, but that only brought them back into a tie. For the first time in the series, a Chicago strategy aimed at probing vulnerable areas of the Leafs began to emerge. With Bobby Baun playing only a handful of shifts in the opening three games, the burden was mounting on the two pairs of Leaf defencemen that were playing all the minutes. Tim Horton and Allan Stanley were one pair, and the surprisingly effective combination of Marcel Pronovost and Larry Hillman were holding up rather well as the other tandem.

The Hawks began to eschew their strategy of carrying the puck through the neutral zone and into the Leaf end, and started to dump the puck and pursue it. This put more pressure on the four Leaf rearguards to turn and retrieve the puck while trying to avoid Chicago forwards with mayhem on their minds. Ken Wharram had scored for the Hawks just nine seconds into the game, tying a Stanley Cup record, a sign that the visitors were not going to be headed at any point in the evening. Pierre Pilote scored to make it 2–1, but Horton replied on a Toronto power-play opportunity to create a 2–2 deadlock going into the first intermission. Chicago went on to win 4–3, surviving a late goal by Mike Walton with Terry Sawchuk removed for an extra attacker.

The series was tied 2–2, but the talk after the game was more about the blood that had spurted all over the Gardens ice after a couple of incidents, one involving Horton, and one involving Chicago goalie Glenn Hall. Horton had been high-sticked in the nose by Hawks winger Dennis Hull after he had tried to cut between Horton and Stanley on a rush. The immediate diagnosis was a broken nose for Horton, putting his suitability for competition in the rest of the series into question. Hall, playing his first game of the series, took a shot from Jim Pappin in the face in the third. After playing 13 seasons without a mask, Hall lost his first tooth, and also had his lip sliced open. The gash required 25 stitches. The Hawks had won the game, but they would be forced to go back to Denis Dejordy for the pivotal Game Five contest at Chicago Stadium.

The Leafs remained well ahead of where they thought they'd be after Game One, but the series was eating away at their lineup. Horton was bloodied, George Armstrong had missed his second straight game with a knee problem, Pappin was walking with the assistance of a cane and an ineffective Frank Mahovlich had been on for three goals against in Game Four. The Montreal Canadiens, meanwhile, had already finished off the New York Rangers in four quick games. Habs coach Toe Blake said publicly that he favoured a matchup in the Stanley Cup final with the Leafs, not the Hawks, because his team would have home ice advantage against Toronto and had been more successful against the Leafs during the regular season. It was a sign of the times that a coach would speak in such a manner. Today, no coach at any level would ever be lured into suggesting one team would be a preferred opponent or an easier touch than another.

The Leaf loss in Game 4 ended the anthem flap, as "O Canada" was played at the Gardens two days later prior to a junior game. The defeat, meanwhile, had come on a Thursday, as had the loss in Game One. Superstition is superstition, but the Leafs would not lose a game on any other day of the week for the rest of the playoffs.

4 *Turnaround*

The Beatles had just broken up, or at least the process had formally begun, with Paul McCartney telling the world from London that he no longer "believed in the image."

An ocean away, as the Maple Leafs gathered for a players-only meeting at a Chicago hotel on January 30, 1967, it seemed their hockey dynasty was fraying at the edges and on the verge of falling apart. Every man—every Leaf—would get his chance to speak that day, and when it was time for Pete Stemkowski to have the floor, he knew exactly what the focus of his thoughts would be.

"That fucking Imlach," he began.

The proud team, loaded with future Hall of Famers and the winner of three Stanley Cups in the early part of the 1960s, had already tasted embarrassment the previous spring when it had been wiped out in the first round of the playoffs by the Montreal Canadiens, beaten easily in four straight games and outscored by a resounding 15–6 count. The 1966–67 season had started in decent fashion, with the club losing only once in its first nine games after Ontario premier John Robarts had dropped the puck on opening night at Maple Leaf Gardens. December, however, had included a weak effort in Montreal that seemed to indicate the team lacked spirit. Kent Douglas had gone to the aid of teammate Eddie Shack, who was in the middle of one of his countless battles with John Ferguson. Ferguson then turned his attention to Douglas and began to inflict a beating on the veteran Leaf defenceman. Afterwards, critics assailed a "gutless" Leaf team for failing to come to the defence of Douglas or to stand up to Ferguson and the Habs. January, meanwhile, had been a miserable month, beginning with a 4–0 loss to the powerful Blackhawks at Chicago Stadium on January 15. By the time the Leafs revisited Chicago two weeks later, they'd lost five consecutive games, and on January 29 were thumped again by Bobby Hull and crew, this time by a 5–1 score for their seventh straight defeat.

Back home, newspapers were surveying readers under the headlines "What People Say about the Losing Leafs." Just three years after their last Cup, no one, including the players, seemed to believe in the blue-and-white image any more. The Leafs were, by that point, the ninth year of Punch Imlach's reign, a distracted team, frayed at the edges and on the verge of falling apart entirely. Imlach himself was suffering from severe health problems. Terry Sawchuk talked non-stop of retirement and couldn't stay healthy. Frank Mahovlich was injured and spent his time running a travel agency and taking a speed-reading course. He had generally lost his zest for the game under Imlach. Shack had been benched—again. Douglas thought he had outfoxed Imlach by having a clause in his contract that said he couldn't be sent to the club's minor league team in Rochester. Instead, he ended up contemplating retirement when the Leaf boss shrugged and gave Douglas a ticket to Tulsa in the Central Hockey League. The team was so desperate for some kind of a boost that 39-year-old career minor leaguer Dick Gamble was called up from the minors for scoring help.

The players, meanwhile, were increasingly preoccupied with their various off-ice endeavours. Red Kelly was finished with politics but intrigued by a future NHL coaching career. Bob Pulford was plotting the creation of the players association with his agent, Alan Eagleson. Tim Horton, after unsuccessfully trying his hand at a hamburger stand and a car dealership, was busily growing a small collection of doughnut and coffee outlets into what would become an icon of Canadian business. Winger Larry Jeffrey was the "Hamburger King of Goderich," spending his summers operating Larry's Beach Bar in that Georgian Bay town. Jim Pappin had become involved working with horses at Woodbine race track, getting up every day at 6 a.m. to work with trainer Jerry Meyer before going home to change and then heading to practice. Players were making money on the stock market and everybody, it seemed, had something going. "We would finish practice and have a phone in each ear and one in our ass," said defenceman Bobby Baun.

The ugly loss to the Hawks on January 29 had dropped the Leafs to a mediocre 17–18–8 on the season—good enough to stay ahead of the youthful Boston Bruins and Detroit Red Wings for the final NHL playoff berth, but hardly the kind of quality season that anyone expected would lead to a championship. Many of the key forwards, including Dave Keon, Pulford and Mahovlich were having poor offensive seasons. Freshman Brian Conacher was one of the lone bright spots up front, finishing third in mid-season voting for the Calder Trophy as Rookie of the Year behind Bobby Orr of the Bruins and Chicago's Ed Van Impe.

At home, the team was far from the headlines, fading from the imagination of a Toronto public preoccupied with other matters. Expo '67 in Montreal was in the news every day. The Beatles were finished, but the Monkees were all the rage and on their way to town. So too, perhaps, was the Boston Strangler, who had escaped from jail, and authorities warned he could be headed north to Canada. The U.S. space program, which had created such a rush of excitement in its space race with the Russians, had just suffered its first tragedy when *Apollo One* had caught fire on the launch pad, killing three astronauts. The cost of new homes in Toronto was out of control, soaring to an average $30,000, up more than $5,500 in one year. The winter had been nasty, veering from bone-chilling cold fronts to messy, slushy greyness. In sports, Muhammad Ali was about to fight Ernie Terrell at the Astrodome in Houston, a controversial fight that had been earlier scheduled for Maple Leaf Gardens. The Green Bay Packers, commanded by the legendary Vince Lombardi, had just won the first Super Bowl and the Edmonton Eskimos and Hamilton Tiger-Cats had completed a spectacular eight-man trade, with quarterback Frank Cosentino heading west and receiver Tommy Joe Coffey bound for Steeltown.

Most of the Leaf news wasn't particularly heartwarming, including a story of how Byers Motors Ltd. was doing a lucrative business towing cars parked illegally outside the Gardens on game nights. Carl Brewer, meanwhile, was attracting attention 18 months after walking away from the Leafs, starring for the Canadian National team in a rousing 5–4 victory over the Soviet Union to capture the Centennial Hockey Tournament in Winnipeg before 10,642 fans. On January 10, Brewer returned to the Gardens for the first time in nearly two years as the Canadian Nats again defeated the touring Russians 4–3 before a raucous crowd of 15,878. "It's good to be with a winner," said Brewer after a reunion with former Leaf teammates such as Baun and Mahovlich.

It seemed the Leafs, in sharp contrast to Father David Bauer's spirited Nationals, were a fading bunch heading nowhere—a club either being snorted at in derision on the home front or ignored altogether. After an embarrassing December 21 loss to Montreal, famed hockey writer Red Fisher looked at the patchwork Leaf lineup filled with minor league call-ups and said, "Expansion had its first test last night and lost." Indeed, the spectre of six new teams and more than 100 new NHL jobs was front and centre as the league prepared for the most fundamental structural change in its history. Five of the new teams had named general managers, including Wren Blair, the man who had acquired Bobby Orr for the Bruins, in Minnesota, Lynn Patrick of the famous Patrick clan in St. Louis and Bud Poile in Philadelpia. These talent-hungry men were in Toronto constantly during the season, and the Leafs and other teams suspected they were cutting deals to lure established players to their virgin hockey territories.

The Original Six clubs would only be able to protect 10 skaters and one goaltender initially, leaving dozens of well-known players theoretically available to the new teams. All season long, it was widely understood that Kelly was headed to Los Angeles, probably as playing coach, as Jack Kent Cooke put the finishing touches on his $14-million Fabulous Forum. The Leafs fumed over the Kelly issue all season, and during one game Imlach had Larry Regan, the Kings first GM, tossed out of the Gardens. To the players, expansion meant new opportunities. "The big question was money," says Conacher. "Would expansion increase our salaries?"

It was just another distraction for the Leafs. With trade rumours in the air, the Leafs continued to plummet, and the situation seemed bleak at best. Imlach couldn't decide whether he wanted to encourage his troops or sneer at them. Asked about the fact that Chicago's Stan Mikita led the voting midway through the season for the Lady Byng Trophy—the award for gentlemanly conduct—Imlach took a shot at the passive nature of his team. "There shouldn't have been a vote," he said sarcastically. "The Maple Leafs deserve that trophy." Three days later, however, the Leaf coach was defiant. "I've never had a team finish out of the playoffs since I started coaching and this won't be the first one," he said.

History, of course, shows that the Leafs not only fixed their problems, they somehow went on to record their 11th Stanley Cup victory. In mid-season, the idea that the Leafs would be doused in ticker tape and confetti and cheered by throngs of fans, as their convoy moved slowly north on Bay Street in their fourth Stanley Cup parade in seven years, seemed utterly ludicrous. But it happened. While most have focused on the extraordinary upset victories over Chicago and then Montreal in the playoffs, the reality is this: The turn-around began much earlier, producing a team that was growing more confident by the time the playoffs rolled around in April, and, thus, was not necessarily the spectacular under-dog it was portrayed to be.

The season was filled with one mini-drama after another, the combination of a hockey-hungry city and a team filled with complex and confounding characters. But three key develop-ments changed the season. The first was the illness that befell Imlach in mid-February and helped alter the tenor of the cam-paign and the mood of the team. The second was a pivotal game, a 9–5 victory over the first place Blackhawks on March 18. It was the Leafs' largest offensive output of the season and infused the team with the sense it could beat the best the league had to offer. The third, it would seem, was that players-only meeting in Chicago back on the penultimate day of January.

Such meetings, of course, have become the cliché of modern sport—the usual reaction to losing, to which good and bad teams in all sports resort, with predictable regularity. When they are seen to work or have a positive impact on the team in question, they are interpreted as pivotal. When the results don't improve, the team meeting is quickly forgotten and the business of specu-lating about the coach's future or contemplating the possibility of major trades commences. Early in the 2003–04 NHL season, for example, Leaf captain Mats Sundin called a team meeting after the squad had limped listlessly through the first five games of a western road trip. That slump created speculation about the job security of head coach Pat Quinn. Two nights later, the club won in Vancouver, then ripped off seven more consecutive wins. Sundin's leadership was, not surprisingly, viewed as inspirational and incendiary. That the winning streak had mostly to do with goaltender Ed Belfour figuring out how to stop the puck again was merely a footnote.

---- ✿ ----

When captain George Armstrong called that meeting in January 1967, at the hotel in the Windy City, he knew he was taking a risk. He knew that there was deep-rooted dissatisfaction with Imlach, but he also understood that such a gathering might turn into just another session of complaining and that the team might be less cohesive afterwards, rather than more so. The '66–'67 Leafs were a very quiet, almost reserved team. They were a club without rah-rah leaders, a team that preferred to go about its business in a serious, low-key manner, with only brash winger Eddie Shack and boorish team vice-president Harold Ballard inclined to generate unnecessary headlines.

Several seasons earlier, pugnacious forward Bert Olmstead had served as the emotional epicentre of the team, one of the key reasons an 11-year Cup drought ended in 1962. Some, like Mahovlich, believed that Olmstead would have been an excellent replacement for Imlach as coach. But Olmstead had retired after the '62 playoffs and was no longer part of the organization. In Olmstead's wake, the club had won two more Cups, but the nagging question of whether the Leafs lacked leadership on the ice remained. Did the team need the kind of gregarious, noisy individual who could rouse the necessary passion one more time? Armstrong, who had played his first game for the Leafs way back in the 1949–50 season and been captain since 1957, was certainly respected, but he wasn't the flamboyant type, and getting this group of aging vets and stubborn youngsters to pull together was a major task. He'd heard the suggestion that he lacked fire many times over the years. Moreover, he wasn't as productive on the ice as he'd once been, and sports history is filled with the stories of players who tried to lead but could not because their inability to play at a high level meant others wouldn't listen and follow. Just as rumours began to circulate that 70-year-old Lester B. Pearson was about to retire as the country's prime minister, whispers about Armstrong's ability to lead the Leafs were again in vogue.

Born of Irish-Algonquin First Nations parentage, Armstrong grew up playing on natural ice in Falconbridge, Ontario, on the outskirts of Sudbury at a time when goal judges still stood behind the nets and signaled goals. Later, he moved 10 miles away to play on the same junior team, the Copper Cliff Redmen, as Horton. He signed a junior playing card with the Leafs organization as a 16-year-old with a deal that included $100 for signing, funds to cover his room, board, laundry, schooling and books, as well as $2.50 spending money every week. As a native Canadian, he was a pioneer in his sport, a forerunner to modern Canadian hockey players like Jordan Tootoo of the Nashville Predators—born of Inuit heritage in Churchill, Manitoba, and the darling of Team Canada at the 2003 World Junior Championships in Halifax—and Jonathan Cheechoo, a Cree from Moose Factory, Ontario, who burst into prominence with the San Jose Sharks in the 2004 Stanley Cup playoffs. Armstrong remembers feeling inferior growing up as "the only Indian kid in Falconbridge."

While Horton joined St. Mike's, a key part of the Leafs' junior chain, Armstrong wasn't even given the chance to play for the Toronto Marlboro Juniors. Instead, he was exiled to Stratford, Ontario, after the team's coach, Dave Pinkney, had asked Smythe if he had any extra players. Smythe took a list out of his pocket and pointed at Armstrong's name. "I have no idea if this guy can play, but if you have a spot for him, he's yours," said Smythe. It was in Stratford that teammates began calling Armstrong "Chief," a nickname that stuck with him his entire professional life. At first, he found the moniker uncomfortable, and today it would be taken as a clearly racist term. But Armstrong was a man of his time and came to take the name as a sign of respect and a reflection of the heritage for which he felt increasing pride. Later, his ability to take

"Indian" jokes as good-natured ribbing went a long way to his ability to lead the club as captain. At one point during the 1966–67 season, he received a letter imploring him to stop the controversial seal hunt in Canada. "Imagine asking an Indian to stop a massacre," Armstrong quipped. Bob Nevin experienced a very different reaction in New York after being traded to the Rangers by the Leafs. He would try out some of the same jokes used with Armstrong on defenceman Jim Neilson, a Cree band member from Saskatchewan. Neilson, predictably nicknamed Chief as well, didn't take the humour well; he would retreat into an emotional shell and wouldn't bounce back for several days.

While in Stratford, all Armstrong did was lead his league in scoring, winning MVP honours. He arrived at the Leaf camp in the fall of 1948 at a time when Toronto still had only five covered rinks, including Maple Leaf Gardens. There was Varsity Arena on the grounds of the University of Toronto, Ravina Gardens, a curling facility called Royals Rink, which reeked of cigar smoke when it was rented out to minor hockey teams in the evening and Icelandia, a 150-foot-long rink used mostly for children's hockey. Already big for pro hockey at a shade under 6-foot-2, Armstrong was the club's hottest young prospect by the '48 camp, and both he and Horton were allowed to skate with the big team for several weeks in the pre-season.

Smythe's son, Stafford, was just taking over the reins of the Marlies at the time, and the patriarch wished to give his son a stacked team and so told Armstrong the Marlies would be his new club. "If I wasn't good enough last year for the Marlies, then no way I'm going to play for them this year," replied Armstrong. "I'll play my junior back in Stratford or nowhere." Every day during camp, Smythe would summon Armstrong to his office. "No way," said Armstrong as the Leaf owner tried to convince him to join the Marlies. Armstrong threatened to quit, although he knew he was taking on one of the biggest names in professional hockey. "I was out of my league," he recalled. Finally, Smythe won the battle of wills, but Armstrong later speculated that their disagreement had convinced Smythe that his new recruit would make a fine captain. Years later, Smythe named one of his beloved racehorses Big Chief Army in honour of Armstrong. Only Charlie Conacher, one of the greatest Leafs ever, was ever recognized in similar fashion by the Leaf founder.

Armstrong never proved to be the scorer he'd been in junior hockey, but after finally cracking the Leaf lineup on a full-time basis in the 1952–53 season, he established himself as a strong positional player and outstanding corner man. For years, he was a fixture in the Leaf dressing room, generally rooming with one of the club's goalies. First it was Turk Broda, then Ed Chadwick, then Johnny Bower. Until 1960, three seasons into his run as Leaf captain, he still worked summers at a nickel mine near Sudbury. That year, he finally bought a home in the quiet, leafy Toronto neighbourhood of Leaside for $22,000 and has never moved.

When it came to hockey, he was a model citizen. "I did everything without complaining," he said. "I put hockey first, I put the team first. I told my wife before we got married that was how it was going to be. I could talk to guys because they knew I was team first. They knew I wasn't jealous of anybody else on the team. I was a damn good player, but not a great player." He learned lessons about leadership from his predecessor as Leaf captain, Ted Kennedy, and also learned to dislike team meetings after sitting through long, boring bitch-and-whine sessions with a series of Leaf teams during the 1950s that were wholly unproductive. To Armstrong, the meetings needed to be few and far between, short in duration and constructive, not filled with complaints.

When it came to the end of January 1967, he realized he needed to do something to try to help a team that was in obvious distress. "The key was for us to help ourselves," he recalled. "Never mind what we couldn't control, like the coach, the owner, the fans—whatever. How could we make ourselves a better hockey team?" Armstrong often kept notes on hotel stationery from around the NHL circuit, self-motivating reminders to help him stay focused on his job. "I've got to skate harder now that I'm older," read one. "Always keep myself between my check and our goal," read another. "Don't stay out on a shift too long," read another. He was no Norman Vincent Peale, certainly not a self-styled positive-thinking guru like Tony Robbins, the big-toothed self-promoter who hung around the Los Angeles Kings when they beat the Leafs in the '93 playoffs. But Armstrong was an intelligent, sensible man, and he knew he needed a plan for the January 30 meeting.

He instinctively understood that this Leaf team, filled with experienced, older players who had enjoyed a great deal of success, didn't need to be led. It needed to be focused and reminded of its abilities. He didn't need to be a charismatic general, or an inspiration to others, or a father figure. He didn't need to tell Mahovlich or Kelly or Sawchuk what to do or where to go. He needed to be a brother, perhaps an older brother, to a group of teammates that had become disorganized and lacked unity.

Instead of turning into yet another Imlach-hating session, he wanted this meeting to be different. So he went first and began talking of his own shortcomings, how he could work harder and contribute more. As prearranged by the Leaf captain, goaltender Johnny Bower went next. "I haven't been playing that well," he started, detailing weaknesses in his game. And so it went, veteran after veteran focusing on himself, just as Armstrong had planned and had rehearsed with his shadow cabinet. When Stemkowski and others jumped in to register their usual complaints about Imlach, his practice regimen and his abrasive manner, a player like Tim Horton or

Allan Stanley would interrupt. "Listen to what Chief said. Stick to how we can help ourselves." It proved to be a helpful, effective meeting that players still remember. "[Armstrong] was the best captain I ever played with," says Marcel Pronovost, who played 15 years with Detroit with captains like Ted Lindsay, Alex Delvecchio and Sid Abel. "His ability to take the pressure off the team was incredible."

Most members of that team vividly remember the meeting and the sense that it galvanized the players. Still, the Leafs promptly went out and lost three more games to run their losing streak to 10 games. The 10th defeat was a 5–2 setback to Gordie Howe and the Red Wings at the Gardens. With Sawchuk out with back problems, Bower also injured his knee, giving way to Bruce Gamble for the third period. The team's goal-scoring seemed to have dried up completely, and the loss dropped the Leafs to fifth place. After the game, a Canadian soldier recently returned from Vietnam, Frank Williams of Kingston, Ontario, approached Imlach and offered him an emblem of the U.S. 101st Airborne Division. "It might bring you luck," said Williams. Imlach put the emblem on his hat, not knowing the unusual nature of the events to come.

The next day, headlines screamed about the lack of choices for the plummeting club. "No Leaf Shuffle—Because the Cupboard Is Bare," blared *The Star*. With Jim Pappin and Larry Hillman already recalled to help stop the slide, none of the three minor pro affiliates, Tulsa of the Central Hockey League, Victoria of the Western Hockey League or Rochester of the American Hockey League, seemed to offer a special player who could single-handedly alter the club's fortunes. Tulsa was last in the Central with only uninspiring forwards Marc Reaume and Gary Veneruzzo in its lineup. Victoria was fifth in the Western league, and its best players were Andy Hebenton and Milan Marcetta. Rochester, meanwhile, boasted a lineup almost as aged as the Leafs, with the aforementioned Gamble on the wing,

36-year-old Bronco Horvath and playing coach Al Arbour, a 34-year-old defenceman. Sprinkled throughout these teams were younger players like Mike Corrigan, King Clancy's son Terry, Jim McKenny, Wayne Carleton and Nick Harbaruk, but they were not yet ready for the big leagues. Brit Selby, who had played so well for the Leafs the previous season that he'd won the Calder trophy as the NHL's top rookie, had come to training camp overweight and been exiled to the Vancouver Canucks of the Western league, taking a 30 per cent pay cut with him. By February, he'd been lost as a possible reinforcement after suffering a serious knee injury.

That absence of eager replacements, suggested *The Star's* Jim Proudfoot, had created a "smug complacency" on the Leafs. There was ongoing speculation that King Clancy was to take over as coach. Clancy, a long-time Leaf stalwart as well as an NHL official, had joined the Leafs in no particular role during Howie Meeker's brief coaching tenure, stayed on through the Billy Reay years and then had become Imlach's assistant general manager in 1958. "If Imlach goes, I go," bellowed the 5-foot-7 Irishman, a teetotaler with an impish grin and ready laugh. The team owned a sorry record of 17–21–8, but Bower came to the defence of Imlach. "What's he ever done except put money in our pockets since he came here?" asked the Leaf goaltender.

Slowly, the Leafs began to improve. At the end of a bitterly cold week in which temperatures dropped to minus 12 degrees Fahrenheit, the coldest days since 1950, they earned a 4–4 tie with high-flying Chicago at the Gardens. The next night in Boston, they squeezed out a 2–1 win over the last place Bruins, their first triumph in 29 days. Bower, forced into action because Gamble had taken a hard shot from Dennis Hull in the arm the night before, was strong in net, although he wondered whether Armstrong's tradition of being the roommate of the club's goalies was worth continuing. "It's a wonder I wasn't too stiff to move out there," said Bower.

"[Armstrong] opened a window last night and it was so cold two oranges on the sill froze solid."

Kelly, who would score only 14 times that season after lighting the red lamp just eight times the year before, came up with one that night in Boston. In an indication of what was to come, Stemkowski potted the winner on an assist from Pappin. Three nights later, a 6–0 romp over the Rangers made the Leafs unbeaten in three, an encouraging string of successes, but that didn't stop the circulation of major trade rumours. The most intriguing was a report that suggested the Leafs and Bruins had all but agreed on a swap that would have sent Pulford or perhaps Stemkowski, Shack and Mike Walton to Beantown for Johnny Bucyk, Murray Oliver and defenceman Ted Green. But an injury to Green on the previous Saturday night had postponed the proposed deal. "The way I'm playing is enough of a problem right now," said Pulford when asked about the rumours.

Beginning with a gruelling 36-day training camp that included 15 exhibition games, the Leaf training staff had its hands full during the season. It all came down to the age of the Leaf team. Bower and Stanley were both in their forties. Five more players were 36 or older. During training camp team physician Dr. Hugh Smythe, son of Conn and brother of Stafford, told Imlach "except for one or two exceptions, your players are soft." This comment motivated Imlach to increase the length of the two-a-day practice sessions to whip the team into shape. The man in charge of the training staff was Bobby Haggert, who worked with his assistant, Tommy Nayler, and non-staff physiotherapist Karl (The Healer) Elieff to keep as many Leafs as possible healthy. At the time, attitudes towards injuries were, to put it mildly, rather medieval. It took several years for Haggert to convince Imlach to let him bring Elieff into the fold on a semi-permanent basis. "You can imagine how hard it was to convince them at a time when a cough for a player could send him to the minors," says Haggert.

Elieff was at the cutting edge of his profession, while Nayler was a canny inventor who, along with longtime Gardens ice magician Doug Morris, could come up with unique solutions to equipment problems. He invented the tendon guard and protective tongue for skates, and the portable skate sharpener. Some of Nayler's ideas actually extended the careers of players. In 1962, for example, the Leafs acquired Douglas in a trade, not knowing his left shoulder tended to pop out periodically and cause him to miss games. Nayler found a shoulder harness from the University of Maryland that he tailored to Douglas' needs. In the 1962–63 season, Douglas played all 70 games and won league honours as top rookie. The following summer, while driving without the harness on, his shoulder popped out when he used his arm to signal a left turn.

No one could match Nayler's expertise at the skate sharpener, and his fame in that area led opposing players to ask him to work on their skates. Famous figure skater Barbara Ann Scott visited from Ottawa to have Nayler shave her blades into shape. Nayler, who was born in West Bromwich, England, and had been with the Leafs since 1927, never sought any patents for his many inventions. In 1972, as Team Canada's equipment manager for the Summit Series against the Soviets, he flew overseas ahead of the team and determined that the ice in Moscow was harder than in Canada. He sharpened Team Canada's skates with deeper grooves, an adjustment that many later credited as being an important factor in the unforgettable series. Haggert left the team in 1968, Elieff closed his clinic at the Gardens in 1974, and Nayler retired in 1977, although Imlach vowed to convince him to return when he came back to manage the Leafs in 1979. When Nayler died in 1981, it was widely suggested that his contributions to the game were so significant that he should be considered for induction into the Hockey Hall of Fame. But that has never happened.

—————— ❦ ——————

With Haggert and his colleagues struggling to keep as many players on the ice as possible, and with the Leafs still not sure whether they had anything left with which to fuel a Stanley Cup charge, lightning struck. On the morning of February 18, a home game against Boston, the 48-year-old Imlach was rushed to Toronto General Hospital. The initial diagnosis was "complete exhaustion," but the fear was the imperious Leaf coach had suffered a heart attack, because he had shooting pains in his left arm. Years earlier, while coaching the minor pro Quebec Aces, Imlach had suffered a "breakdown" in mid-season, forcing his pal Joe Crozier to do his job for the remainder of that season. In February 1967, Crozier was working for the Leafs' top farm club in Rochester, but instead of asking to him to stand in for Imlach, the Leaf brain trust turned to Clancy.

At 63 years of age, Clancy had no coaching record to speak of. But he knew the team and its array of personalities and took over behind the bench to face rookie Bobby Orr and the Bruins. Already having recovered from their 10-game losing streak, the Leafs nonetheless seemed energized by their new coach rather than buffeted by the shock of Imlach's sudden departure. Pappin, unable to secure a steady role with the Leafs to that point in the season, scored the winning goal in a 5–3 victory over the Bruins. Meanwhile, the mercurial Walton was the best Leaf on the ice after having been on the verge of demotion to the minors. Suddenly, everything felt different in the Leaf camp. The atmosphere was lighter, the practices were easier with fewer wind sprints—"We couldn't believe it," says Stemkowski—and players who had fallen out of favour with Imlach were once again given an opportunity under Clancy.

Imlach was initially expected to miss only a few days, but the immediate success of Clancy spawned a flurry of speculation as to whether Imlach would return at all. Four days after beating Boston, the Clancy-led Leafs won again, this time beating the Stanley Cup champion Montreal Canadiens by a 5–2 score. Bower was left slightly miffed with the result, since a local butcher had promised him three free steaks for every shutout he registered. After an experiment in practice, meanwhile, Clancy had gone with a hunch and put together Pulford, Pappin and Stemkowski on a line that would prove to be crucial to the rest of the season.

The next day in Detroit, Clancy took a walk after breakfast with Jim Gregory, a young executive in the Leaf organization who had been summoned to help out in Imlach's absence. As the two men strolled, a bird flew by and deposited its contents on Clancy's hat. "He was swearing and cursing, but I reminded him that it was good luck to have that happen," recalls Gregory. With Sawchuk back in net after a lengthy absence, the Leafs beat the Wings that night, with Walton again outstanding on the attack. The win moved the Leafs back up to third and improved Clancy's record to three wins against no losses. "He injects his own enthusiasm into us," said Ron Ellis. "And he gives everybody a chance, sends them out and roots for them. You have to go for a guy like that." After the win, team president Stafford Smythe indicated Clancy would coach only two more games.

Reports from hospital, meanwhile, suggested Imlach was suffering from a hiatus hernia, not heart problems. Suspicious writers began to wonder if Imlach was really still running the team from his hospital bed, using a "hot line" to instruct Clancy on his every move. "Instead of the hot line, you should call it 'information, please' because I do most of the talking," responded Clancy. Clancy, however, did reveal one direct order from his boss. "He told me to check and see if his new car was ready," said the interim Leaf coach.

McKenny, a flamboyant young defenceman just a year removed from junior hockey, scored his first NHL goal in the next game, a 4–0 win over Detroit. The next night in New York with Stanley hurt, Clancy made the unusual decision on his 64th birthday to shift Horton to left defence from right defence and partner him with McKenny. The Leafs won again 4–2 with goals from Walton and Pappin, pushing Clancy to a perfect 5–0 and giving the Leafs their seventh straight win. The daily grind had now given way to a more relaxed atmosphere, and the wins were certainly helping. "They went from Punch to King, who basically just let them do whatever the hell they wanted," said Gregory. Clancy even handed the practice whistle over to Gregory one day. "A real Imlach protégé—same sweet disposition," grumbled Stemkowski after the 30-minute workout.

Clancy appeared headed for his first defeat March 1 in Montreal, but Pappin tied the game with 11 seconds to go to salvage a 1–1 draw. Clancy, meanwhile, had refused to clean the bird poop off his hat after winning in Detroit, and he'd also worn the same shirt and socks throughout his six-game unbeaten streak. Clearly, there was at least the possibility that Clancy would continue to coach the team, and that Imlach wouldn't return anytime soon. The more Clancy won, the more speculation it fuelled. Horton came to the defence of his ailing coach. "Aww, Punch had us straightened out before his health gave out," said Horton. "He proved he was a real man during that 10-game losing streak. He could have blasted us in the news media, made wholesale line changes and taken us apart verbally behind closed doors. He did none of those things." While many of the younger players, not to mention the sensitive Mahovlich, were happier with Clancy than Imlach, Horton's statements made it clear that Imlach still had his loyalists in the dressing room, including Horton, Bower and Armstrong. "It didn't matter if it was Imlach or anyone else," recalls Armstrong. "The players had to do it for themselves."

On March 4, two weeks after being admitted, Imlach was released from hospital and immediately made the 10-minute drive to the Gardens. "I made the doctors a lot of promises to get out of that hospital," said Imlach. He stayed at the Gardens for two hours, shuffling some paperwork, and then drove home in his shiny new car. He didn't stay for that night's game against the Hawks in which the Leafs triumphed again by a 3–0 score, a game that included Armstrong's 250th career goal and the 100th shutout of Sawchuk's dazzling career. After the game, Sawchuk circulated in the Leaf dressing room, "totally nude and eternally grateful," according to *The Toronto Telegram*, shaking the hand of each teammate.

The next night in Chicago before a jammed stadium of 20,000 fans, Clancy finally lost, with the Leafs going down to a 5–2 defeat. Imlach returned to the office two days later, immediately making a slew of minor-league roster moves, sending goalie Gary Smith from Rochester to Victoria, moving Red Armstrong and Corrigan from Rochester to Tulsa, and directing Douglas to get himself from Oklahoma to New York State to join the Americans. Clancy moved to 7–1–1 the next night against Montreal, with the Leafs victimizing a leaky Rogatien Vachon in the Montreal net, a story that would be revisited in the coming months. Imlach watched from a north end perch usually reserved for Clancy, and was approached by Montreal GM Sam Pollack after the game. "How you feeling?" asked Pollock. "Better than you right now," responded Imlach with a chuckle.

Clancy's notion to create a line of Stemkowski, Pulford and Pappin had given the club offensive firepower it had lacked earlier in the season. Clancy coached his final game that season on March 11 against the Rangers, with the Leafs earning a 2–2 tie to complete Clancy's run with seven wins, one loss and two draws. Harold Ballard, on behalf of Smythe, unsuccessfully tried to convince Imlach to stay away for another two weeks. Imlach, however, returned to the Leaf bench the next day in Chicago, and the Leafs were slaughtered 5–0 as the Blackhawks clinched first place in the NHL for the first time in 40 years. After Clancy departed, Imlach would guide the team to a mediocre 6–5 record the rest of the season, perhaps an indication that the team wasn't that happy to see him back.

But three weeks without their taskmaster had clearly bene-fited the Leafs and given them a mid-winter break in the dog days of the NHL season that leave even the most motivated players short of inspiration. "It was a breath of fresh air," recalls Mahovlich, who was already hoping that it would be his last season under Imlach in Toronto. Whether the Leafs would have gone on to win the Cup with Clancy as coach, or whether Imlach would have been just as successful if he hadn't fallen ill, are hypothetical questions that tickle the imagination. But 10 games with Clancy clearly helped some well-worn veterans prepare for one last gasp of championship quality and demon-strated that a group of young, unproven players—Stemkowski, Pappin and Conacher, specifically—were ready to be trusted with primary roles in the post-season tournament.

———— ❦ ————

Armstrong's January meeting in Chicago had helped to re-unite a fractured team, and Clancy's infectious laugh had provided them with a new sense of joyful energy. Two March games, the 19th at home against Chicago and the next day in Detroit, gave the Leafs a final confidence boost that would carry them into the first round of the playoffs. Against the Hawks, the Leafs rolled to a rollicking 9–5 triumph, ripping six goals past all-star goalie Glenn Hall and another three past his backup, Denis Dejordy. The team that had managed to score only 15 goals while losing 10 straight games had once again found its scoring touch. "Those were nine important goals for us," said Imlach. The always analytical Keon suggest-ed afterwards that the Hawks' blueline corps had seemed vulnerable to the heavy forecheck the Leafs had thrown at them, a strategy that would appear again in the playoffs.

Conacher, meanwhile, delivered thundering bodychecks on both Stan Mikita, the league's leading scorer, and Chicago rearguard Doug Jarrett—a hint of the physical role he would play in the games ahead.

For Reay and the Hawks, meanwhile, it was a blow to their collective ego. That loss was a worrisome result for a team that had beaten the Leafs and captured the Stanley Cup for the first time in 23 years in 1961, but had since stumbled repeatedly in big games despite a talented lineup. Quite clearly, the Hawks were hoping to play the Rangers in the first round of the play-offs, but they would end up playing the Leafs under the quirky, illogical system that in those days saw the first-place team play the third-place team in the first round, while the second-place team played the fourth-place squad. Rewarding the team that finished second in such a way, however, was probably no more absurd than the following season when the NHL herded all six expansion teams into one division and allowed the winner of that grouping to advance to the Stanley Cup final.

The next day after demolishing the Hawks, the Leafs fell behind 4–1 in Detroit but stormed back to win 6–5. The win gave them 15 goals for their weekend's work, the same offensive total they'd mounted during that ugly 29-day drought earlier. "What's all that guff about that gang not giving out for Punch?" demanded Gordie Howe after the game. "If they weren't giving 120 per cent in that game, I'm a singer midget." The Leafs still had seven games left to play in the tumultuous '66–'67 season, and they would win four of them. Despite repeated overtures from, among others, Boston GM Hap Emms, they had declined to make a blockbuster trade as they had three years earlier by acquiring Andy Bathgate from the Rangers.

Ron Ellis had led the team with only 22 goals, just ahead of Pappin, who had roared to the finish to end up with 21. Stars like Keon and Mahovlich hadn't even managed to pot 20 goals, while Armstrong had scored just nine times in 70 games.

The goalies, Sawchuk and Bower, had been repeatedly injured as had Baun, the hero of the '64 Cup chase. The success of the team under Clancy had brought into question Imlach's coaching skills. There were tensions within the team that exploded at a March 31 practice when Stemkowski and Bower exchanged angry words. Later, Pappin, who earlier in the season had injured Gamble in practice with a shot to the throat, also argued with Bower. Keon and Baun exchanged shoves, and Jeffrey and Hillman dropped the gloves and fought at practice. But the team had clearly rebounded from many of its troubles and believed it still had the ingredients to create a championship finale.

Keon was one player who understood that much was going on behind the scenes at the Gardens. He had caught the scent of decay in the air that might make this the last serious Cup challenge for a long time. "It was the last stand for a group of veterans as they forged a quiet spirit within," recalls Keon. "We wanted to be successful and win. " By the early days of April, the Leafs were poised to prove their team could yet again be more than the mere sum of its parts.

Alexandra Studios/Courtesy of the Stan Obodiak Collection

Three originals leaving for training camp in the 1930s: Conn Smythe (centre) with trainer Tim Daly (left) and publicist Frank Selke. During the Second World War, Selke showed outstanding hockey acumen in overseeing the team in Smythe's absence, something the Major would resent upon his post-war return. Ultimately forced out of the Leaf organization by Smythe, Selke would go on to success as the general manager of the Montreal Canadiens from 1946 to 1964.

Graphic Artists Photographers/Courtesy of the Stan Obodiak Collection

Red Kelly and the
Stanley Cup in 1963.

Toronto Maple Leaf dressing room as the team prepares for a third consecutive run at the Stanley Cup in 1964. Left to right: Kent Douglas, Allan Stanley, Bob Nevin, Carl Brewer, Red Kelly, Tim Horton, Don Simmons and Johnny Bower. A few weeks later Nevin would be involved in a trade to the New York Rangers.

Graphic Artists Photographers/Courtesy of the Stan Obodiak Collection

Dave Keon with the Conn Smythe Trophy he won as the Most Valuable Player in the 1967 playoffs. Though the Leaf organization honoured Terry Sawchuk with an internal award as the playoff MVP and Jim Pappin's mother on her deathbed still believed "her son should have won the award," no player inside the Leaf dressing room could dispute the selection of Keon.

Graphic Artists Photographers/Courtesy of the Stan Obodiak Collection

Bob Pulford sips from one of the four Stanley Cups the Leafs won in the 1960s, while Alan Eagleson looks on. Their friendship would stand the test of time and circumstances. While most Leafs of that era view Eagleson with disdain or in a negative light, Pulford has remained a friend and ally four decades later.

One Canadian institution, the Dionne Quintuplets, wearing the sweaters of another Canadian institution – the Toronto Maple Leafs.

Lineup around Maple Leaf Gardens for playoff tickets in the early 1960s.

Future Leaf captain George Armstrong, with Harold Ballard and Leaf coach Joe Primeau on a promotional visit to an "Indian Reservation" in 1950. The 20-year-old Armstrong was given the honorary title "Chief Shoot the Puck." He would play that season for Pittsburgh in the American Hockey League and crack the Leaf lineup for good a year later.

Bob Pulford (left) and Frank Mahovlich give team president Stafford Smythe an impromptu shower after winning the 1963 Stanley Cup. Mahovlich would later become alienated from Leaf management, specifically GM/coach Punch Imlach, while Smythe personally engineered Pulford's trade to Los Angeles in 1970.

Brian Conacher, one of the unsung heroes of the 1967 playoff drive. He never again participated in a Stanley Cup playoff game.

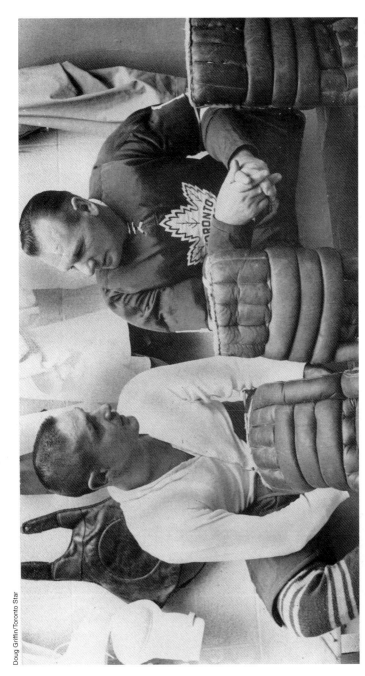

Terry Sawchuk and Johnny Bower confer in training camp, September 1966. Bower was injured five different times before Christmas. Sawchuk had had off-season surgery he believed had solved his back problems, but by mid-season he was hobbled again.

DEFEAT DOES NOT REST

...LIGHTLY ON THEIR SHOULDERS

Courtesy of the Stan Obodiak Collection

Four generations of the Smythe family (Conn with son Stafford, grandson Tommy and great-grandson Tommy Jr.) in the Leaf dressing room in 1970. Conn would have no idea that in a year's time his son would be dead and the "house that Smythe built" would be in the control of Harold Ballard.

GAME FIVE
MAPLE LEAFS AT CHICAGO, APRIL 15, 1967

By the spring of 1967, Leonard (Red) Kelly was no longer a Member of Parliament, having relinquished his seat and the gruelling schedule that went with it two years earlier. He'd never make it to the Senate, as teammate Frank Mahovlich would one day, but he would have made a perfect addition to that snoozy upper chamber of sober second thought. Kelly, after all, had perfected the art of napping while on the job, including catching a few winks in between periods of important hockey games. After a 20-minute period of intense NHL activity, Kelly would lean back on his seat in the Leaf dressing room, one leg slightly crossed over the other, and sleep. "It was a quiet group," recalls Peter Stemkowski. "Red was especially quiet. He never said anything. I wondered what he did in Parliament if he never spoke. He would fall asleep during intermission and someone would nudge him when there were two or three minutes to go. He was just so quiet. The exception would be in places like Montreal where we would have an hour or so to kill at the train station before we had to board. We'd gab a bit and have a few beers. Red would have one, maybe two beers, and then he'd never shut up once we got on the train."

————— ⚜ —————

For Game Five of the 1967 Stanley Cup playoffs against the Chicago Blackhawks, a first-round series that had turned into a surprisingly tight competition, Kelly and the Leafs were poised to experience another awakening, a summons back to the determined, never-say-die greatness of Leaf teams of the past. That, after all, was how the Leafs had defined themselves as a franchise, particularly in the post-war years of the 1940s and early 1950s, as NHL stars were gradually coming back from Europe and Asia to reassert themselves as professional athletes. Some suggest that the success of the Maple Leafs during that period, which included six Stanley Cup victories from 1942 to 1951, was largely the result of being the best team in a league diluted by the departure of so many talented players to the Second World War, some of whom never returned to play.

That it became a time when the Leafs defined themselves to the nation, however, cannot be denied. Conn Smythe presented himself as the consummate patriot, seeking active duty in the Second World War after having been involved in the First World War. The Leafs developed a group of players and a team concept that appealed to the Canadian public. The 1941–42 Leafs fired the imagination with one of the greatest comebacks in NHL history, storming back after losing the first three games of the Cup final to Detroit to win in seven games. Stars like Gordie Drillon and Bucko McDonald were benched at the turning point of the series in favour of less heralded players, establishing in the hero-starved public's mind the ideal sense of a true team.

As Canada and the world were recovering from the spasms of inter-national conflict, Leafs like Syl Apps and Ted Kennedy were perceived as honest, clean-living professionals, men who epitomized the concept of gentleman-athlete. Chubby Turk Broda was an everyman character in net with his public battle of the bulge. After being seriously injured in the European theatre, Howie Meeker, an NHL rookie-of-the-year before the war, came back to the league and resuscitated his career. It was the golden age for the Leafs, a team in which Canadians, particularly English Canadians, saw a reflection of their best instincts and possibilities. After the great conflict, ordinary people began to reorganize their lives, which included a blitz of family growth that became known as the baby boom. The Leafs were a championship hockey team, but even more important, a Canadian institution worthy of admiration at a time when people didn't ask probing questions of such institutions.

As the 1950s wore on and further success eluded the Leafs, that image and mystique largely held, but began to chip at the edges. When Stafford Smythe took over as team president in 1961 from his father, Conn, the Leafs and the business of hockey began to take centre stage in the public's mind. That was partly because the Leafs were changing, and partly because the explosive cultural changes of the 1960s were fanning out into all walks of life. People were starting to look at everything in a different way.

On March 21, 1964, Canada's national magazine, *Maclean's*, published a story written by Peter Gzowski, who would later find fortune and fame as a beloved broadcaster on the CBC. Titled "The Maple Leaf Money Machine," Gzowski's piece chronicled the extensive business success of the Leafs, from selling out all of their games from 1946 on to being the darlings of *Hockey Night in Canada* to having players make money from sponsoring products they didn't even use. "In the world of sports promotion, where nearly everyone loses money and where even the winners have off-years, this makes the Gardens—whose profits are unaffected by war, peace, the economy or how many goals they score—appear to be the original money machine," wrote Gzowski.

The article caused a sensation, and the Leafs reacted with outrage. *Maclean's* advertising executives, meanwhile, were none too pleased that

Gzowski had poked fun at Schick razors as part of his story. An ad by the company claimed that all the Leafs had one day received a comfortable shave using a single razor, but Gzowski nosed around and found none of the players had actually used the product. It was indicative of the clashing cultures between editorial and advertising at the magazine, and several months later Gzowski and several of his superiors all quit in a huff after a different piece was killed while virtually on the presses and without consultation. In his summary of the incident and the problems that had been brewing at *Maclean's* for months, Gzowski wrote a piece for *The Canadian Forum* entitled "The Day the Schick Hit the Fan."

With respect to the "Money Machine" piece, the Leafs were not used to being portrayed in this way, and they didn't much like it. "In that period, the media treated the Maple Leafs and their leadership as almost beyond criticism," says acclaimed journalist Robert Fulford, who worked with Gzowski at *Maclean's* when the feature article was published. "I myself had started at *The Globe and Mail* in 1950 when the publisher of the newspaper was on the board of the Leafs. So we just said nothing against Conn Smythe or the Leafs. *The Globe and Mail* ran as a branch press office of the Maple Leafs, as far as I could tell. With the Gzowski piece, well, it was the way he treated the Leafs. He treated them in a light-hearted way, not as this serious institution." Gzowski left the magazine of his own accord, but the Leafs, when challenged, had earlier demonstrated a willingness to intimidate members of the media. When *Globe and Mail* columnist Scott Young, the father of legendary rock star Neil Young, told a *Hockey Night in Canada* audience that the stories of selling Frank Mahovlich to the Chicago Blackhawks in 1962 were, in his estimation, phony rumours designed to grab newspaper headlines, he was bounced from the program as a regular commentator. The sense of the Leafs in the community was clearly evolving into something new, something other than a symbol of pure national pride and patriotism.

Over the past four decades, it can be argued, the Leafs' carefully sculpted image has disappeared entirely, and has been replaced by something less warm and homespun. Yet it can also be argued that the Leafs have never been more popular nor profitable than they are today. They're a team that always plays to capacity audiences in a glittering lakeside playpen, owns its own television outlet and rakes in millions and millions of dollars in annual profits despite decades of on-ice disappointments. Even during the disgraceful years in which Harold Ballard controlled the franchise, some of which ended with the Leafs holding the worst record in the NHL, fan interest never wavered, at least not to the point where there were substantial numbers of empty seats or silenced television sets.

We have seen over the course of the 20th century and into the 21st that the impression professional sports teams leave in their community changes and morphs as time goes by. Lovable losers become efficient champs. Long-established teams like the Brooklyn Dodgers and Cleveland Browns pick up stakes and move elsewhere. Titans become also-rans, ignored in the same buildings that once were filled with screaming, adoring patrons. It would be a mistake to see the mystique of the Leafs from the Second World War to today as a simple continuum. Rather, it seems apparent that while undeniably popular, the manner in which the Leafs are viewed in Toronto and across Canada has changed fundamentally.

As NHL teams have taken root in cities like Vancouver, Calgary, Edmonton, Winnipeg, Ottawa and Quebec City, the passion for the Leafs across the nation has become diffused. At the same time, the hockey team has become more of a parochial interest, a weird

Toronto-kind-of-thing—the target of local spite after defeats and public missteps. But the Leafs are also something that those who define themselves as Leaf fans will aggressively defend from outside attacks. Thousands of Leaf fans will still show up to cheer on their favourites when the club visits western Canada, Buffalo, Ottawa or Montreal. More often than not they are either transplanted Torontonians or Torontonians who, because they couldn't afford or acquire tickets at the Air Canada Centre, have bought plane and train tickets to travel to see the Leafs.

Over the decades, the Leafs have become less a focus of intense admiration, and more the beneficiaries of an extraordinary devotion, drawing an almost cult-like support from what has come to be described in both affectionate and derogatory terms as the Leaf Nation. Tickets to Leaf games are easily sold for well above their face value. Season ticket holders willingly pay expensive "seat licences" just for the privilege of controlling tickets, and the team has become accepted more as a band of rock stars than a hockey club. The more outrageous the behaviour, the greater the depth of blind, unconditional devotion. The Leafs have endured the Ballard years, near constant losing, an unimaginable pedophile scandal in the mid-'90s and relentless gouging of their customers—and have still emerged as popular and profitable as ever.

The corporate community—often reluctant to support sporting ventures in Canada and particularly those with controversial elements—has flocked to the Leafs with millions of dollars in seat and luxury suite sales. Toronto's cultural mosaic, meanwhile, has changed drastically since the 1960s, but that hasn't hurt the Leafs. A 2003 census said almost 37 per cent of Greater Toronto's 4.6 million residents were visible minorities, up 15 per cent from just five years earlier. Many of those minorities are from non-hockey cultures or countries, yet in Toronto many have been drawn to the traditionally lily-white sport of hockey and the Leafs.

In theory, the changing nature of Toronto's cultural composition should have shifted allegiances to other sports and teams, but it hasn't. Members of these same ethnic groups didn't flock to the Argonauts of the Canadian Football League or the Blue Jays of Major League Baseball. Both franchises saw their attendance drop off drastically in the mid-1990s at the same time that Toronto's cultural composition became more diverse. The Raptors of the National Basketball Association offered a new and different challenge to the Leaf dominance of the Toronto sporting scene, and the Leafs solved that challenge rather neatly by purchasing the Raptors in 1998 and installing them as co-tenants at the Air Canada Centre.

This cultural dynamic, which still places the Leafs and hockey at the top of the sports pyramid, was probably best symbolized when Anson Carter, a flamboyant, dreadlocked Canadian, who was born of Barbadian immigrants in the Toronto suburb of Scarborough, scored the goal in overtime that won the 2003 World Hockey Championship for Canada. Later that year, a young black man named Anthony Stewart emerged from the tough environs of a downtown Toronto housing project, known as Regent Park, to become a first-round draft pick of the Florida Panthers and then to grab one of the highly coveted positions on the Canadian National Junior Team heading to the world championships in Finland. The city had changed, but the dream of being a pro-hockey player had survived and reached new cultures, as had the soaring appeal of the Leafs.

Different cultural and ethnic groups have thus become part of the Leaf Nation, which contains members so dedicated to the glorification of the Leafs that they will argue passionately that Ballard wasn't such a bad guy, and that 1970s enforcer Dave (Tiger) Williams truly belongs in the Hockey Hall of Fame. There are those who view Lanny McDonald's semifinal overtime winner against the Islanders in 1978 on the same level as Paul Henderson's winner against the Soviets in the '72 Summit Series, and recall referee Kerry Fraser's non-call of a high stick by Los Angeles centre Wayne Gretzky on Leaf centre Doug Gilmour in the 1993 playoffs as one of the great sporting crimes of all times—right up there with the Black Sox scandal of the 1919 World Series. The Leafs are like a hockey version of baseball's Chicago Cubs—being the butt of jokes from all corners has not diminished the support of the Leaf Nation.

Those who bleed blue and white may accept the inevitability of defeat, rarely honestly viewing the Leafs as a team capable of actually winning a Stanley Cup championship. But that realization does not diminish their passion. Interestingly, as the city has grown gradually more diverse, cosmopolitan and outward-looking, the affection for its hockey team has become more of a local phenomenon. During the 1990s, as the NHL exploded from a 21-team league to 30 teams, with established teams in Winnipeg and Quebec City moving south of the border, there was a tangible change in NHL interest across Canada. Kids collected hockey cards for profit, not to trade them among friends and treasure those of their favourite players as they did 30 years earlier. Whereas once fans understood the various minutiae of NHL statistics, now they knew what the big names of their favourite teams like Gretzky and Yzerman were doing, but the activities of clubs in far-flung places like Dallas and Nashville seemed remote.

After peaking with the exciting 1993 and 1994 playoffs, the league devolved into a style that featured low-scoring, clutch-and-grab games that drained the game of style and creativity at the same time that the cost of tickets was skyrocketing. By the 2003–04 season, an average of only 5.1 goals was being scored per NHL match, a figure that dropped another 15 per cent in the playoffs. In the 2004 Stanley Cup final, Tampa Bay and Calgary went the seven-game distance, with Tampa winning, but only managed to score a combined 27 goals.

Fifty-goal scorers, the players that make the imagination soar, became rare. At the 2004 NHL entry draft in Raleigh, NC, Wayne Gretzky suggested that the league might never again see a 50-goal scorer. At the same time, an influx of players from countries like Sweden, Slovakia, the Czech Republic, Russia and Finland brought undeniably talented athletes who were far more distant figures to Canadian fans, accustomed for years to watching boys who had grown up in Toronto, Timmins or Winnipeg. Somehow, however, as affection for the league seemed to decline temporarily in different parts of Canada, with sagging attendance for a time in Calgary, Edmonton, Vancouver and even Montreal, interest in the Maple Leafs seemed to intensify in the Toronto market. Where once stars like Frank Mahovlich and Darryl Sittler dominated the head-lines, now the quality of the last man on the roster was cause for serious and relentless debate.

The arrival of 24-hour TV and radio sports outlets in the city fed the monster, giving Leaf fans a daily voice that they'd never had before. They could publicly critique men like Cliff Fletcher and Pat Quinn in a way they'd never been able to sound off about Punch Imlach. As interest in the NHL sagged, and concern over the long-term financial stability of other Canadian-based teams surfaced, interest in the Leafs intensified. When teams like the Flames, Canucks and Canadiens recovered by 2003 or 2004 to again sell out their arenas, it seemed as though the Leafs, despite an inability to win the Stanley Cup, had provided a standard of devotion and enthusiasm for other Canadian teams to match. The extraordinary explosion of civic enthusiasm that greeted Calgary's charge to the 2004 final was an expression of this revitalized interest in many of the Canadian markets that followed a period of malaise in the late 1990s.

The change from the old Leaf reality to the new was probably right around the 1967 season. Indeed, the city hall reception that greeted the Leaf champs that spring was the smallest of any of the previous three that decade. The reduced city hall gathering for the Leafs, however, was not a sign of an impending fade in popularity; it was more likely a sign that the meaning of the Leafs and the place they held in Toronto was changing and about to be replaced by something entirely different. Indeed, a story from that spring's playoffs seemed to suggest a new level of commitment by Leaf fans that went beyond straightforward appreciation. Ernie Blochlinger, a 28-year-old baker, attended Game Four of the opening round series with Chicago while his wife, Marjorie, sat in Scarborough General Hospital with the couple's two-day-old son. Blochlinger's plan was to name his son after the first Leaf goal-scorer of the night. That turned out to be Dave Keon at 3:42 of the first period, on assists from Brian Conacher and Frank Mahovlich. The young child was thus named David Brian Frank Blochlinger, and several days later the Leafs sent the child a "contract," dated 1987, along with an autographed Keon stick, a miniature Leaf sweater and a puck. What was once the object of intense admiration was becoming the object of utterly blind and forgiving devotion.

Blochlinger had also been one of the disappointed thousands who had watched the Leafs lose Game Four that night, allowing the Hawks to deadlock the best-of-seven series at two games apiece with Game Five set for Chicago Stadium on April 15th, a rare Sunday afternoon game in a league that was beginning a search for greater TV exposure in the United States. The Leafs, meanwhile, realized this was the opportunity that had seemed so distant during the problematic regular season. "We knew if we were going to be Stanley Cup contenders, this was the critical game," said winger Brian Conacher.

As the NHL has expanded, it eventually became necessary to win four consecutive best-of-seven competitions to win the Cup. In 1967, however, it still took only two series to take the Cup, and so after putting together two wins in four games, the Leafs could detect that familiar smell of a championship, knowing that six more victories would get them there. But there were problems. The aforementioned Kelly, for example, had not been a factor against the Hawks, despite the respect his name held across the league. The same was the case for Mahovlich, who was drawing to the close of his usefulness as a Leaf, at least to Imlach. George Armstrong hadn't played since the third period of Game Two, while the club's most productive right winger, Jim Pappin, was on the limp. Shifty Mike Walton had been able to supply the club with sporadic offence during the season, but he had only skated a few shifts against Chicago. Terry Sawchuk had struggled in Game Four, so Imlach decided to take a gamble and put Johnny Bower in goal for Game Five, despite the fact Bower had been injured before the series opener and hadn't played a minute in the playoffs. The good news was that veteran defenceman Tim Horton would play in Game Five, despite taking a high-stick that had broken his nose from Chicago forward Dennis Hull in the previous game. The storied Horton toughness was on display at the most critical juncture of the playoffs.

The story that would emerge for public consumption from the 4–2 Leaf victory was that Sawchuk, who came on in relief for Bower after the first period, stole the game with brilliant goaltending—an incident of outright larceny in the middle of the Stanley Cup playoffs. The record shows that Sawchuk did face 37 shots over the final two periods, including 22 shots in the third, without allowing a single goal. But a careful analysis of that game tells a very different story. It was a contest, yes, in which a shot by Bobby Hull that temporarily downed Sawchuk very early in the second period provided a crucial moment. But the overall contest really showed that the personality of this Leaf team was truly unfolding. It was not a team driven by a bunch of old guys, by two veteran goalies or by Imlach's genius, although all of those were elements in the final triumph. This team managed to surprise the hockey world by riding a group of surprise performances by players like Pappin, Conacher, Peter Stemkowski, Larry Hillman and Marcel Pronovost: A review of Game Five against the Hawks proves that to be true.

Walton, of all people, provided the Leafs with a 1–0 lead in Game Five at 6:10 of the first period on a power-play goal, snapping a shot from the high slot past Denis Dejordy, who had returned to play after Glenn Hall had been injured by a Pappin shot in Game Four. That lead didn't last long, however, as first Lou Angotti deflected a point shot past a shaky-looking Bower at 9:31. Then Hull flicked an innocent wrist shot from 30 feet past the Leaf goalie to bring the Chicago Stadium crowd—certain that the Hawks were now on their way—to its feet. Before the end of the period, however, the Leafs got another power-play goal, this time an easy tap-in for Mahovlich on assists from Dave Keon and Walton.

The second period began with Sawchuk in the Leaf net, replacing Bower; what proved to be a decisive moment for the series quickly followed. The two teams resumed play with four skaters a side after a tussle between Leaf forward Bob Pulford and Hawks winger Eric

Nesterenko in the dying seconds of the first had sent both players to the penalty box with minors. Shortly after the faceoff to begin the period, Hull charged down the left boards into the Leaf zone and circled the net behind Sawchuk. Hull worked the puck back to Pierre Pilote at the right point, and after head-faking the Leafs into thinking he was going to move the puck towards the net, Pilote relayed the puck back to Hull low in the Leaf zone. Stanley had bit on Pilote's fake, leaving Hull wide-open. Finally given the time and space in prime scoring territory that the Leafs had denied him for most of the series, Hull drew the wicked curve of his blade backwards in an arc and slammed it forward, driving a rising slapshot at Sawchuk from 25 feet. At first, as Sawchuk jumped to defend himself against the shot, it seemed it had hit him square in his flimsy mask. But then it became clear it had hit him in the left shoulder, sending him to the ice like he'd been pistol-whipped. "The bench just took a big gulp," recalls Conacher. "At that point in the game, there was really no chance to go back to [Bower]." Pappin was first on the scene, quickly falling to his knees to slide his right glove under the fallen goalie's head. Stanley and Hull both stood in the crease watching Sawchuk, as Leaf trainer Bobby Haggart, dressed all in white like a surgeon, arrived to tend to the goaltender. After lying on the ice for a minute, Sawchuk sat up, then stood up, skated a few tentative steps away from the net, then back to his crease. After donning his mask, he stayed in goal, providing the Leafs with a wake-up call.

Keeping a man between Hull and the net had been a priority, and now Sawchuk had been inflicted with a frightening blow because the Leaf defenders had given Hull room. It wouldn't happen again. As the game started up again, the inability of the Hawks to deliver a killer blow to their supposedly overmatched opponent was glaring. In fact, what was striking was how few good offensive chances the Hawks were able to generate the rest of the game against Sawchuk. The Leaf goalie was treated like a war hero afterwards, but the reality was that after facing that shot from Hull, he was only seriously tested a handful of times. His performance, while flawless, was nothing like that which Ken Dryden turned in against the Big Bad Bruins in the 1971 playoffs, or even the sensational work delivered by Jean-Sebastien Giguere in the 2003 playoffs while leading the Anaheim Mighty Ducks to the Cup final. Sawchuk showed incredible bravery to stand up unflinchingly to Hull's blast, but after that, his teammates took over. They were even able to overcome the flawed strategy of Imlach to repeatedly use his defencemen, particularly Horton, Hillman and Pronovost, to take defensive zone faceoffs. The strategy seemed designed to create a scramble, which could then turn in the Leafs favour as the centre, Kelly, Keon or Stemkowski, moved up from behind the faceoff circle to grab control. More often than not, however, the Hawks simply won the draw, and more often than not, Leaf checking quickly snuffed out an offensive opportunity.

At 2:11 of the third, Stemkowski gave the Leafs a 3–2 lead, finishing off a sequence in which it was clear that the Winnipeg native's rambunctious, ornery forechecking style had left the Hawks blueline crew of Pilote, Doug Jarrett, Pat Stapleton and Ed Van Impe totally flustered and looking over their shoulders. With Hull and Esposito wandering back nonchalantly after Hillman flipped a high backhander into the Chicago zone, Stemkowski and Pappin combined on a play that left Stemkowski with an empty net to shovel home the go-ahead score. Stemkowski, Pappin and Pulford had clearly established their line as Toronto's Number 1 scoring threat, and that unit had come through again.

The inability of the Hawks to put serious pressure on Sawchuk, despite their mounting shot totals, was striking. Sawchuk made solid stops on Mikita in tight, on Hull from the point and on Doug Mohns from 40 feet. Really, however, the only top-flight save he had to make was another on Mohns after a faceoff in the Toronto zone, a draw taken and lost by Horton as Imlach's peculiar strategy failed again. Both Horton and Stanley somehow lost track of Mohns off the draw, allowing the converted defenceman to walk in alone, with Sawchuk delivering a sprawling stop. The Hawks weren't able to generate another quality attempt for the final six minutes, and with less than three minutes to play, Pappin struck, again off persistent forechecking by Stemkowski. After Pulford batted a puck out of the air off Dejordy, Pappin swept in the insurance goal from the edge of the crease, the third Leaf goal from five feet or less that afternoon against a crumbling Chicago defensive wall. In the final moments, Imlach deployed three defencemen and two forwards to fend off the Hawks, and Pulford and Mikita dropped their gloves in the final seconds, symbolizing Chicago's frustration with the Leafs' checking. Hawks coach Billy Reay seemed equally exasperated, saying, "American television is going to ruin hockey." He was referring to his annoyance with the nine, one-minute breaks inserted during the game for TV purposes that always seemed to give the Leafs a chance to catch their breath.

Heading back to Toronto, the underdog Leafs were ahead three games to two. Sawchuk had stood up to the Hull challenge, but goaltending hadn't won the game. It was won by a collective team spirit that seemed to reach back in time, back to the 1941–42 series when an unknown player, Ernie Dickens, had come off the bench to help save the Leafs. At a time when the place of the Leafs in the culture of their city was changing, the Game Five victory proved that despite everything that had gone wrong and was going wrong, this was not a team that had lost its sense of history.

GAME SIX
CHICAGO AT MAPLE LEAFS, APRIL 18, 1967

Stan Mikita saw his chance, recognized an opportunity to make the kind of impact play he'd not been able to make the entire series and to get back at his Maple Leaf tormentors for all the pain and frustration they'd caused him over the previous five games.

And he went for it.

Early in the third period of Game Six of the 1967 Stanley Cup semi-final series between the Leafs and Chicago Blackhawks, Mikita spotted rookie Leaf forward Brian Conacher cruising in from the right boards with the puck and closing in on Hawks defenceman Pat Stapleton, with the game tied 1–1. Mikita, hounded by a variety of Leafs throughout the series, saw Conacher dip his left shoulder and prepare to shoot, dropping his head just slightly. A simple stick check would have sufficed, but Mikita had other plans. He remembered being flattened by a Conacher hit in Game One 13 days earlier, and here was his chance to even the score. Mikita jumped at Conacher, going for his head, going for the big hit that might energize his team and save the series for the floundering regular season champs from the Windy City, who trailed the series 3–2 and were on the brink of elimination. The Hawks had carried the play in the second period of Game Six, and early in the third only a spectacular, sprawling chest save by Leaf defenceman Larry Hillman on the Golden Jet, Bobby Hull, had prevented Chicago from taking a lead that might force a decisive Game Seven match back in the Hawks noisy home rink. Hawks left winger Doug Mohns, standing in the Chicago goal, had stopped Dave Keon from scoring in a similar way late in Game Five, and Hillman proved even more acrobatic on his save. The Hawks had lost two of three at Chicago Stadium in the series, and they believed if they could force Game Seven against the Leafs, the law of averages would come around for a Chicago team that had lost only five of 35 home starts during the regular season.

Conacher had already scored in the first period, sweeping in from the right side to accept a pass from Frank Mahovlich and snap a shot past Glenn Hall in the Chicago net, a goal a nation-wide TV audience didn't see because, in those days, the first period of games didn't always make it to air. Conacher, voted the NHL's third-best rookie that season, had replaced captain George Armstrong on a line with Mahovlich and Dave Keon late in Game Two. For the most part, he'd been a thorn in Chicago's side from that point on, using his tall, lean frame to forecheck aggressively and cause chaos around the Chicago crease. With this game tied in the third, he again delivered an important hit, knocking down Hawks blueliner Ed Van Impe as he attempted to skate the puck out of the Chicago zone, creating a loose puck that dribbled just outside the blueline. Conacher quickly retrieved the puck and swooped back into the Chicago end with Mahovlich screaming in from the other side looking for a pass.

Mikita, moving back to cover, was looking for Conacher's head. But he missed. Conacher went to the ice after slipping the brunt of Mikita's attempted hit, but not before whipping a rising shot that glanced off the top of Hall's left pad and into the net. It was a brilliant solo effort of which his father, Lionel (The Big Train) Conacher, would have been justifiably proud. It was also the winning goal as the Leafs won the game 3–1 and the series four games to two, upsetting the powerful Blackhawks and moving on to the Stanley Cup final against Montreal. "It ended up being the most important goal of my career," said Conacher, who never again played an NHL playoff match after that glorious spring. For Mikita, it was a fitting end to a lamentable performance by the Hawks and the Scooter Line he centred. The Hawks centre had scored two goals and added two assists, but the Scooter Line with Mohns and Ken Wharram didn't manage a goal in the final two games of the series and Mikita never seemed anywhere close to as dangerous as he was while leading the NHL in scoring during the regular season. Hull had managed four goals, but by the end it was clear that too much of the Chicago offence was funneled through the powerful left winger. In the dying seconds of the clinching game, Eric Nesterenko had a wide-open chance from 25 feet but inexplicably glanced towards the slot, looking for Hull, before losing the puck altogether. "Against Chicago, we just worked at shutting down their stars," recalls Hillman. "Everything revolved around their star players, Mikita and Hull. You shut them down, you shut the team down. With the Leafs, we had the team concept."

Phil Esposito was another Hawk forward who had failed to support Hull and Mikita, going scoreless in six games. At a post-season gathering a few days later over countless beers, Esposito and Hull were recounting the failure of the team. "We're never going to win with those two assholes in charge," said an inebriated Esposito, pointing across the room at coach Billy Reay and GM Tommy Ivan. Hull mischievously challenged his 25-year-old teammate to tell Reay and Ivan to their faces, and to his surprise, Esposito sauntered across the room and did just that. Three weeks later, the Hawks unloaded him to Boston along with Ken Hodge and

Fred Stanfield in one of hockey's most one-sided blockbuster deals, a deal that altered the balance of the Original Six heading into expansion and armed the Bruins for their two Stanley Cups in the 1970s.

Long gone from Maple Leaf Gardens by the time Conacher potted the winning goal was Leaf president Stafford Smythe. On a cool, blustery night with the threat of rain in the air, Smythe exited the arena in his overcoat after the first period, spending the final two periods, as was his habit in tight matches, walking the streets outside the famous building his father had built, pacing north on Church, west on Wellesley, down Yonge Street and back across the north side of the Gardens along Wood Street, and worrying over his team, which had experienced so much adversity that season. There was vindication for Smythe, but also intense relief. The team wouldn't be eliminated in the first round for a third straight year, and there would be more Gardens gate receipts to be counted. This was helpful for the Leaf president at a time when he and partners Harold Ballard and John Bassett were heavily leveraged with bank loans, and he and Ballard were skimming money from both the Leafs and the Marlies to pay for personal expenses. The wave of triumph that enveloped the city and team served as a helpful smokescreen for Smythe, a canny hockey man troubled by the onset of alcoholism, his own shady business practices and the burdensome legacy of his family name.

Inside, winger Larry Jeffrey was finished for the rest of the playoffs after suffering a knee injury late in the game. He'd been a regular on a line with Red Kelly and Ron Ellis. Punch Imlach, meanwhile, was greeting members of the media in a storage room near the Leaf dressing room, uncharacteristically pushing himself out of the limelight while his players basked in the glory of their stunning upset victory. With players like Conacher, Hillman,

Peter Stemkowski and Jim Pappin leading the way, along with Terry Sawchuk's standout goaltending, Imlach had squeezed the most surprising playoff victory of his career out of his team. Could he squeeze another four victories?

5 *The Union*

At 70, more than a decade removed from being one of the most powerful figures in NHL history, Alan Eagleson remained far from humbled, still a vibrant, fast-talking ball of energy. Despite his trials and convictions and incarcerations, despite his dishonorable discharges from the Hockey Hall of Fame and Order of Canada, he declined to openly buy into bitterness or regret or apologies and still personified ambition, if not quite as intensely as he once did. He certainly didn't hide. When he showed up in the spring of 2004 for a Maple Leaf playoff game at the Air Canada Centre as the guest of Philadelphia executive Bob Clarke, it made news. "Ken Dryden asked me why I had waited to come to a game until Clarke called," he said. "I told him, 'Well, you never asked me.'"

By then, he'd purchased a condo in downtown Toronto, but spent most of his time living in a century-old farmhouse near Collingwood, Ontario. On a drizzly day in August 2003, he exuded vitality as he guided visitors on a tour of the sprawling township that had become his new kingdom. The tour was supposed to be 15 minutes and ended up being almost two hours as he told listeners who made how much off the sale of which chunk of land, who nobody liked and how much cash was generated from which property. Through all the success and disgrace, Eagleson still loved the feel of being the ultimate insider with the confidential lowdown.

Peering back through the mists of hockey history, one can only imagine the unusual figure Eagleson presented to the most powerful men in professional hockey when he took aim upon their game in the mid-1960s. The very men who brought him down later in his controversial career were the same who were dazzled by his charm when he first hit the hockey scene. He was extraordinarily engaging and charismatic, an elected member of the Ontario Legislature who could cross cultural and class lines with ease, the son of Scottish settlers who wore expensive suits but could curse and scrap like a fourth-line enforcer.

Back in 1966, he was not yet The Eagle, the man who wore all the hats, the man whose name, accurately or not, would become synonymous with the greatest hockey series ever played and the game's greatest financial scandal. He was an ambitious, thirty-something Toronto lawyer who had just begun to parlay a few friends in the game and a couple of star clients into a modicum of influence, but still also a politician with decidedly non-hockey dreams of scaling the highest legislative towers.

Perhaps it was the voters of the Lakeshore riding who decided hockey's future back in 1968 when they rejected Eagleson as their provincial candidate after a single term, dumping him in favour of a New Democratic Party politician after some had accused Eagleson of not spending enough time on riding business. Given that he was considered cabinet material at the time, and given that he was politically influential enough to win the federal Progressive Conservative presidency several years later, Eagleson certainly could have climbed the political ladder had he chosen to put his energies in that direction. But the voters of Lakeshore set him back and the intrigue of hockey drew him in.

Back in the mid-1960s as the Leafs were coming off three consecutive Stanley Cup triumphs, Eagleson was just figuring out hockey, but he already knew politics. His instincts told him that a foothold with the Leafs, hockey's most famous team, was desirable. As his empire began to expand, he quickly understood that influencing players from the other five teams would be a great deal easier with the Leafs as his base of power. With that, gaining control of the exploding player market, as the NHL doubled in size in one year, would be a snap. He identified the Leafs as the team crucial to his most audacious plans.

That the men who ran hockey's most famous team were not interested in being part of the Eagleson plan was no surprise. Ultimately the Leafs couldn't resist Eagleson and the growth of player rights. Instead, the man and all he stood for ended up playing a pivotal role in the process that turned the team from a model of NHL success into a laughingstock. The Leafs had always won and believed that winning was part of the sport's natural order. The arrogance with which they made destructive decisions before and after their 1967 championship season demonstrated that they believed that there would be pauses in their successes, but never a time when they would not win the Stanley Cup on a regular basis. The Leafs believed they were indestructible. As far as Eagleson, they believed that he and his union had to be destroyed, and that became an obsession.

Fighting the development of the players union, and fighting Eagleson, played an important role in the deterioration of the franchise—an instructive example of the way in which the changing forces that controlled Maple Leaf Gardens were in no way equipped to deal with the explosive changes to come in the industry or to efficiently turn the Leafs from a team with a glorious past into a team with an exciting future. By itself, straightforward opposition to the players union would not have been the destructive force that brought the once proud Leafs to the competitive mediocrity that followed the 1967 championship. But the Leafs were singular in the ferocity with which they opposed Eagleson, and decisions that were made to strike out at the new union clearly undermined the short-term future of the team and came back to haunt the organization more than a decade later. In 1966, nobody in NHL ownership circles welcomed the union. But nobody fought it quite like the Leafs did. Specifically, no NHL administrator wanted to kill the union baby before it grew like GM and head coach Punch Imlach. "Punch would work the [players association] guys harder," recalls Eagleson. "He let his arguments with the PA interfere with his assessments of the team. He resented anybody else coming in and having authority over his team. He brought it all on himself." If opposing Eagleson didn't lead to the undoing of the franchise, it became symptomatic of the sickness that would transform a team that had always won into a team that couldn't quite figure out how to win again. By misreading the churn of history, the Leafs sentenced themselves to a competitively bleak future.

By the time the Leafs had fashioned the 11th Stanley Cup victory in team history in May 1967, they were no longer the game's best, most efficient operation. Not surprisingly, they proved unable to make the transition from the days when they controlled all of the talent of hockey-mad Canada's most populous province to the new order, which had harvested new franchises in places like Los Angeles, Oakland, Pittsburgh and Philadelphia, ushered in a universal draft and was slowly opening to international hockey. That lack of progressive thinking would be even more costly with the creation of a rival league, the World Hockey Association (WHA), as the Leafs were arguably more badly damaged than any other established team by WHA incursions. The Leafs' mindset to resist change, rather than adapt to it, had been formed years earlier.

To Imlach's chagrin, and that of many crusty administrators in various pro sports, the roles and rights of the professional athlete in North America were changing—with astonishing speed. Interestingly, the NHL was in some ways on the leading edge of this change, and some of that had to do with the aggressively ambitious Eagleson and his key clients. By the time the NHL players association was established in

1967, unions were already in existence in Major League Baseball, the National Basketball Association and the National Football League, but the pivotal individual legal challenges that would change those sports and the business of sports in the United States and Canada were still several years away. The public was just beginning to look at athletes in a new way, eschewing the one-dimensional, athlete-as-hero model and understanding these warriors of the fields as rather more complex, human and flawed, capable of brilliance on the field but also greed and stupidity away from their chosen sports.

For decades, the idiosyncracies and true nature of athletes had been glossed over and sanitized for the consumption of all, and in many cases deliberately hidden from the eyes of the public. To some degree, the public liked it that way, loved thinking their favourite stars played for the pure love of the game and lived apple-pie lives. Business had long been a part of the landscape, and icons like baseball star Joe DiMaggio had staged repeated holdouts in efforts to get more money to play. But as the tumultuous 1960s broiled and turned into the 1970s, the combination of societal change and the sense that the status quo could and should be challenged created a latticework of momentous events involving the independence of athletes that forever altered the manner in which they were viewed by a once unquestioning public.

In April 1967, for example, boxer Muhammad Ali refused induction into the U.S. Army on the basis of his religious beliefs, evoking his famous "I ain't got no quarrel with those Viet Cong" quote. Ali's determination to fight the system reverberated around the world and was certainly felt in Canada and in Toronto. Stories of the Canadian government sending increased medical aid to southeast Asia juxtaposed with headlines of U.S. bombs falling on churches and villages left many Canadians troubled by the military involvement of their American friends. Ali, who had fought George Chuvalo at

Maple Leaf Gardens 13 months earlier in a bout that had sparked Conn Smythe's decision to resign from the organization, was punished heavily for his decision to mix his political and religious conscience with his brutal profession. He was sentenced to five years in jail, stripped of his heavyweight title, fined and barred from boxing.

The Ali controversy didn't emanate from his activities in the ring, but soon athletes would begin flexing their muscles of independence in ways that impacted their sports in more direct ways. In 1969, for example, St. Louis Cardinals outfielder Curt Flood took on baseball and its vaunted reserve clause, which essentially bound players in perpetuity to the team that held their contracts. Flood, then a $90,000-a-year, 31-year-old African-American outfielder, balked at a trade from St. Louis to Philadelphia for a variety of reasons, including the fact the Phillies were a bad team and he considered Philly to be an overtly racist city. He asked baseball's commissioner, Bowie Kuhn, to have him declared a free agent, free to choose his next employer. Kuhn refused, and Flood took baseball to court, ultimately losing his case at the U.S. Supreme Court and in the process ruining what was left of his career. Five years later, however, pitchers Andy Messersmith and Dave McNally picked up where Flood had left off, again testing the reserve clause by playing without contracts in their option years and ultimately successfully loosening baseball's grip on its players when arbitrator Peter Seitz ruled that they were free agents.

At around the same time, Spencer Haywood, one of 10 children from a Mississippi family of cotton pickers, mounted a challenge to the NBA's rules of entry, rules that stated a player could not be eligible for that league's draft until four years after the graduation of his high school class. Those regulations were intended to wed players to the NCAA college system, essentially a free feeder system to the NBA. Haywood had led the U.S. national team in scoring as an 18-year-old phenom at the 1968 Olympics in Mexico City and then turned pro with the rival American Basketball Association the next year, winning that league's rookie-of-the-year and most valuable player honours. When he sought, along with the co-operation of an existing NBA team, the Seattle Supersonics, to be drafted into the league the following year, NBA powers blocked his attempt with a long series of court challenges and injunctions. Haywood argued that the NBA was in violation of anti-trust laws in not allowing him to pursue a living in the sport, and in 1971 the U.S. Supreme Court agreed and cleared him to play for pay in the NBA.

In 1970, former major league pitcher Jim Bouton wrote *Ball Four*, a seminal treatise on professional sport and an insider's look at baseball that rocked the foundations of the game and forever removed the veil of secrecy owners had used to conduct their businesses—ways that were plainly unfair and, in some cases, illegal. For his efforts, Bouton became for years afterwards a virtual pariah in the game he loved, although the book was extremely popular and was reprinted twice. "I believe the overreaction to *Ball Four* amounted to this: People were simply not used to reading the truth about professional sports," wrote Bouton in an updated preface released in 1990.

Against this backdrop, it's striking and instructive to understand that Eagleson's pivotal involvement with the NHL actually began in the early 1960s, and that he participated in the same type of fight for athletes' rights for which players like Flood and Haywood became famous. Eagleson's later acts, including some ultimately determined to be criminal in nature, have understandably come to dominate his entire record. But it's fair to argue that back in the early 1960s, back before he could have been accused of turning the NHL players union into a "house" union, he was publicly perceived as an advocate for players' rights, a revolutionary, of sorts.

Eagleson came to know several of the Leaf players on a business and social basis in the late 1950s and early 1960s, partly through his connections at the University of Toronto. He established The Blue and White Group, involving Bobby Baun, Carl Brewer, Bob Pulford and Billy Harris, among the brightest and most articulate Leafs, along with a local car dealer, a jeweler and three other lawyers. The concept was to get the players to learn about stocks and investments and how to more intelligently use the funds they were making as pro hockey stars. Each member of the group contributed $50 a month to the group plan. "I exposed them to business people they otherwise wouldn't have met," says Eagleson. "Most hockey players back then would use their money to open a bar or something. I persuaded these guys to look beyond their careers."

There was, at that time, a different type of athlete moving through the Toronto hockey culture, young men who had the ability to play pro hockey but also saw futures in education and other pursuits. They were very different from those who had come along even a decade earlier. Good local junior players like Ron Casey, Bill Kennedy, Mike Elik, Dunc Brody and Jim Murchie all chose to go to university rather than pursue professional hockey opportunities. This was particularly true of those that began with minor league contracts, which didn't pay even as well as jobs they already had. Casey, for one, was offered a deal that paid less than he was making to sell cars part-time. Brian Conacher was another who, after a quick taste of the pro game, decided to head to university. Jimmy Keon, brother of Dave, eventually followed a similar path to Conacher. The captain of the Toronto Marlboro team that won the 1964 Memorial Cup title, Grant Moore, chose school over hockey and became a well-known Toronto lawyer. "We were all Toronto boys playing junior hockey in Toronto," says Harry Neale, who went on to become the top analyst on

Hockey Night in Canada. "Many decided pro hockey was not as attractive as other things they could do."

Neale, a defenceman with the Marlies in the late 1950s, had been the property of the Maple Leafs for years because of the sponsorship hold the NHL team had on the Marlboro chain. In 1958, he attended the Leaf pro camp held in Sudbury, Ontario, and then was shifted to a shared minor pro camp between the Leafs and Canadiens in Montreal. "I felt I could play at that level because many of the guys I played junior hockey with were able to make it. But I had to decide by September 28th of that fall whether I was going back to school because I had to enroll by then." With two years at the University of Toronto already under his belt, Neale was offered a $3,000 signing bonus by the Leafs and a two-year contract that would have paid him $7,000 a year if he made the Leafs and $3,500 if he played in the minors. "I thought I should make $20,000 over two years if I played for the Leafs," he says. Neale headed back to school. A year later he was making $3,700 a year teaching and moved on to play in university, and later, senior hockey in Galt, Ontario, where he won the prestigious Allan Cup with that team.

Meanwhile, players like Pulford, Brewer and Harris earned university degrees after turning pro, unprecedented in those days. It wasn't surprising that a new breed of hockey players, more inclined to have their own opinions and less inclined to simply take arbitrary orders from their hockey masters, ruffled feathers and helped to fuel the sense of unrest with established practice that was already growing in NHL circles. "I don't know that the system adjusted all that well to people like me, and others," says Jimmy Keon. "The system had a difficult time adjusting to educated people."

Some of the Leaf players, particularly those in The Blue and White Group, became close friends with Eagleson. Brewer, for example, became the godfather to Eagleson's daughter, and

Eagleson's stature in the game began to grow because of his Leaf connections. "The Leaf players gave me credibility, and it gave me an introduction to the NHL," recalls Eagleson. "As different Leafs got traded, I then had an in with other teams." Andy Bathgate helped Eagleson wedge himself into the Detroit Red Wings dressing room after Bathgate had moved on from the Leafs in 1965, a key development given that a similar players' uprising had been squashed with the Red Wings a decade earlier. Bob Nevin, meanwhile, helped introduce Eagleson to all the Rangers players after he was traded from Toronto to New York in February 1964. Eagleson also developed close ties with the Leaf trainer, Bobby Haggert, thus gaining full access to the inner sanctum of the Leaf operation.

In 1963, established as a lawyer in the Toronto enclave of Thistletown, Eagleson ran for the federal seat of York West against the sitting Liberal member, and Brewer helped out with the campaign. In that election, Eagleson's opponent was none other than Leonard (Red) Kelly, then in his third season as a star with the Maple Leafs. In fiery partisan spirit, Eagleson attacked Kelly for not being attentive enough to the riding, the same charges that would be fired at Eagleson himself five years later. Saying the riding needed "somebody who works and lives among us, not some imported name figure," Eagleson ran hard against Kelly, charging him with "not uttering a single word in the House," not knowing that Kelly would be one of the established Leaf stars he would need to persuade to buy into the players union concept down the road. Kelly romped to an easy victory in a bitterly contested race that left the losing NDP candidate so outraged by the process he labelled Canada a "sick society" and promised to leave the country as soon as possible.

Eagleson did capture a provincial seat a year later, but that political success did not conclude his involvement in pro hockey. Instead, it accelerated. Over the course of the 1966–1967 season, three monumental events in which Eagleson was a central character would begin to change the shape of the NHL and pro hockey, and set the stage for his showdown with the Leafs.

First, young Bobby Orr and his family stood up to the bully tactics of the Boston Bruins and insisted that Eagleson negotiate Orr's first pro contract. Second, Brewer fought to have his amateur status reinstated so he could join Canada's national program a year after abruptly quitting the Leafs. Third, the Springfield Indians went to war with gnarly owner Eddie Shore in one of hockey's most famous off-ice battles, blazing a new path for players' rights on the way—a path that would lead to the formation of the NHL Players Association. "It was those three things that did it," recalled Eagleson. "It will never be totally understood by people retrospectively. But the most important factor was the Toronto Maple Leafs. My relationship with those players was the factor that got me to Orr, for example. The Leafs were a really big factor in the formation of the union."

Back in the summer of 1966, professional hockey players had lawyers and advisors, but the word "agent" had yet to be an accepted term within the rules of the game as set down by owners. Boston had established ownership of Orr in 1962. When it came time to negotiate a contract with the 18-year-old Oshawa Generals star four years later, Bruins GM Hap Emms was determined that he would not be forced into changing established practice or handing over unprecedented sums of money. Moreover, he was bound and determined not to negotiate with Eagleson, who had emerged as the Orr family's representative earlier in the year. "We're prepared to be fair, I might say most generous, with Orr," said Emms. "But we have no intention of dealing through a lawyer." Emms and the Bruins must have assumed that Orr would eventually back down, come to his senses and do business the way they wanted it done. Orr, however, continued to insist that Eagleson was to do the contract, and on September 2, 1966, there was Eagleson by the side of Orr and his father, Doug, in Barrie, Ontario, as the game's next supernova signed a two-year contract with the Bruins.

The rumour was that the deal was for $50,000 a season, an extraordinary amount for a first-year player, at a time when the mayor of Toronto made half that amount and a first-class firefighter in Toronto was earning the princely sum of $6,245 a year. Orr, however, says that the exact deal he signed was for one year at $10,000, with a $5,000 bonus if he played 40 games, and a second year at $15,000, with another $5,000/40-game bonus. But the significant breakthrough was that a precedent had been set that would alter player–team relations drastically in a remarkably short period of time. Orr had insisted on an agent, and the Bruins had blinked.

Over the ensuing decades, Orr would eventually break with Eagleson on bitter terms and would play a pivotal role in the events that ultimately sent Eagleson to prison for his activities as head of the players union. It is a truly compelling historical coincidence that more than three decades after that first contract, Orr emerged in the late 1990s as one of the most significant and powerful player agents in the sport. For two decades after that first contract was signed, however, the Eagleson–Orr connection was as high profile as Orr's famously battered left knee. In April 2004, with his friendship with Eagleson a distant memory, Orr underwent surgery in Boston for a total knee replacement.

The story of Brewer was unusually complicated, at least partly because Brewer was an unusually complicated sort. He cracked the Leaf lineup as a 19-year-old directly from the ranks of the Toronto Marlboros in 1958, culled from the same blueline herd as Neale, and he quickly became a fixture on the Leaf clubs that won three consecutive Stanley Cups in the early 1960s. Though not large in stature, perhaps 5-foot-9 or 5-foot-10 and only about 175 pounds when he started out, Brewer had both immense skill and a tenacity that intimidated and often enraged others. "For an hour before and after every game, he's on a different planet," said one teammate. Brewer would take on much larger men and instigate brawls inside even the quietest games, spitting in opponents' faces and breaking his arm in the 1963 Stanley Cup final while throwing a check. Yet his puck-moving skills and keen understanding of the game made him a first team all-star once and second team all-star twice. As the 1965-66 season dawned, Brewer was 26 years old, married with a six-month old son and perhaps headed for the Hall of Fame one day. Then, seemingly out of nowhere, he packed it in after a period of an exhibition game—just quit and walked away from the game.

There was media speculation that fear of flying had grounded the high-strung Brewer, or perhaps it was the pressures of the game, which explained why he was prone to strange rashes and had lost chunks of his hair. Ten months earlier, Brewer had been involved in a spectacular night of fights at Maple Leaf Gardens in a game against the Chicago Blackhawks. In separate scraps with Hawks forward Murray Balfour, which many believed substantially altered Brewer's attitude towards the game and his status with his teammates, he was beaten twice. Once he fell through the door on the Leaf bench, which inspired Toronto Argonauts star running back Dick Shatto to charge down from the seats to intervene. Balfour later accused Brewer of biting him, but more important was the widespread sense that Brewer had backed down and behaved like a frightened schoolboy, a stigma he couldn't shake. Brewer's fragile psyche, many of his teammates believed, was enormously affected by this humiliating sequence of events.

Many also pointed to a seething hostility towards the controlling Imlach that crystallized Brewer's overall philosophy towards pro sports, and it is that factor that is the most compelling. All that he saw was wrong and unfair in pro sports, all that he saw that stole the dignity of athletes, he personified in Imlach. "Brewer thought hockey players, even though they were well paid, were slaves to the profession," says Neale. "In his own way, he wanted to correct that." Years later, Brewer summed up his own difficult relationship with the sport. "I love the game, but it hates me," he said.

Neale said that even in junior hockey, Brewer was multi-faceted and unique, his own man, hardly the simple reflection of callow youth often associated with apprenticing shinny artists. "He wasn't a normal Junior A hockey player," said Neale. In one game, Neale recalled, Brewer was called for a penalty and while the other team controlled the puck prior to a whistle, he skated to the Marlie bench and hid under the bench itself. When the referee skated over to call the foul, Marlie coach Turk Broda waved his arms helplessly. "He's not even dressed!" argued the former Leaf goaltending great. The official then said, "You've got 15 seconds to find him," and soon Brewer emerged to serve the penalty.

That oddball, sometimes clownish, outlook on hockey never changed. When he joined the Toronto Toros of the WHA in the 1970s, Brewer was bumped up to first class on a flight to California. He took out his bathing suit from his carry-on bag, went to the bathroom and splashed water on his face and hair. He then walked back to economy wearing only the bathing suit exclaiming, "You guys don't know what you're missing. The pool in first class is great!"

When he announced his retirement on September 18, 1965, Brewer denied it was a holdout or a negotiating ploy, and also rebutted suggestions that his young wife, Marilyn, was behind his decision. "I'm going to miss hockey," he said. "But my wife will miss it more than I will. This isn't a case of a wife talking her husband into retiring." Brewer spoke in riddles, leaving sportswriters and fans mystified as he started to attend classes at the University of Toronto and later formally enrolled. "Hockey opens many doors," he said. "But so many have closed." Later, he indicated the decision had long been in his mind, and that financial considerations had kept him in the Leaf lineup. "I almost quit two years ago. I wish now that I had," he said. "If I'd gone into business rather than college, it would have been more gradual. It's a jolt to cut off any income and I was very well paid for playing hockey. We all were."

It may well have been that Brewer himself couldn't pinpoint the reason he wanted out —he just knew he did. Behind the scenes was Eagleson, his friend and advocate, and the university option selected by Brewer became one of the themes that would pop up time and time again in the succeeding years as Eagleson sought to create new forms of leverage for hockey players who had traditionally been utterly at the beck and call of their NHL bosses. The following June, after Brewer had sat out the entire 1965–66 season, only occasionally appearing to run hockey clinics and continually deny any interest in returning to the NHL, the defenceman showed up at a workout with the semi-pro Toronto Rifles of the Continental Football League, sparking stories that he might be considering a switch in sports. The stunt would have appealed to the mischievous bandit in Brewer. Eagleson, not surprisingly, was the president of the Rifles. "He hit one punt 100 yards—50 yards up and 50 yards down," recalled Eagleson.

On September 5, 1966, at a press conference with Eagleson and Father David Bauer, the head of the reborn Canadian National Team Program, Brewer announced his intention to be reinstated as an amateur so he could join Bauer's team. Whether it was an exercise in youthful idealism or a practical means of breaking the NHL's hold on his freedom, it was unprecedented, and Eagleson was prominent at Brewer's side, answering many of the questions posed by a skeptical media. For the Leafs and the NHL, this was a brazen challenge to their powers of total cradle-to-grave control, an effort by an athlete to come up with a strategy to slide outside their influence and no longer be their property. If Brewer could go to the nats, couldn't he then come back to the NHL with another team? Didn't this strike at the very heart of the league's ability to dictate every step of a player's professional livelihood, even in retirement?

Not surprisingly, NHL president Clarence Campbell did not respond graciously to Brewer's request to be cleared of any NHL encumbrances, and the Leafs declined to lift the suspension they'd imposed when Brewer had walked out of training camp the year before. "[Brewer] and Eagleson must know it's impossible," said Imlach of Brewer's attempt to repatriate himself as an amateur. Interestingly, another Eagleson client and an unsigned Montreal draft pick, Danny O'Shea, also appeared at the press conference and professed an interest in joining the national team, a clear indication, perhaps, that this was not Brewer's idea alone.

For weeks, the Brewer saga played out to bold headlines from coast to coast as the NHL refused to alter its rules to clear the path for the AWOL blueliner. Some sounded notes of outrage that a Canadian could be denied the right to play for his country by a league controlled by a majority of American owners. Prime Minister Lester B. Pearson chimed in, saying it was "deplorable when a Canadian who wants to play on Canada's national hockey team has to get permission from clubs in the U.S." When Campbell announced in late October that the NHL was finally willing to let Brewer go, *The Toronto Star* published an editorial under the headline "NHL Springs a Slave." By December, Brewer was free to join Bauer's barnstorming band of amateurs, and his unusual journey would take him to international competition, then to the minors with Muskegon. He would have a stint as a player/coach in Finland before he returned to the NHL with the Detroit Red Wings for the 1969–70 season after the Wings had acquired his rights from Toronto. When he did return to the NHL, he was still good enough to be named to the NHL second all-star team, and he mused many times over the years that he should have been on the first team ahead of New York's Brad Park.

Through Orr and Brewer, Eagleson had firmly established himself as an energetic and sometimes mischievous advocate for players' rights, just as he'd earned a reputation as a maverick member of the Ontario Legislature for backing controversial reforms in divorce laws and fighting to drop religious barriers for adoption in the province. One can speculate upon Eagleson's motivations, whether they were for a sense of truth and justice or simply ego, ambition and greed, but that he was regarded as an agent for change, both popular and unpopular, is clear. Orr and Brewer stood up for themselves, but Eagleson was the mouthpiece. With hockey, he understood before others that while skates were still $14.98 a pair and you could play shinny in Toronto from 8 a.m. to 4 p.m. for $2, there were potentially much larger sums up for grabs in the professional game, with colour television becoming increasingly popular and expansion to new cities on the way. Each of six cities had paid $2 million to join the league for the 1967–68 season, and CBS had announced a three-year, $3.6 million contract to broadcast some regular season games, the all-star game and the playoffs. The entire Leaf payroll at the time was estimated by Imlach to be the largest in the sport at $400,000, less than half the amount that Bobby Hull would get to sign with the WHA Winnipeg Jets just five years later. Leaf tickets, meanwhile, were becoming so valuable that when ex-Leaf and Toronto lawyer Windy O'Neill had his overcoat stolen at a political rally, he complained to police only because he had two Leaf ducats in the pocket of the pilfered garment.

His involvement with Orr and Brewer introduced Eagleson to the sporting public. Then, as Eagleson was looking to expand his hockey business while still considering his future as a politician, Eddie Shore and history came calling. Shore, one of the most compelling legends in NHL history, was by then the crusty, idiosyncratic 64-year-old owner of the independent Springfield Indians of the American Hockey League. Shore was a man who had earned a frightening reputation as one who treated his players with little respect, preferring to subject them to various forms of abuse disguised as discipline and training, as they sought to escape his control and graduate to the NHL.

Just before Christmas, 1966, after Brewer had shaken the NHL by being cleared to join the Canadian Nationals, Shore's reign of terror became more than hockey's dirty little secret when his entire 23-man roster went on strike. The protest had been sparked a few days earlier when Shore had suspended Bill White, Dale Rolfe and Dave Amadio without pay for "indifferent play" in a 5–4 Saturday night loss to the Quebec Aces. When the players reported back to work on Monday, they practised in the morning but then refused to go back on the ice for an afternoon session until they received an explanation for the suspensions meted out to the three players and the opportunity to voice various grievances with Shore's operation. Shore refused, instead suspending spokesmen Brian Kilrea and Gerry Foley. He was backed in his efforts by AHL interim president Jack Butterfield, who also happened to be Shore's nephew. Eagleson was summoned to act as a mediator, apparently after White contacted Brewer for help. Eagleson headed south to do battle with one of hockey's biggest names and to resolve the first major rebellion in pro hockey in 40 years. Shore initially refused to speak to Eagleson but eventually relented, and Eagleson's first advice to the striking players was to end their walkout and go back to work while he negotiated with Shore. They did, but Shore still refused to reinstate four of the suspended players, encouraged as he was by the support of other minor pro owners in Tulsa and Memphis who happily agreed to send him replacements. The defiant Springfield owner told disgruntled fans they could cancel their season tickets if they found fault with his decisions and he would be happy to offer a full refund.

By early January, the Springfield situation had exploded again, and this time Eagleson arrived in a far less conciliatory mood. On behalf of the players, he threatened legal action at the same time two more players, goalie Jacques Caron and Mike Corbett, were suspended—again for "indifferent play." Corbett's crime was his failure to complete a set of intricate skating routines designed by Shore for practice purposes, and he was docked $400 from his next paycheque, forcing him to borrow from friends and teammates for food and rent. In exasperation, coach Harry Pidhirny quit and was replaced by Shore's son, Ted. Shore's unusual training methods continued, including insisting that the players sit on the ice for 30 minutes kicking their legs as a means of improving their speed and conditioning. When a player named Roger Cote protested, he was suspended.

Shore was increasingly defiant, but he was also isolated as Eagleson turned up the pressure. Soon, Eagleson issued an ultimatum that Shore would have to step down and set a deadline, and on January 22, after waiting a few minutes after the deadline, Shore relinquished day-to-day control of the team for "health reasons." The players, and Eagleson, had won. "Eddie Shore was a great hockey player and his departure now means an end of an era, and for this, I am sorry," Eagleson told reporters. In a sign that the NHL either understood that times were changing or didn't understand that Shore's demise would bring new problems to their doorsteps, none of the six existing clubs rallied to Shore's aid. "The players union might not have happened at all if the NHL had interceded for Shore," says Eagleson. Emboldened by his string of successes, Eagleson told a New York writers' luncheon a month later that "a players association will be formed," news which must have resounded like a thunderclap to NHL owners who had easily put down a similar movement a decade earlier.

———— ❧ ————

For the Leafs, already irritated by Brewer's unwillingness to toe the line, there was a sense of betrayal that accompanied Eagleson's rise to prominence, an uncomfortable sense that they'd been blindsided by an uppity lawyer they all knew well and had invited into their inner circle. Relationships between agents and teams were just forming back then, and while now it would be unimaginable for an NHL club to invite an agent along on a road trip, that's where Eagleson had found himself a year earlier in late November 1965 as the Leafs journeyed to Manhattan for two games with the New York Rangers, a Sunday–Wednesday double-header that was a popular scheduling peculiarity at the time. It was Pulford who had managed to get Eagleson invited, possibly because Dave Keon had been permitted to bring his financial advisor, Dan McLeod, along on an earlier trip. Eagleson and longtime pal Bob Watson, the best man at his wedding, ended up on the town with team vice-president Harold Ballard, sliding into various after-hour clubs before returning to the team's suite at the Commodore Hotel to experience the remnants of one of the legendary parties thrown by the Silver Seven, the kind of booze and broads parade for which that privileged group of influential Leaf executives and directors had become famous. The evening included a few scantily clad women and was punctuated by one of the participants ordering breakfast at 5 a.m., then passing out face first into his poached eggs. Headed by Ballard and Stafford Smythe, the Silver Seven used their position as custodians of the Leafs to revel in the high life, indulging in every sort of joyful debauchery, and Eagleson was trusted enough, or not feared enough, to be invited in as a witness and participant.

What the Leafs didn't know was that the push for a players union was beginning and that the wheels were turning quickly. By December 1966, Eagleson was meeting with Orr and Eddie Johnston at their team hotel in Montreal to aggressively begin planning for the new association. As the movement became public knowledge, Leaf officials, Imlach in particular, appeared to decide that they'd been double-crossed. "A large part of it was me," says Eagleson. "They'd known me for 20 years. I was just this goddamn lawyer. Punch had control of the dressing room, and then here was this Eagleson guy coming in and he was losing the dressing room again. They probably all took it too personally."

Initially, Eagleson's organization attempts hit obstacles, even within the Leafs. George Armstrong and Johnny Bower initially declined to sign up, feeling they were being disloyal to Imlach, and when they agreed to join, Dave Keon opted out, according to Eagleson. Keon, however, disputes that version of events. "We never saw [Eagleson]," he says. "We heard things through Pulford about how it was going to be a good thing for the players, but we weren't provided with any information. Eagleson was never in our dressing room, which in hindsight was probably a good thing because he screwed us all." But, by June 1967, virtually all the players on all six teams had signed union pledges. "They told us we'd be farting in silk pajamas," says Leaf winger Eddie Shack, referring to the bold promises of pension improvements from union organizers.

On June 6, at the Queen Elizabeth Hotel in Montreal at a meeting of the players/owners council, just five weeks after the Leafs had captured the Cup, Leaf forward Bob Pulford read a statement to the owners announcing the formation of the play-ers association, an entity that would be represented in all matters by Eagleson. It was a turning point for all NHL players, one many would come to regret years later when Eagleson was charged with a variety of offences relating to mismanagement of the union, put in jail and kicked out of the Hockey Hall of Fame. "I know he's not popular with most of the players now, but the players owe Alan Eagleson a big thank-you," says Pulford. "We would never have got off the ground without him. The medical benefits, the requirement of waivers so guys couldn't just be sent down to the minors—those are a couple of the hard fought battles that Eagleson waged on behalf of the players."

That it was Pulford who made the announcement that day in Montreal, not a member of the Habs, Rangers or Red Wings, just added another layer of betrayal in the minds of the men who ran the Leafs. Three minutes after Pulford spoke, Stafford Smythe stormed out of the boardroom and screamed to Imlach, "You won't fucking believe it. They've formed a fucking union and they won't talk to us without that fucking Eagleson. No fucking way!" Unnoticed by Smythe in his anger was Eagleson, standing just a few feet away. "I don't think the Leafs ever agreed to accept the union," says Eagleson, revelling in the memory of that exciting day. "But they got outvoted."

It was a vote Imlach refused to accept. While progressive thinkers like Emile Francis of the Rangers looked to accommodate the new order, Imlach and the Leafs fought back, or tried to. Bobby Baun had helped teammates negotiate better contracts, and through that and his own salary fights, had seen his relationship sour with Imlach. He was also a strong proponent of the union and succeeded Pulford as president. Despite being only 30 years old and still a very capable rearguard, Baun was exposed in the '67 expansion draft and lost to Oakland. The following September, according to Eagleson, Imlach tried unsuccessfully to get all the Leafs to quit the union. "There were several issues in the 1967–68 season. I was always putting out fires in Toronto," says Eagleson. "It was

Mickey Mouse shit. There was always a problem. Imlach put a heavier burden on himself and hurt the team."

Imlach decided he would fight the new union on his own turf—the Leaf dressing room. "Go out there and fucking skate around until we're finished," Pulford was told one day during the September 1967 training camp as Imlach prepared to address the team. With Pulford out of the room, Imlach then lit into the team over "this stupid fucking association" and the "traitors" on the team who had joined the union. Mid-rant, Tim Horton stood up and skated out to join Pulford. Most of the others soon followed, but young players like Ron Ellis remember feeling torn between sticking with their teammates and listening to the feared coach who had coached the team to the Stanley Cup just four months earlier. "Imlach wanted to break the union and he knew his chances were better with me out of the way," recalls Pulford of that day. "So I skated by myself for what seemed like a long time and started to wonder how things were going to play out. After what seemed like an eternity I saw Tim Horton coming on the ice, and a few seconds later out come Dave Keon. God bless them. If they hadn't joined me on the ice, that might have been the end of the union right there."

It was, to many, the day Imlach lost his control and power over the dressing room, but the resulting tension and upheaval tore the team apart. Even Armstrong, "the absolute greatest captain ever," according to a veteran like Marcel Pronovost, could no longer see his skills as a liaison between players and management used constructively: the barrier between Imlach and his team was now too great. The natural rivalries that always exist between teammates jostling for their share of ice time became exaggerated and poisonous. When Jim Pappin couldn't get a spot in the lineup, he held a grudge against Ellis, whom he viewed as one of Imlach's boys. When Imlach traded Frank Mahovlich in March 1968, he blamed the union for the nervous problems that had twice landed The Big M in hospital. Armstrong warned youngster Jim McKenny and other young players to be careful with their choices. "He told us to stay away from that shit, that we didn't need to get on Imlach's bad side because of the union," says McKenny.

Baun, meanwhile, came to resent Pulford over the years for handing over the reins of the new association just a few months after making that announcement to the owners in Montreal. By then a member of the Seals, Baun accepted the presidency of the union after Pulford told him the position had made him a "marked man" in Toronto. "I think that was the first indication of the way Pulford really operated," said Baun, who ultimately broke with Eagleson while Pulford remained friends with the former union boss. "From being a guy we believed was looking out for the players, history shows he was a guy who was really just looking out for Pulford," said Baun.

Peter Stemkowski, meanwhile, said he and his teammates all viewed Pulford as the player who led the fight against Imlach and watched in confusion over the years as Pulford became a dedicated, tight-fisted management man with the Blackhawks. "It's interesting that Pulford was the guy who most detested Imlach, yet he is the one guy from that team who has become the most like Imlach," says Stemkowski, Pulford's linemate in those '67 playoffs. Pulford remains unapologetic for his continuing friendship with the disgraced Eagleson or his switch to the management side. "When I was a player, the players needed help," he argued in the winter of 2004 as the NHL and players union prepared for another in a series of labour showdowns the following fall. "Any reasonable request was always shot down by the owners. It was complete unfairness. I was always active on the players' behalf. I was a vice-president of the pension society committee and as active a player as possible on behalf of players as it related to NHL affairs. Now, it's gone too far the other way. The pendulum has swung too far. We have to bring it back. The players long ago didn't need the kind of help that we needed in the 1960s. We have to bring some sanity back into the game."

————— ⚜ —————

The union, unquestionably, was the grenade in the dressing room that helped destroy that '67 Leaf champion at a time when the tide of sports history was moving relentlessly in new directions. The old system was breaking down and there was nothing Imlach, Shore or any other executive could do about it. Unionism spread to the minors. By May 1968 the NFL Players Association was bracing for a major showdown with the league, and in June baseball experienced another round of player independence when various players refused to play on the day of assassinated politician Robert F. Kennedy's funeral. The average salary in hockey was said to be $15,500, about 50 per cent below that of baseball, and when Orr went to negotiate a new contract he asked for $100,000, a salary the likes of which Gordie Howe and Jean Beliveau did not then command. Eagleson began making unprecedented noises about the union wanting a piece of the NHL's television revenue.

The Leafs, with four Stanley Cups in the previous six seasons, should have been better positioned than any other club to move forward and meet the new challenges of professional sport. They and the Canadiens, after all, had kept all Canadian TV revenues to themselves for years and the less-than-generous terms of the expansion agreement should have allowed them to protect enough talent to stay at the top. Indeed, Montreal had won Cups in 1965 and 1966, and after falling to the Leafs the following year, the Habs were still so well-stocked and organized that they carted off eight Cups in the next 12 years. The Leafs, however, squandered talent, sold their farm teams to generate cash and profits and fought changes in the game. Player after player went to war with Imlach over salaries and was sent packing. Every negotiation was bitter, and good players were lost because they stood up for themselves. Imlach left a twisted wreckage when he was fired in the spring of 1969.

Incredibly, the manner in which the Eagleson–Brewer–Imlach wars affected the Leafs was not yet over. Ten years after being fired, Imlach returned to Maple Leaf Gardens as the successor to Jim Gregory, who had taken over from Imlach. The Leafs had come full circle. Under Gregory's leadership, the Leafs had once again become a solid hockey club that had made the league semi-finals a year earlier. Quickly, however, the Imlach influence turned the Leafs into a circus, and part of that circus involved bringing Brewer back from five years of retirement to once more skate for the Leafs at age 41, fully 15 years after he had mysteriously bolted the club. Also signed were 38-year-old defenceman Larry Carriere and 30-year-old Darryl Maggs, both of whom had played for Imlach's coach and confidant, Floyd Smith, in the disbanded WHA. The two former Cincinnati Stingers and Brewer were regarded as Imlach spies in the dressing room, a rather strange accusation against Brewer given his previous tussles with Imlach. Their presence, however, fuelled the growing chasm between Imlach and team captain Darryl Sittler, one furthered by Imlach's refusal to let Sittler participate in the popular NHL "Showdown" intermission series. Sittler was represented by Eagleson, and to Imlach that meant that Eagleson had influence within the team in the same way he had influenced the Leaf dressing room in the final seasons before Imlach's first firing. It was the same fight all over again.

This time around, Imlach's spite knew no bounds. Sittler had a no-trade contract, so instead he dealt Sittler's linemate and best friend, Lanny McDonald, to Colorado for Pat Hickey and Wilf Paiement on December 28, 1979. After telling the classy McDonald he'd been traded, McDonald asked where he was going. "None of your business," growled the Leaf GM.

McDonald asked the identity of the players he'd been traded for. "That's none of your business either," said Imlach. Imlach also concocted the idea of giving Paiement Number 99 to wear, the same as the growing legend that was then Wayne Gretzky, to create the perception that he had traded McDonald for a "star" player.

Imlach also fought with another Eagleson client, goalie Mike Palmateer, who was playing out the option year of his contract in the 1979–80 season and wanted a no-trade clause in his new deal like Sittler. "Why is the standard NHL contract that was collectively bargained with the NHLPA and doesn't include the right to no-trade provisions good enough for everyone else in the NHLPA except for the client of the head of the NHLPA?" Imlach fumed. Palmateer, the best goalie the club had employed since Bernie Parent, was dealt to Washington the following June and the Leafs went into the 1980–81 season with the unproven Jiri Crha as their starting goalie, an experiment that had predictably bad results. When Eagleson arrived in the Leaf offices that fall to negotiate contracts for Rocky Saganiuk and Robert Picard, Imlach bellowed, "I'm ready for you, you prick." On Imlach's desk when Eagleson poked his head in were a half-dozen vials of medication Imlach was taking for his heart condition. While that exchange seemed lighthearted, Eagleson was often heard to boast, "I told Punch Imlach I'd piss on his grave. And I did."

A promising Leaf team was thus destroyed by Imlach's enmity for Eagleson just as Imlach's hatred for the players association had undermined a championship Leaf team in 1967. In the 1980 playoffs against Minnesota, the club arranged for two hotel shuttle buses to pick up the team as it arrived in Bloomington. As Imlach sat on one bus and cursed his players, each and every one of them walked past and got on the other bus. Brewer, who by then had become a malcontent and more welcome in the dressing room, made a shoulder fake as though he was about to get on to Imlach's bus and then strode to the other vehicle. Ultimately, Imlach dumped Brewer, Maggs and Carriere, believing their contracts had been only for the 1979–80 season. But by failing to do the proper paperwork, specifically failing to sign the three players to termination contracts, the Leaf GM inadvertently gave all three an option for the following season. Maggs and Carriere walked away, but Brewer pursued the matter despite dressing for only 20 games in his comeback season. The fight raged for years until Brewer finally received a cheque for $27,418.52 in 1987 as compensation for Imlach's oversight. The defenceman's appeal to his former agent, Eagleson, for help in the matter went unheard, and many believe that further motivated Brewer in what became his historic fight to investigate the abuse of players' pensions. Imlach's stupidity on Brewer's contract, in a weird historical twist, may have inadvertently been a crucial factor in the series of events that finally toppled Eagleson.

Interestingly, hearkening back to Eagleson's experiences with Ballard and the Silver Seven in New York back in 1966, Ballard had a much better relationship with the players union boss. After Ballard was convicted of 47 fraud charges in 1972, Eagleson called both the crown attorney and the judge to plead for a lenient sentence. When no TV partner could be found for the 1972 Summit Series, Eagleson called Ballard and convinced him to form a company with him that would find a sponsor and sell the TV rights. Years later, Eagleson boasted that if he needed $100,000 in a hurry, he could call Toronto boxing impresario Irving Ungerman for half and Ballard for the other half. Finally, when Ballard was searching for a new general manager in 1989, he offered the job to Eagleson, who turned it down. The Leafs had finally warmed to Eagleson by the time he was about to become an NHL pariah.

Through all the tangles with the NHL union and the explosive growth of athletes' rights, the Leafs never quite got it right, always reading the current incorrectly. After winning it all in 1967, that lack of insight into the sport's changes meant the Leafs had, without question, disembarked from hockey's train of manifest destiny.

Stanley Cup Final, Game One
Maple Leafs at Montreal, April 20, 1967

On any successful hockey team, and particularly on any championship team, there emerges a debate over the contribution of the coach. There are those members of the Montreal Canadiens teams that won four straight Stanley Cups in the 1970s, for example, who will argue that Scotty Bowman's prime contribution to their victories was to open the gate and make sure he didn't accidentally trip the players as they headed out on to the ice. Not surprisingly, there are still those who argue that George (Punch) Imlach was never the master strategist he was portrayed to be, never the brilliant mind who brought the Leafs back into contention after the dismal 1950s. "Imlach was a great motivator, but he did a lot of things that were wrong in the way he handled players," says Bob Pulford, who went to war with Imlach as the first president of the NHL Players Association in 1967 but eventually became a hard-nosed NHL executive himself. "I can tell you this. We had no strategy whatsoever when it came to things like X's and O's and the power play. But when it came to the 1967 final, he outcoached Toe Blake."

Blake and the Montreal Canadiens were, after the collapse of the first-place Blackhawks, a new and very different opponent for the Leafs that spring when the two clubs met in the last Stanley Cup final of the Original Six era. Unlike Chicago coach Billy Reay, who had been unsuccessful during his time in Toronto and had inherited a championship team from Rudy Pilous in 1963 but been unable to coax that jittery squad to another title, Blake was by then the dean of NHL coaches. He had already won seven Cups with the Habs, and was going for a third straight against the Leafs with a powerful club that had routed Toronto in four straight games the previous spring and looked even more formidable this time around. Montreal hadn't been able to match Chicago during the regular season, but injuries to Jean Beliveau and Henri Richard had been part of the problem. As March rolled into April, however, the Habs had taken off, and came into the playoffs having won 15 straight games, including four consecutive wins over the New York Rangers in the opening round of the post-season. Les Habitants were strong in a classic sense down the middle with Beliveau, Richard and Ralph Backstrom, and had a fearsome power play. Yvan (The Roadrunner) Cournoyer had scored 25 goals during the season, and 20 had come with the Habs holding the man advantage. Ten of those power-play scores had come against the Leafs.

The Canadiens were good, but not great, on the back end, certainly nothing like the defence corps of the '70s dynasty that included The Big Three: Larry Robinson, Serge Savard and Guy Lapointe. Defencemen like Jacques Laperriere, Terry Harper, Jean-Guy Talbot, Ted Harris and J.C. Tremblay manned the Montreal blueline in 1967, and they played in front of a surprise goaltender. Rogatien Vachon, just 21, had emerged from obscurity and the Thetford Mines Junior Canadiens to steal the starting job from veterans Gump Worsley and Charlie Hodge that season after the Worsley–Hodge tandem had provided the essential netminding in '65 and '66. Due to injuries, Vachon was promoted from the Houston Apollos partway through the season; he lost only three games during 19 appearances for the Habs as they got on their late-season roll. He was a good goalie who would have an outstanding NHL career, but as a rookie he was the most obvious potential weakness the powerful Habs appeared to have.

So Imlach zeroed in on Vachon. He understood that if he made Vachon the centre of the debate, rather than the Leafs' ability to slow the Montreal power play or the matchup between Beliveau and Dave Keon, it might portray the series in a very different light. Rather than wondering whether George Armstrong would play after missing the final five games of the Chicago series, or if the defence combo of Larry Hillman and Marcel Pronovost could continue to thrive against the speedy Habs, Imlach wanted to make this a series about Vachon, first and foremost. Reporters might ask whether the wonky knee of aged Leaf defenceman Allan Stanley could stand up this time around after giving out on him 30 seconds into the previous year's playoff test against Montreal, and they could wonder whether Blake would make good on his threat to use Claude Provost to shadow Frank Mahovlich as Provost had done to an infuriated Bobby Hull in previous years. But Imlach wanted every story to begin and end with questions about Vachon.

Vachon helped out by suggesting the Canadiens were pleased to be facing the Leafs, not Chicago, in the final. "Tell that cocky Junior B goaltender that he won't be facing New York Ranger peashooters when the Leafs open up on him," snapped Imlach. The phrase "Junior B goaltender" exploded into controversy, becoming one of the most memorable utterances and pieces of psychological warfare in Stanley Cup history. "I hope Blake doesn't disappoint me with Worsley or Hodge," taunted Imlach. "After we get through with [Vachon], he may be back in Junior B." The Canadiens, naturally, suggested they had no reason for concern. "What's the difference between stopping the puck at Thetford Mines or at the Forum?" asked Vachon. "Why should [Vachon] be nervous?" wondered Blake.

It was the first time the two teams had met in the Cup final in eight years, a matchup made doubly meaningful by the opening of the world's fair at Expo '67, which further accentuated the sense of rivalry between the two cities and Canada's French–English populations. Unlike today, the teams were accurate reflections of their home towns. More than half of the Canadiens' roster was composed of Quebec-born players, but also included players from Ontario and Saskatchewan at a time when the Montreal establishment was still dominated by the Anglophone elite. The Leaf roster included one athlete who spoke French in Pronovost, who had only been a Leaf since 1965. Keon was from the border town of Noranda, Quebec, but from the English-speaking part. Otherwise, the Leaf team was filled with either Toronto-born boys or players who had come to the city in their teenage years to go to school at St. Mike's or play for the Junior Marlboros. The sense of city versus city, French versus English, was vibrant and real. "We were the underdogs so we didn't feel the pressure," says Mahovlich, looking back. "Montreal was just going berserk about Expo, and we wanted to do something to deflate a city that assumed the Stanley Cup was going to be a part of Expo."

It didn't happen that way in Game One at the Forum. The opening contest of the Stanley Cup final featured a Canadiens team that looked very much like it had been resting for seven days while the Leafs were incurring fresh bruises and wounds with their tough six-game series with Chicago. Vachon, seemingly dismissing any doubt, made an excellent early save on Jim Pappin while the game was scoreless, and then another on Tim Horton with the Habs cradling a 2–1 lead. It was all Montreal the rest of the way, with Richard potting a hat trick with his famous brother,

Maurice, in the stands cheering him on. Cournoyer snapped home two power-play goals as the Canadiens cruised to an easy 6–2 win for their 16th consecutive victory. "I thought they would come out hitting, but they didn't," said the Pocket Rocket. *Toronto Star* columnist Red Burnett said the game appeared to be "a duel between modern jet fighters and World War One Sopwith Camels."

While Hillman and Pronovost fared reasonably well, the tandem of Horton and Stanley was torn to shreds, with Horton on the ice for five Montreal goals and Stanley victimized on four occasions. Terry Sawchuk suffered through a lamentable night in the Toronto net, and when Johnny Bower replaced him for the final 15 minutes, he ended up with a bruised ankle and bloodied nose. The Montreal victory had been complete, and after the game the relaxed Vachon, who had snoozed on the team bus to the game that night, joked with reporters about looking forward to improving his upper-body strength in the off-season at a brewery, "slinging cases of beer around to build up my muscles."

The mood had changed on the Leaf side from the elation that followed the victory over the Hawks, but there were some promising signs. Pappin had scored another goal and assisted on Hillman's first-period goal, maintaining his torrid pace as the club's top post-season attacker. Armstrong had returned after missing most of the series against the Hawks with a knee injury, and the lopsided game allowed Imlach to give his captain extra shifts along with other little used players like Bobby Baun, Aut Erickson, Eddie Shack and Mike Walton. With any rust gone, Armstrong was now ready to go back to his regular line with Keon and Mahovlich, while Brian Conacher would find a permanent spot on the left side with Red Kelly and Ron Ellis to replace Larry Jeffrey, who had blown out his knee in the final game against the Hawks.

Two off-ice stories, one before Game One and one after, served as titillating hints of what lay ahead. On the day the Leafs took the midnight train to Montreal before the opener, Pappin was walking his dog in his west-end neighbourhood, when an acquaintance named Jimmy Black intercepted him. Pappin loved the horses and Black owned a few at Woodbine Race Track. He was also a serious gambler, and they had forged a friendship. Black told Pappin that he had bet $2,000 on the Leafs to win the Cup at 15-to-1 odds and was already halfway to winning $30,000. As they parted, Black told Pappin that if the Leafs beat Montreal, he would have an in-ground swimming pool built at Pappin's home.

Meanwhile, with her fiancé, Brian, out of town with the Leafs, the future Mrs. Susan Conacher took the opportunity to have their Don Mills home painted. The day after the resounding Montreal triumph in Game One, she returned to survey the work that had been done. The quality of painting was good, she decided, until an unfinished wall caught her eye. One of the painters, an obviously disturbed Leaf fan, or perhaps a triumphant Habs supporter, had painted 6–2 in bold numerals. "Half-amused and half-annoyed," she wondered what might be written about her husband and his team if the tone of the final didn't change in the days ahead.

6 *Owning the Empire*

In 1999, the Maple Leafs abandoned the only home they'd ever known, the yellowed brick edifice at the corner of Church and Carlton Streets that Conn Smythe had somehow managed to build and open in the depths of the Great Depression. Maple Leaf Gardens had almost always been busy and usually full, particularly for NHL hockey games, but it had outlived its usefulness, at least to the Leafs. Baseball's Boston Red Sox might still want to operate out of tiny, historic Fenway Park, but the sparkling new Air Canada Centre south of the Gardens near Lake Ontario was everything to the Leafs that the Gardens wasn't—air-conditioned and extremely revenue friendly. The Leafs, never a team to clutch their history too tightly, seemed anxious to leave the site of their 11 Stanley Cup triumphs and start fresh in a new home.

No wonder, then, that by June 2004, the Leaf ownership group signed a contract with Loblaw Cos. Ltd., approving a concept to pave the famed ice rink at the Gardens and convert the building into a giant supermarket. The longtime homes of their Original Six partners in Boston, Chicago and Detroit had been flattened by the wrecker's ball, and Montreal's famed Forum had been turned into an entertainment complex filled with theatres, bars, restaurants and video game parlours. By comparison, the Leafs' plans seemed no more heartless or crassly commercial. The public relations problem, however, was that somebody else had a much more appealing plan.

That spring, Eugene Melnyk had just absorbed his first crushing playoff loss to the Leafs as owner of the Ottawa

Senators, the fourth such post-season defeat for the Sens in the Battle of Ontario. That setback, however, didn't diminish Melnyk's interest in buying Maple Leaf Gardens and turning it into a modern hockey and business complex. Melnyk, who also owned the St. Mike's Majors of the Ontario Hockey League, the same junior team that once supplied the Leafs with oodles of hockey talent, proposed to maintain the Gardens as a 10,000-seat hockey arena for the Majors and local minor hockey teams, complete with a Canadian Amateur Hockey Hall of Fame. The new complex, under Melnyk's plan, would also house a restaurant, retail space and two 12,000-square-foot penthouse lofts. "I want to restore the property to its former glory and keep it intact as a shrine to Canada hockey," said Melnyk in a statement. "Growing up playing ball hockey on the streets of Toronto, I could never afford to go to a game at the Gardens. I want to restore this building so our kids and Toronto families can watch the excitement of minor hockey at affordable prices. I want to expose more Torontonians to the skills and talent of tomorrow's NHL stars."

Leaf officials, bound by their deal with Loblaws, denied that Melnyk's proposal was worthy of serious consideration. Even before signing the deal with the grocery giant, the Leafs had refused to negotiate a deal with Melnyk. "We are not interested," reiterated senior vice-president Bob Hunter in May 2004. Still, the choice had long seemed clear. The hockey club could either discard its history, allowing cars to be parked and watermelons to be sold where Syl Apps once skated, or find a new way for that history to be cherished and embraced.

The grocery store plan, at least symbolically, was a means for the hockey club to bury the past, and to get everyone else to forget it as well. The plan was about profit and use of a complicated real estate property, of course, but it also seemed a subconscious attempt to make modern times more important—to physically erase the horrors of a sexual abuse scandal that had its genesis in the hidden rooms of the Gardens in the 1960s and stained the ownership of two old men who had come to control the building and the team by controversial means.

As much as the Leafs' past and connection to Maple Leaf Gardens was something to be cherished by millions of Canadians, by 2004 it was also something to run from as the club was eliminated in the second round of the Stanley Cup playoffs, marking a 37th straight spring in which the Leafs had failed to even return to the final, let alone win the Cup. The myths of the 1967 Cup victory loomed larger than ever as an old Leaf team, modelled in some ways after the '67 winners, filed off the ice after being eliminated in the sixth game by the Philadelphia Flyers on Jeremy Roenick's overtime winner.

As always, however, references to 1967 were warm and syrupy, hardly in rhythm with the truths of that last championship season. By the time George Armstrong's long shot had skimmed into an empty net to clinch the '67 final over Montreal, for example, the process of ripping the Leafs from the hands of the legendary Smythe family was well underway. Founder Conn Smythe had already been shoved aside after a bitter dispute with the manner in which the organization was being run and his son, Stafford, was soon to be erased from the picture as well.

It remains the subject of considerable debate as to the nature of the plans that were swimming ambitiously through the mind of Harold E. Ballard as he sat in a sparkling convertible beside Armstrong on a chilly May 5, less than 72 hours after the Leafs had clinched the 1967 Stanley Cup. The trophy was in the car with Armstrong and Ballard as it turned into Nathan Phillips Square, where 30,000 admirers had gathered to fete the surprise champions, a team that had recorded stunning upsets over Chicago and Montreal to walk away with hockey's most famous hardware. It was the fourth such celebration in six years, and four different mayors had presided over the proceedings amidst turbulent political change in Toronto, including William Dennison in 1967. That it was Ballard waving to the crowd from the car that carried the Cup was striking, given that it was his partner, Stafford Smythe, who was still seen to be the hockey brains at the Gardens.

Then, few viewed Ballard as the future emperor of the Maple Leaf realm. As he approached his 64th birthday that summer, he was generally viewed as Smythe's bombastic side-kick. "I never thought in my wildest dreams that Harold would ever take over," recalls Alan Eagleson. "Stafford ran the joint. Harold didn't have the heart for the franchise that Stafford did." Smythe was the president of Maple Leaf Gardens Ltd., while Toronto businessman John Bassett was the chairman of the Gardens board and Ballard the executive vice-president, in charge of many things, but not of the famous hockey team itself. That was Stafford's job, and he'd had significant success since taking over in 1961: the team had captured four Cups. Ballard was a showman and a huckster, and seemed too old to be seriously considered as the future of the Leafs. Stafford, after all, had children who believed they were the future heirs of the Leafs, particularly his son Tommy. But as the Stanley Cup parade of 1967 wound its way through the heart of down-town Toronto, Ballard knew he and Smythe had been diverting monies from the Gardens for their own interests and needs, binding the two men together in their crimes.

They were close friends who had enjoyed the fruits of being part of the infamous Silver Seven and now shared important secrets that could bring both of them down. The Gardens was more profitable than it had ever been, and Ballard must have coveted it and dreamed of owning the entire operation. Within five years, he would. The Smythe hockey empire would be his, and the desecration of a national hockey institution would be the result. So twisted would the relation-ship between the team and its past eventually become that

Ballard would even besmirch the legacy of the '67 champs. In an attempt to refashion history, he would superimpose a picture of his son, Bill, over that of his former partner, Bassett, in the official '67 team picture when it was reprinted for a Leaf calendar in the mid-1980s.

It's open to speculation whether the Leafs would have been better off had the Smythe family never lost control. But ever since the Smythes were pushed out, it has been as though ownership of the team has brought with it a curse. By the mid-1990s, Ballard's longtime lawyer, Rosanne Rocchi, described ownership wrangles surrounding the team as akin to the pursuit of the legendary Hope diamond—bringing only misery, bad luck, defeat and financial destruction.

When the chance came to grab the Gardens, Ballard wasn't interested in prolonging or honouring the Smythe hockey legacy, just as his friend Steve Stavro would have his own plans for the Leafs when Ballard's will declared the team should be sold off to a group of charities in 1990. The ambition of both men to own a Canadian hockey institution ultimately proved successful, at least in the acquisition. But in both cases, their reach exceeded their personal wealth and certainly their skills as hockey entrepreneurs. Ballard, with the team heavily leveraged, died an angry, pathetic old man, estranged from his children during many of the final years of his life and widely reviled as the person who had destroyed the honour of the Leafs.

Stavro's personal financial empire, meanwhile, buckled under the weight of trying desperately to maintain his hold on the hockey jewel. It was as though the sheer power of angry Leaf legends was dragging him down. Although Ballard had wanted proceeds from the sale of the Gardens to go to organizations like the Salvation Army and various hospitals, the transaction that put Stavro in control of the Gardens left little for the charities, perhaps only $3 million to $5 million.

(Interestingly, the exciting Leaf playoff run of 1993 that came within one game of putting the Leafs in the Cup final occurred when nobody was truly the owner of the Leafs. It came at a time when Stavro and his pals were having fun operating a team that was still owned by the Ballard estate.) Immediately, Stavro found himself the target of government investigations, lawsuits and howls of protests from Gardens shareholders, who protested that Stavro had used his position mostly to benefit himself. Eight tumultuous years after using his position as executor of Ballard's will to seize control of the Gardens and the Leafs, he was forced to close his entire 10-store Knob Hill Farms grocery chain, long a fixture in the Toronto area, and to sell about $60 million worth of real estate to generate funds to support his stake in the Leafs.

By 2003, with no obvious heir to hand the team to and no ally left to save his position, Stavro ended up selling his stock in Maple Leaf Sports and Entertainment Ltd., the corporate entity that he had created to take the club private after years as a publicly traded company. He was forced to do a deal with his bitter rival, construction magnate Larry Tanenbaum. That put Tanenbaum at the helm of the team that has since become controlled by multiple corporate interests. Over four decades, the franchise has, with a few changes in the current, gone from the hands of one man into the hands of many, both individual and corporate. It has never been sold to the highest bidder on the open market; instead, it's always been purchased under controversial circumstances.

The headlong rush from the dignified, if idiosyncratic and dictatorial, days of Conn Smythe to utter disgrace began in early 1961. Under Smythe Sr., the Leafs had at that time gone an entire decade without winning a Stanley Cup. For seven years during that period, they didn't win a single playoff series. A young Stafford Smythe, then 40, was chomping at the bit to prove he could do better than his father, a no-nonsense man who commanded respect through terror and his no-drink, no-smoking ways. Four years earlier, in 1957, Stafford had accepted the chairmanship of the Gardens hockey committee after Hap Day had been ousted as the club's hockey boss. At the time, he insisted he had no intention of succeeding his father as president of the Gardens. "Sand and gravel is my business," he said, a reference to the family's non-hockey enterprise.

The hockey committee, designed to get young voices heard in the organization, included Stafford, Ballard, Bassett, and other prominent Toronto businessmen. This marked the beginnings of a group that would come to be known as the "Silver Seven," a group ostensibly created to collectively chart the course back to hockey glory. But over time the Silver Seven became better known for a wild, raucous lifestyle of parties, women and alcohol. In the terms of the day, the Silver Seven was referred to as a glorified "glee club" for its penchant to join the team on the road and cheer. But that term cloaks the group in a kind of happy innocence, when in reality for many it was a welcome diversion from their families and businesses for sexual romps and all kinds of bizarre antics. In fact, their behaviour extended to the home front, as an apartment was rented within sight of the Gardens and registered as the "Marlboro Athletic Club." In fact, it was used for all kinds of activities and parties. The lease was made out to "S.H. Marlie," besmirching the name of the organization's junior affiliate in a rather lurid way.

Stafford Smythe had developed a solid reputation in hockey, particularly after he managed the Marlboros, owned by the Leafs, to consecutive Memorial Cup titles in the 1950s. But he had another side to his character that, to all accounts, his father did not, including, according to longtime Toronto sportswriter Dick Beddoes, "an insatiable appetite for oral sex." In his biography of Ballard, entitled *Pal Hal*, Beddoes quoted Chicago Blackhawks owner Jim Norris' assessment of Stafford. "He was a good hockey man," said Norris. "But he was always looking to get laid." Those proclivities for wild living and an increasing attraction to the bottle would be part of the sad elixir that destroyed Stafford Smythe.

In November 1961, Stafford forced his father's hand, suddenly announcing he was resigning as chairman of the hockey committee. "I don't want to pressure Stafford into any position which he is unwilling to accept," said the elder Smythe, stunned by his son's decision. "But I'm hoping some solution may be worked out. Nothing would make me happier than to see my son take over my job." It seemed on the surface that Stafford was backing away from the hockey business, but the truth was he was angling to take over his father's empire. To Stafford and his cronies, the Gardens was a sleeping giant, capable of generating more business and profits than had been the case under Conn Smythe's conservative leadership, a reign primarily dedicated to developing strong hockey clubs and generating consistent, reliable profits. To the young turks the old man was sitting on a gold mine but wouldn't take advantage of all the possibilities. Plus, he was standing in the way of his son's various ambitions.

Stafford's strategy worked beautifully. Ten days after his bold resignation, Stafford became the new president of Maple Leaf Gardens, pushing aside his father 30 years after the opening of the building. Along with Ballard and Bassett, Stafford bought his father's 45,000 shares for an estimated $2 million, giving the troika 60 per cent controlling interest and changing the direction of the company and the hockey team forever. At the time, Conn Smythe was still vibrant at 66, still capable of running the operation. The waiting list for season tickets was 6,000 names long, and while the team hadn't won a Cup since '51, there was no public outcry for Conn Smythe to be removed. Instead, handing the club to his son seems, in retrospect, the act of a man trying to smooth the way for his own ambitious child's success, rather than the decision of an elderly businessman sensing his time had passed. What he didn't realize immediately was that Ballard and Bassett were also involved. In fact, the Smythe patriarch didn't find out his son had partners until several days after the sale, and that served to poison the waters between father and son immediately. Conn Smythe felt deceived, and he certainly must have felt worried over the future of the company he had built from the ground up now that large chunks of equity were held outside the family. Ballard's intentions as Stafford Smythe's partner had little to do with getting the Leafs' hands back on the Stanley Cup. "I was going to make the Gardens take off at a million miles an hour," he told Beddoes.

With Stafford Smythe, Harold Ballard and Bassett in control as president, executive vice-president and chairman of the board, respectively, there was immediate on-ice success. Cups in 1962, 1963 and 1964 were evidence that a successful transition had taken place. Under the new owners, it appeared the Leafs would remain a hockey powerhouse, a team that didn't always win but was never far from winning again. In truth, however, the business of the Leafs was changing, and fast. That was never clearer than in the unusual events of October 1962, when the Leafs agreed to sell star winger Frank Mahovlich to the Chicago Blackhawks for a cool $1 million, an amount roughly equivalent to a single season's gate receipts at the time and half the value of the sale of Gardens shares a year earlier. Indeed, the three Leaf owners had taken out a $2.5-million loan from the Bank of Nova Scotia to finance their ambitions, and selling their top star would have helped to retire a major chunk of that debt.

Mahovlich had just come off a 48-goal season but wouldn't sign a new contract, at least not for what the Leafs were offering. The proposed deal had its genesis in a late-night drinking session between Ballard and Hawks owner Jim Norris, a man who knew the value of a box office attraction from his boxing enterprises. Norris wanted to put Mahovlich and Bobby Hull together as the greatest set of left wingers the game had ever seen. The Norris family had an interest in four of the six NHL teams, so the idea of cornering the market on brilliant left wingers appealed to Jim Norris. The Hawks had won the 1961 Cup while the Leafs had won in 1962, meaning it was an audacious and unusual deal between two keen rivals for an outrageous amount of money. Why would the Leafs do it? For starters, they couldn't get Mahovlich to sign a new contract. Secondly, the new ownership group had some different priorities than the old, and suddenly selling off stars for income seemed like a good idea.

The tale gets a bit foggy with the retelling, but the most accurate version probably appeared in a column by Milt Dunnell in *The Toronto Star* on February 28, 1966, almost four years after the deal. When the news first hit the headlines, the Leafs were able to laugh it off successfully as a bit of a lark, as though the alcohol-inspired auction between Ballard and Norris had been a bit of late-night nonsense that others had foolishly taken seriously. After all, this was at a time when players made an average of about $12,000 a season. "This is the greatest publicity stunt since the Regency Rockets," sniffed Stafford Smythe when the Mahovlich sale reached the papers, comparing the rumoured transaction to that of a Toronto contractor who had offered to buy the Leafs if they changed the name of the team to reflect his business interests. In the next breath, however, Smythe suggested that Norris could yet make the offer in the sobriety of the next business day. "I am interested," said Smythe.

The true story was that Ballard had indeed cut a deal with Norris to sell The Big M, and both men believed it was a binding agreement. In the boozy party that followed the all-star game in Toronto, Norris had peeled off $1,000 in $100 bills as a down payment and written on a piece of hotel stationery, "I will pay $1,000,000 for Frank Mahovlich." He then asked Ballard and another Gardens director, Jack Amell, to sign the document, and both did. Ballard didn't seem inclined to back out of the deal. "One million dollars is more than we could get for the whole hockey team, including the Stanley Cup," he said. On the night of the deal, however, a worried Bruce Norris, Jim Norris' brother and owner of the Detroit Red Wings, called Conn Smythe at home to voice concerns that Mahovlich had indeed been sold.

According to Dunnell, Smythe frantically tried to contact his son, and by 3 a.m. he did. Stafford confirmed the deal. The father told his son that no player was worth that kind of money, and making such a transaction under the influence of alcohol was bad business. As well, Conn told Stafford that if any player was worth that amount of money, he should be playing for the Leafs. Suitably scolded, Stafford refused to accept a cheque for the remaining $999,000 when Blackhawks GM Tommy Ivan arrived at the Gardens to seal the deal the next day. "We never rolled a drunk yet and we don't have to start now," the Leaf president told reporters.

Conn Smythe, then, had foiled the attempt of Ballard, with the apparent agreement of Bassett and Stafford, to turn the Maple Leafs into an auction house, with prime talent available to the highest bidder. That probably just made Ballard and his cronies more anxious to get the legendary patriarch out of the way. Indeed, some of the directors of the Gardens were enraged to learn that The Major, with no significant stock in the team, had killed the deal, and a second inquiry was made to Norris a week later to see if he might still be interested. He wasn't, and Mahovlich stayed a Leaf, foiling what, in hockey history, would have rivalled the $15-million-plus players trade of Wayne Gretzky to the Los Angeles Kings in 1988 as the most expensive transfer of an NHL player.

Within four years, however, Conn Smythe would be out of the way, resigning from the Gardens board in disgust. It was probably not surprising, since he was a hockey man through and through from the start—the coach of the New York Rangers who was abruptly fired by team executive Colonel John Hammond in a brief meeting at Union Station in Toronto and replaced by Lester Patrick, another hockey legend. Smythe received $2,500 in severance, and parlayed that and a connection with mining entrepreneur J.P. Bickell into the Gardens empire. Smythe bought the Toronto St. Pats for $165,000 and built the hockey arena when electrical workers agreed to take Gardens stock in lieu of paycheques. By the time the arena opened in 1931, the new hockey business was $2 million in debt, but over the decades Smythe paid that off, issued an estimated $2.7 million in dividends to stockholders and built a championship hockey team.

If Conn Smythe doubted his son's intentions in November 1961, he didn't reveal them publicly. "It's a great satisfaction to me that my son, who not long ago as a stick boy congratulated me on winning the Stanley Cup, now has a chance to do the same thing as president," said Smythe Sr. There was no talk of a family legacy, but Smythe's intention seemed clear: his son would rule the Gardens for as long as he had and then pass it on through the family. The Gardens, still fairly compact with 12,583 seats, was flush with cash, owned several parking lots around the arena and had a lengthy season-ticket waiting list, but it now had renewed debt. It soon would go on a wild ride from stability and conservative profitability down a path of wild expansion and questionable practices that would land those who ran the Gardens in serious legal jeopardy.

By 1963, the new Gardens owners remodelled the building, installed a smoky refuge called The Hot Stove Lounge on Church Street, and opened stores on the front of the building to attract new customers. The Beatles played the Gardens in

September 1964, with Ballard coercing the Fab Four into playing two shows when they had initially agreed to play only one. Music was changing North American culture in an explosive way, and Ballard courted the controversy, putting the Gardens squarely in the limelight. The Beatles arrived on Labour Day, but not before many in the city had voiced their misgivings about the musical group. Nine hundred police officers were set to ensure security and six city blocks had been cordoned off for the event. "I think we are quite unjustified in disrupting traffic in the heart of our city for these young misfits, completely lacking in talent, whose contribution to the youth of the nation is the absolute negative of all that is desirable," read one letter to *The Toronto Star*, expressing an opinion that was widespread.

Ballard, of course, loved it. The Beatles dominated the headlines for weeks, and on the same day separatists were burning Union Jacks in Montreal, the Beatles arrived to a crowd of 10,000 at Malton Airport. They played to more than 33,000 fans in two concerts at a top ticket price of $5.50, snubbing Toronto Mayor Phil Givens after one concert when Givens and his wife dropped by the King Edward Hotel to pay their respects. By the fall of 1965, the Leafs had failed to win the Cup for the first time in four years, but the organization was soaring to new heights of profitability, issuing the largest dividend in company history. Maple Leaf Gardens was now about much more than hockey.

Ballard's next carnival would be even more controversial, and would prove to be pivotal to the future of the Gardens and the Leafs. In March 1966, the news broke that Ballard had cut a deal with Bob Arum, the lawyer for Main Bouts Inc., to hold a heavyweight fight between Ernie Terrell and Muhammad Ali, although most media outlets declined to acknowledge Ali's Muslim choices and continued to refer to him as Cassius Clay. Ali's controversial, "I ain't got no quarrel with those

Viet Cong," statements were perceived as unpatriotic comments on both sides of the Canada–U.S. border. Consequently, the proposed fight had bounced around from New York to Chicago to Montreal until finding a promoter in Toronto, namely, Ballard. The announcement caused an immediate uproar, with one provincial politician claiming Toronto would lose prestige in the world because of its willingness to host the fight. The bout came with a top ticket of $100, unheard of in Toronto entertainment circles.

Not surprisingly, Conn Smythe, a veteran of two World Wars, was bitterly opposed. "A fight that isn't good enough for Chicago or Montreal certainly isn't good enough for Maple Leaf Gardens," he said. The elder Smythe had been forced to accept Ballard's ownership position, the Mahovlich mess and the arrival of the Beatles, but he refused to stomach Ali. He resigned from his position as a director with the Gardens on March 8, 1966, sold his remaining 5,100 shares but kept his office, a secretary, two phone lines, a car and a $15,000 annual salary. An era was over, and Smythe Sr. punctuated his retreat with a famous quote that would ring for decades. "I cannot go along with the policy of present management to put cash ahead of class," he said. He felt betrayed by his son and utterly alienated from the company he had built. Years later at a Hockey Hall of Fame luncheon, he told reporters, "You fellows know what it's like to be traded. I was traded for a Black Muslim minister and $35,000." The dollars represented the fee charged by the Gardens to hold the fight.

The Leafs again failed to win the 1966 Stanley Cup tournament, and the team was growing old and ineffective. Expansion was coming, doubling the size of the league to 12 teams from six, but instead of preparing for the new NHL, Ballard and Smythe were losing their grip on the hockey operation at the same time the business of the Gardens was booming. There was still debt on the team and building, but NHL expansion fees and the sale of the Leafs' minor league affiliates netted the club almost $3 million. The Marlies were still very profitable, drawing crowds in excess of 14,000 fans during the 1966–67 season, while the players were making only $60 a week. A new three-year $3.6-million TV deal in the U.S. with CBS promised new sources of revenue. In 1965, the Leaf owners struck a six-year $9-million deal for the club's local broadcast rights, and in the same year Gardens stock hit $93 a share and was split, five for one.

When the players arrived to begin the 1966–67 season, they were greeted by a refurbished Gardens, which had been redesigned again at a cost of $750,000 to embrace commercial needs over tradition. More than 600 seats had been added to hike capacity to 15,461 seats for hockey, and the enormous portrait of Queen Elizabeth II that had been a fixture at one end of the arena had been ripped down to make room for a mezzanine. Colour television was all the rage, as the CBC had announced 85 percent of its programming would be available in colour, and bright, new television lights had been installed to enhance the picture emanating from the building. Players complained about the glare, and Kent Douglas wore stripes of burnt cork under his eyes to deflect the brightness until Imlach ordered him to stop.

Behind the scenes, meanwhile, Ballard and Smythe were starting to play games with money and taxes, games that would land each man in serious legal trouble and destroy the proud reputation of the franchise. Conn Smythe was out of the way and the Gardens was profitable, but Stafford Smythe was becoming increasingly erratic and both he and Ballard had begun the process of diverting Gardens monies for their own personal use.

In 1965, the Cloke Construction Company began doing work on the Gardens. At the same time, the company began work on Ballard's home on Montgomery Road in Etobicoke and on the construction of Stafford's new home at 15 Ashley Park, also in the west Toronto suburb. The invoices from Cloke, paid in full by the Gardens, indicated that some of the work on the hockey arena was actually for work on the two homes. In this way, monies were diverted from Gardens shareholders to the wallets of Smythe and Ballard. In March 1967, just two months before the club would stun the hockey world by somehow capturing an 11th Stanley Cup, Ballard illegally used Gardens money to pay for limousine services at his daughter's wedding, according to court documents.

This was the dark underbelly of the Leafs. While the team was crafting a stunning championship run, Ballard and Smythe were stealing money from company coffers, displaying a callous disregard for the national institution they had purchased. "Harold orchestrated most of it," said Jim Gregory, who was a key hockey insider with the organization through the 1960s. The Gardens had expanded and become more profitable, but the primary owners had twisted the company into a trough for their own purposes. The hockey team would soon be the toast of the town again, but that only served to mask from public eyes, at least temporarily, the illegal activities going on behind the scenes.

The company had become increasingly focused on non-hockey businesses, the minor league system was being sold off piece by piece to give the club badly needed cash and Stafford Smythe, once regarded as a solid hockey man, had become hopelessly derailed in his personal and professional life. He was a complicated character, a man who once responded to a *Toronto Telegram* story on the need for an outdoor rink in a small Canadian town by writing the entire $1,000 cheque himself. "Stafford ended up with a brutal reputation that wasn't deserved," says Gregory. "People don't know what a good hockey person he was." By 1971, Stafford Smythe would be dead of a bleeding ulcer, dogged to the grave by charges of tax evasion and fraud filed in 1969. "Stafford knew he was going to die young," said his father in a 1973 *Toronto Star* interview. "I don't know why. He would always say he wanted to live as much as he could because he was not going to live as long as I lived." Stafford Smythe had squandered his hockey inheritance, ultimately ceding it to the boorish and ill-advised generalship of Ballard.

The Stanley Cups of the 1960s hadn't provided the club with the infrastructure to tackle the new challenges of the post-expansion era. Winning a surprise Cup in '67 just encouraged the arrogance that was already deeply embedded in the company and diverted attention from meaningful hockey matters that needed to be addressed but were ignored. Interestingly, Stafford Smythe hosted a victory party at his new Ashley Park residence two days after the Leafs won the '67 Cup. All three of the previous Cup wins that decade had been celebrated at his former residence. The '67 party, then, was held at the very home that would prove pivotal in the process that would see the Smythe family lose control of the Leafs.

Sometime around this point, and nobody seems quite sure exactly when, an even darker spectre of criminal activity began to take root inside Maple Leaf Gardens. To be around the famous rink then, or to be an employee inside the building, was to exist within an unusual world of tiny kingdoms, insider deals and scams, a world filled with curious characters, an odd gang of rounders, drifters and ex-cons. There was a smoky charm to it all. Two of famous Leaf goalie Turk Broda's brothers, Stan and Lou, worked at the Gardens. Colourful characters abounded—including Straw Hat, Yogi, Freddie Cigar, Banana Joe, Popcorn Millie and George the Towel Guy. Many of the workers were laid off in the summertime. Some would find work at the Canadian National Exhibition for the final weeks of August and early September before returning to the Gardens for their winter chores. There was the public side of the Gardens dominated by the players themselves, the management team led by Punch Imlach and the ownership of Smythe, Ballard and Bassett. Well below that, however, existed a seedy, sloppy environment filled with some honest men and some very dishonest ones, men paid low wages to do menial jobs while others gradually built mini-domains that came with surprising levels of responsibility. The Gardens was home to many who knew the angles, knew when to look the other way and when to have their hand out when somebody came to the Gardens looking to do business.

The Gardens was a building of nooks and crannies, but even more important, of many doors, and behind those doors an individual could exist outside any controls, behave in ways that others would not see. Players who skated for the Marlies but weren't in school could work on the maintenance staff, but mostly they would know where they could go to sleep and not be found by their supervisors. This look-the-other-way environment gave the Gardens a very relaxed feel, one without security, one in which restrictions were at a minimum. While Ballard and Smythe were concocting their own schemes of petty thievery, others were operating their own little kingdoms. A man named George Hannah, meanwhile, was doing something else entirely, something that would forever besmirch the hockey shrine at Church and Carlton.

The history is sketchy, but Hannah, born in Toronto in 1923, came to be involved in minor hockey during the 1950s and as far back as 1954 was involved in the handling and purchasing of hockey equipment for teams playing out of the Gardens. He coached a little, managed a little, and as the 1960s moved along, he became a fixture around the building. Hannah was known more for his work with the Marlies than the Leafs. He gained a large, main floor office at the corner of Wood and Church Streets, adjacent to the entrance the Leaf players used and where autograph hounds and young hockey fans would gather to catch a glimpse of their idols. It was from this position, acting within the lazy, theft-ridden underworld of the Gardens, that Hannah spread his sickness and committed his crimes.

When it all came to light years later in 1997, 13 years after Hannah had died from kidney failure, it was suggested that he was a little-known, harmless fellow of whom little notice was taken. That wasn't true. In the second tier of Gardens authority below the Ballards, Smythes and Imlachs, Hannah was a person with responsibilities, primarily with the equipment needs of various teams in the Marlboro chain. More importantly, he knew Ballard, an acquaintanceship struck when Hannah worked for a car dealership that Ballard used. Hannah was generally regarded as a friendly, harmless old codger, well known by sportswriters and hockey players. He would learn a corny joke and retell it thousands of times. Playing off the name of defenceman Borje Salming, for instance, he would tell anyone willing to listen that the Leafs had signed a Chinese defenceman, "Sah Ming," always cackling generously as he reached the punchline.

In the mid-1970s he appeared in local newspapers as the contact person for local families wishing to billet Marlie players. He was a fixture in the press box at Leaf games, usually sitting in the south end, where time clocks kept track of the ice time of individual Leaf players. "I knew of him and I knew he had a cubicle or something to work out of with the Marlies," says former Leaf trainer Bobby Haggert. "But I had no idea what he did and he had absolutely nothing to do with the Toronto Maple Leafs." Hannah's office was located at the north-east corner of the building, about 20 feet from the door through which members of the media entered the arena every day. In 1978, Hannah was honoured by a dinner held at the Hot Stove Lounge. When he died in 1984, the flags at the

Gardens were lowered to half-mast, clear evidence that this was a man well known and closely tied to Ballard. That honour came nine years after he had started destroying the life of Martin Kruze.

It's unclear when Hannah began committing his sex crimes, preying on young boys willing to do almost anything to gain admittance to Canada's hockey shrine. Police later reported that the crimes involved dozens of boys in incidents that took place as far back as the 1960s. During that time, including the period around the club's last Stanley Cup victory in 1967 when Ballard and Stafford Smythe were increasingly distracted by their own side interests, it now seems plausible that a man like Hannah could have weaved his wicked web away from unwanted scrutiny. This was the period when he established himself at the Gardens, when the disgrace that was to become one of the country's most significant pedophile scandals was to grow.

As the years went by, the door to his office was often locked. Hannah used the excuse that he was undergoing kidney dialysis treatments. While the Leafs were winning their last championship, and while Ballard and Smythe were building their homes with Gardens funds, Hannah was building the foundations of the nightmare he was to visit on unsuspecting children. Without the reflected glory of his close association with the Gardens and the Leafs, he would never have enjoyed the easy access to his victims that he did. While most of the evidence that later emerged and sent three former Gardens employees to jail on sexual assault convictions involved crimes from the 1970s and 1980s, police believe Hannah was involved in similar activities in the Leaf glory years of the 1960s. He just died before anyone knew, or at least before anyone was willing to tell.

Kruze was an easily influenced, hockey-mad Toronto teenager who got a pass to see the Leafs play in 1975 from his older brother, who had received the gem from none other than

Turk Broda, the former Leaf goaltending great. In the murky mist of the backrooms that filled the Gardens, Kruze met Hannah, who sexually assaulted the teenager dozens of times before handing him over to another sexual predator, a Gardens maintenance worker named Gord Stuckless. Stuckless, a sometime teacher and community worker, organized parking and directed traffic on Wood Street behind the Gardens, where Leaf executives kept their cars. In a truly bizarre twist, he was one of the pallbearers in 1977 for Emmanuel Jacques, a 12-year-old shoeshine boy who had been raped and murdered by a group of men in one of Canada's most heinous sex crimes. By that time, a full-blown pedophile ring was operating out of the Gardens, organized by Hannah and Stuckless.

All of this might well have remained a secret forever had Kruze not contacted members of the Toronto media in 1996. "He walked into my office one day and laid his life on my desk," says *Toronto Star* reporter Dale Brazao. Ben Chin, a television reporter with City-TV, was also hot on the story. In February 1997, Brazao, known as a super-sleuth among Toronto reporters, tracked Stuckless down at a Scarborough apartment, and soon after he was arrested by police and charged with more than 600 acts of sexual assault against 26 victims. "Maple Leaf Gardens was a sex haven of abused boys— lots of them," Kruze said. Later that year, after Stuckless was initially sentenced to two years less a day for his crimes, Kruze ended his life by jumping off the Bloor Street viaduct. Stuckless' sentence was later increased to five years, and he was released in 2001.

Another Gardens usher, John Paul Roby, was later charged with multiple counts of sexual assault. Roby was a pathetic soul who boasted to anyone willing to listen that, as an usher in the north-end reds and blues, he had started the first "wave" at the Gardens in the 1980s. Like Hannah and Stuckless, he had lured young boys with promises of Leaf tickets and free hockey sticks. In May 1999, Roby was accused of assaulting 27 children between the years of 1967 and 1983. He was convicted and died in prison. Another former Gardens worker, Dennis Morin, was convicted of similar crimes in December 2002 and sent to jail.

That the Gardens had been used as a base for such depraved crimes as far back as the mid-1960s, apparently undetected behind the veneer of Leaf popularity and success, came as horrific news to the millions who had long viewed the arena as a sacred hockey shrine. The story mushroomed, however, when it was revealed that Kruze had been paid $60,000 in "hush money" by an insurance company after threatening a $1.75-million lawsuit in 1993 against the Gardens and its owners. "They paid me off with petty cash," Kruze later told reporters.

When the Kruze story exploded in 1997, the Leafs were on a western road trip. GM Cliff Fletcher, who would soon be dismissed, bravely stood in the line of fire as Stavro and his lieutenants scrambled for cover before finally addressing the matter in an awkward press conference, one that Stavro ducked. His key lieutenant, Brian Bellmore, received public criticism for insensitive, arrogant comments in defence of the Gardens and the hockey club. Then came reports that the Gardens had been warned of the activities of pedophiles working inside the building as early as 1988 during Ballard's final years. Since then, Maple Leaf Sports and Entertainment Ltd., the private company formed by Stavro in the mid-1990s, has paid hundreds of thousands of dollars, much of it covered by insurance, in compensation to the dozens of victims harmed by Gardens employees. It was as though Hannah, long dead, had reached up from the grave to curse those who had succeeded the Smythe family as custodians of Toronto's NHL team.

When Stafford Smythe died of a bleeding ulcer in October 1971, he and Ballard were in total control of the Gardens and the Leafs: Bassett had been forced out a month earlier. Bassett sold his shares to his former partners for $5.8 million, more than six times the amount he had paid for them. Without the cash to do the transaction, Ballard and Smythe once again went to the bank and borrowed the money, this time from the Toronto-Dominion Bank, which remains the Leafs' primary banker today. In January of that year, Stafford Smythe signed a will that made Ballard the executor of his estate and included a clause that allowed Ballard to buy Smythe's shares upon his death.

In his 2000 book *Centre Ice: The Smythe Family, the Gardens and Toronto Maple Leafs Hockey Club*, Smythe's son, Tommy, accused Ballard of taking advantage of his father's drinking problems by tricking him into signing the will. "Ballard slipped the will to Stafford late one night after Dad had had far too much to drink," wrote Tommy Smythe. "With a cursory glance, my father signed it on January 4, 1971. The witnesses were staff from the Hot Stove Lounge. And oddly, the will was not legally registered until after my father's death. The signed legal will was put away and never discussed with anyone in the Smythe family. Dad never gave the document another thought until it was too late. This single incident was the most serious error of Smythe family history." Had Stafford knowingly passed on his business holdings to his close friend and associate, bypassing his family's legacy? Or had Ballard pulled a fast one? The most straightforward explanation may be that Smythe, 15 years younger than Ballard, never dreamed he would die first, and that he always assumed that an agreement to give the other partner the first right of refusal would eventually keep the Gardens in his family's hands.

"When Ballard, Smythe and Bassett owned the Leafs, Ballard was invisible as far as the Leafs went," said Gregory. "I would have always thought the Smythe family would keep the Leafs." Ballard was certainly aware that Bassett had tried to buy the Gardens empire the previous year after voting to force out Ballard and Smythe because of their legal issues, issues that came to a head in July 1969 when both men were formally charged with income tax evasion. So he may well have been acting in concert with Stafford Smythe to thwart any potential hostile takeover by getting Smythe to include the buyout clause in his will. That said, he quite likely viewed the other members of the Smythe family, Tommy and Stafford's brother, Hugh, as threats to his hold on the Gardens. While Hugh was a successful physician, 25-year-old Tommy had been very involved with the junior Marlboros, who were still owned by the Leafs. Without question, Ballard had no intention of allowing the Smythes to continue holding a controlling stake in the company after Stafford's death.

In the end, how Ballard came to be put in such an advantageous position without having to put the Gardens up for public auction didn't matter. Stafford Smythe died less than two weeks before he was to go on trial. Through the will, Ballard had the right to buy Stafford's shares and he exercised it. He brushed aside a mild attempt by Tommy and Hugh Smythe to buy the team and instead eventually purchased his late partner's shares for a cool $7 million in February 1972. He financed this transaction, as he would again in the future, with a bank loan. As Ballard increased his indebtedness to the banks, he would gradually cut back on hockey expenses like scouting and player salaries, making the Leafs vulnerable to raids from the upstart World Hockey Association.

After Ballard seized control, Hugh Smythe offered to sell his final 1,200 shares to Ballard, and Ballard agreed, providing Hugh also relinquished his season tickets. Tommy stayed on to run the Marlies, but that July he arrived at the Gardens to find that he'd been fired, with his office emptied and his personal belongings and memorabilia left in the hallways of the Gardens. "How could Harold have done this to me?" wrote Tommy Smythe in his book. "He'd been a second father to me for most of my life. Was it because the Marlboros had earned more than the Leafs in the prior few years? Was it because I was the last remaining link to the Smythes? Or was it because I was so much more involved in Maple Leaf Gardens than [Ballard's] sons? I don't think I'll ever know the real reason for my firing." In the top left corner of the team photo of the 1967 Memorial Cup champion Toronto Marlboros is a picture of a young junior executive, dark-haired and smiling Tommy Smythe, wearing a suit and tie, the next generation of the Smythe dynasty that never came to power.

The Leafs, of course, won the Cup that year as well, and in the victors' dressing room Conn Smythe made his first appearance in years to congratulate the players. "The Smythe name is now on the Stanley Cup 11 times! Who else can say that?" he bubbled. It never would be again, however, and years later the sire of that dynasty declared he had never had much respect for Ballard. "I wouldn't give him a job at 10 cents a week around here," said Conn Smythe in a _Toronto Star_ interview in 1973. "I wouldn't have him around because I don't like his way of doing things." Surveying the scene at that time, Smythe said the deal that saw the Gardens fall into the hands of his son, Ballard and Bassett 12 years earlier was "a lousy deal, the worst business mistake that's ever been made in the world." Ballard must have taken The Major's criticisms to heart. When Conn Smythe died in 1980, Ballard immediately had his office cleared out the day after the funeral, removing all evidence of the old man who had founded the Leafs.

With the 1972 transaction, the Smythes were officially erased from the scene, 41 years after Conn Smythe's entrepreneurial genius had opened the Gardens for business. Court documents showed that, starting just before that unforgettable 1967 championship, Ballard and Stafford Smythe had combined to misappropriate close to $1 million of Gardens monies. On August 15, 1972, seven years after Conn Smythe had complained his successors were putting "cash ahead of class," Ballard pleaded guilty to 47 counts of fraud and was sent to prison. It had been only five years since Ballard had sat beside Armstrong and the Stanley Cup in that victory parade through the streets of downtown Toronto. Behind that trophy lay hidden the tragedy and disgrace that was to come.

Stanley Cup Final, Game Two
Maple Leafs at Montreal, April 22, 1967

If it was all about a missing tip, John Ferguson sure knew how to carry a minor grudge for a long, long time.

As Johnny Bower surveyed the various new welts and bruises over his 42-year-old body—one on the forehead, one on the nose, one on the collarbone—he certainly must have wondered just why Ferguson, the resident tough guy of the Montreal Canadiens and a man who never found a goalie he didn't like to fall on, had to take the ferocity of a Stanley Cup final game to such high levels. "They say I should stick my stick down his throat," grumbled Bower. "But that way I might miss the puck as well as pick up a foolish penalty." For several seasons, the Leafs had used Eddie (The Entertainer) Shack as an antidote to Ferguson, deploying Shack whenever it seemed Ferguson might be prepared to create a little mayhem. "I respected Fergie," says Shack. "He used to skate by our bench and yell at [coach Punch] Imlach, 'Okay Punch, let him out,' as a signal he wanted me out on the ice." In the 1966 playoffs, Ferguson and Shack had clashed repeatedly while the Habs were sweeping the Leafs, four games to none. By Game Two of the '67 Stanley Cup final, however, Shack had found himself mostly chained to the bench, leaving the Leafs—and Bower—without their anti-Fergie deterrent.

Bower never could figure out why Ferguson seemed to have it out for him and loved crashing his crease, but he had his suspicions. More than a decade earlier, Bower had played one season for the Vancouver Canucks of the Western Hockey League, and the 16-year-old Ferguson had been the team's stickboy the season before he headed to the Saskatchewan junior league to play for the Melville Millionaires. The practice for decades in hockey has been, and still is, for players to tip the stickboys and other dressing room attendants at the end of the season, as extra compensation in addition to the tiny paycheques they picked up from their teams. Ferguson, rightly or wrongly, believed that year in Vancouver that Bower hadn't tipped him. Bower felt certain that he'd given the tow-headed boy $10. By late April 1967, it didn't matter why anymore. Bower just knew that every time Ferguson was in the area, he was getting a stick in the noggin or a knee to the chest as the rambunctious Canadien forward fell on him during a scrum.

In Game One of the series, Montreal goaler Rogatien Vachon ignored Imlach's "Junior B goaltender" taunts and backstopped the Habs to an easy 6–2 win in which Leaf starter Terry Sawchuk was driven from the net. Imlach tabbed Bower to start Game Two even though "The China Wall" hadn't contributed much to the post-season run since injuring his finger in a pre-playoff boot camp in Peterborough. Sawchuk had survived a frightening Bobby Hull blast and the restrictions of his own badly bruised body to get the Leafs past Chicago, and now he was being sent to the bench in favour of Bower, who had started only one game against the Hawks and had been pulled after one period.

The Habs drove 31 shots at Bower that afternoon, a matinee clash televised by the CBC and CBS in the United States, and none of them found twine, even with Ferguson whacking away at Bower at every opportunity. While the feared Montreal power play came away empty-handed on seven chances, the Leafs scored twice with the man advantage, one by Peter Stemkowski in the first period and another by Mike Walton in the second. Tim Horton made it 3–0 later in the middle frame and the Leafs rode Bower's goaltending the rest of the way while pelting Vachon with 43 shots. The Leafs were starting to see a weakness in the young goalie's game, an inability to control low shots with his skates. In modern times, of course, the butterfly style of goaltending has negated that style of save almost entirely, but in the 1960s, standup goaltending was still the most popular style, kick-style saves were common and low shots were lethal. "Aww, he's not a bad kid, but he won't win any games if they don't get him any goals," said Imlach of Vachon, whom he upgraded to a "Junior A" goalie after the game.

The other development was Dave Keon's effectiveness against 33-year-old Jean Beliveau, who had scored only 12 goals during the regular season. "Le Gros Bill" had come on strongly in the final weeks but now seemed befuddled by tight Toronto checking. "Everybody's got a different idea about who's leading us," shrugged Keon. It was the first loss after 16 straight wins for the Habs, and Bower took home $100 for the shutout and his goalie pads for a little bit of home repair before Game Three. After all the lumps he had taken at the hands of Ferguson, he mused that he might have to look at trying to wear a mask like Sawchuk the next season. At 42 years of age with some serious miles on his chassis, Bower was only looking to the future.

7 *The Artists*

It would be a severe understatement to suggest the string of championship teams produced by the Toronto Maple Leafs in the 1960s were primarily defensive teams. Defence was the first, second and third game plan of Punch Imlach's teams, and the formula worked brilliantly for a quartet of Stanley Cup victories. Dynasties that came later, like the Montreal Canadiens of the late 1970s and the New York Islanders of the early 1980s, were also miserly defensive teams, but both also sported glamorous offensive players and teams that could score with the best in the league. Not so, the Leafs of the 1960s. When they won, it came by choking the life out of the game, reducing more offensive-minded opponents to frustration and ineptitude. Between 1961 and 1965, the Leafs put together an astounding streak in which they successfully took a second intermission lead to victory 158 consecutive times (135–0–23) times without losing. The 1962 Leaf winners potted a fairly modest 232 goals for 70 games, and that total went steadily downwards until the last year of Imlach's reign in 1968–69.

During that low-scoring era, a time when many incorrectly presume offence was king because of standout stars like Gordie Howe and Bobby Hull, the Leaf offence usually ranked in the middle of the pack, never at the top but never at the bottom. What set the club aside, however, was the manner in which it valued, or didn't value, offensively gifted players. Since 1938, the Leafs hadn't had a league scoring champion, and Gaye Stewart in '46 had been the last member of the blue-and-white to manage even a second-place finish in the scoring derby. The

Leafs had traditionally built strong, balanced teams with sturdy forwards, courageous defencemen and excellent goaltending, and the teams of the 1960s did not stray from that model.

But one could have been forgiven during the Imlach era if one came under the impression the Leafs not only prized defence, but despised offence. The most skilled offensive players produced by the organization from the mid-1950s to the mid-1960s were winger Frank Mahovlich, defenceman Carl Brewer, centre Dave Keon and, in a lesser but nonetheless pure sense, forward Mike Walton. All ended up bitter and disillusioned with the organization, feeling underappreciated and abused. Perhaps all were simply mercurial and moody artists, prone to delicate sensibilities as a reflection of their finesse-first approach to the sometimes violent sport. But other teams employed players with similar personalities and seemed less inclined to bully them and more likely to carefully massage their egos and talents as a means of getting them to produce offensive results that more limited athletes could not.

The Leafs, or Imlach, seemed to resent having to pay such special players a premium in wages, and fought with them over salaries and bonuses. Imlach's favourites—Tim Horton, George Armstrong and Johnny Bower—were straightforward, no-nonsense personalities, grinders who simply went about their business and handled setbacks with even dispositions. That players like Mahovlich, Brewer and Walton were more delicate or fragile was something to which Imlach couldn't effectively adapt. Keon, on the other hand, hid his discontent more effectively, or perhaps concealed it more carefully as a point of personal pride. But in the end, his estrangement was more complete

———— ✥ ————

Brewer, of course, was the most extreme case of the disaffection felt by players who didn't fit the Imlach mould. He had walked out on the team in September 1965, taking his superb skating and puck-moving skills to the Canadian national team. Looking back, however, it seems but a twist of good fortune that the immensely talented Mahovlich didn't also refuse to play for Imlach. By the time the Leafs were making their run to the '67 Cup, The Big M had not only had enough of Imlach, he was about done with the NHL. Early in the season, he had opened the Frank Mahovlich Travel Agency, and had started to contemplate the possibility that he might retire to it at the conclusion of the 1966–67 season. Primarily, he had needed an outlet to release him from what he viewed as the oppressive and highly stressful environment of playing for the Leafs.

It had all started out happily, of course, when the Leafs outbid five other teams for the services of Mahovlich and moved his entire family south from Schumacher, Ontario, to the Toronto neighbourhood of Leaside. His father, Peter, ran the pro shop at Leaside Arena from 1957 until his death in 1981, giving Mahovlich and his family the sense they had roots in the community despite the fact they'd been transplanted from northern Ontario. "I always get a kick out of people who told me my dad sharpened their skates, people like [actor] John Candy," says Mahovlich. "I know if you told my dad you were a fan of The Big M, sometimes he wouldn't charge you." After graduating from St. Mike's, Mahovlich quickly became the team's top left winger, and in the 1960–61 season he set a team record with 48 goals. But soon after, it began to go sour, and the entire city watched the very public destruction of the relationship between the Leafs and the last superstar they ever discovered.

Twice during his Leaf career, in 1964 and 1967, Mahovlich was hospitalized with stress-related problems. Once, a doctor had told him he was suffering from allergies, primarily an allergic reaction to Imlach, who loved to intentionally mispronounce the proud winger's name. Despite the fact he was clearly the most explosive scorer in team history, Mahovlich became dispirited to the point he scored only 18 goals during the 1966–67 regular season. The playoffs wouldn't be much more productive, even though the Leafs won the Cup. When he finally escaped the following March via a boneheaded trade with Detroit, Mahovlich found it a "great relief." When he was moved on to Montreal three years after that, he found the hockey home of his dreams. "The team allowed you to express yourself," he says. "Too many teams are overcoached. It was a nice feeling, how hockey should be played. It was nice playing for good management. If I'd played my entire career with Montreal things would have been much different. I would have thrived much more personally."

The mystery, of course, remains the same years later. Why did Imlach degrade and abuse his most prolific offensive player for so many years, particularly when it was clear Mahovlich was regressing as a player and being less helpful to the Leaf cause? Part of the answer lies in the fact Imlach was more in tune with the needs and personalities of players from the 1940s and 1950s, and less capable of understanding, let alone catering to, the changing notions of the professional athletes that began to emerge in the 1960s. He didn't like the idea that players could have options and choices and opinions, and he fought tooth and nail against the formation of a players union. An athlete that was different was, by Imlach's definition, a spoiled baby. Morever, Imlach was a reflection of Leaf founder Conn Smythe, the man who had hired him. To Smythe, players were strictly employees and workers, and some even drove trucks at his gravel pit during the off-season. Players didn't get a say, they didn't share in the profits of their labour and they were, always, replaceable. Imlach fit perfectly within this environment. Armstrong stands alone as a player who believes Imlach didn't ride Mahovlich too hard. "Punch was told to lay off Frank because he was sensitive, and he laid off him," says Armstrong. No other member of those teams agrees with that assessment, however. Even Bower, Imlach's staunch supporter, recalled the team being resentful over the ridiculously harsh treatment of a fragile athlete. "Frank was like a radio," recalls Brian Conacher. "The moment he hit the dressing room door it was like he was turned off, that all life and fun were sucked out of him."

To be sure, Imlach's attitude and techniques were to some degree a reflection of his peers and the prevailing hockey culture. But Toronto was still very, very different than other NHL teams. Winger Larry Jeffrey came to the Leafs from Detroit in 1965 as part of the deal that sent Andy Bathgate packing after his short stay with the Leafs. Jeffrey had suffered a serious knee injury during the 1964–65 season and had surgery in the spring. He was stunned to realize that the Leafs and Imlach knew nothing of the seriousness of the injury when he showed up in Toronto. He immediately got a taste of the Leaf management style when he negotiated a new contract after being paid $24,300 in Detroit the season before. Imlach offered a $500 increase with the advisory, "Take it or play in Siberia." That, however, was nothing compared to the surprising atmosphere he experienced at his first Leaf camp.

"I couldn't believe how life as a Leaf was," says Jeffrey, who eventually took a regular shift in the '67 playoffs before being hurt. "We had fun times in Detroit. In Toronto, that wasn't the case. And I couldn't believe how Punch picked on some of the guys. He left me alone, but guys like Walton, Mahovlich and [Jim] Pappin, they couldn't do anything right according to Punch.

"I couldn't stand the pressures Punch put on the team. I couldn't take it anymore so at Christmas I met with [King] Clancy and told him I had to get out of there or I was going to quit the team. They sent me to Rochester, where I really enjoyed things. At the end of that season, Joe Crozier told me, 'When I'm up [in Toronto], you're coming.' There was some talk about Crozier coaching the Leafs the next season but that never came to fruition."

The overriding temptation over the years has been to describe and understand Imlach as a Lombardi-esque character, a coach who fervently believed in the same "winning is the only thing" philosophy as the great Green Bay football coach, Vince Lombardi. There are similarities, particularly in the military bearing both men assumed at a time of great cultural shifts in North America. Lombardi, of course, actually did coach at West Point. The crucial difference, however, is that many who played for Lombardi with the Packers during the glorious 1960s later spoke in reverential terms of the man, even while describing how difficult Lombardi had often made their football lives. Lombardi was harsh, sometimes unduly so, but he also preached team unity, teamwork and loyalty like a priest from a pulpit. Like Imlach, he pushed his players hard and demanded a high level of physical conditioning, but Lombardi was also an educated man from Fordham who had a brilliant defensive mind with an intricate understanding of the strategic side of the game. Imlach was no scholar, and players claim he had little or no system at all. Finally, Lombardi knew some players were different than others and had to be treated accordingly. He may not have liked the way Paul Hornung, for example, lived his life, but he always gave the Golden Boy another chance.

With Imlach, his players never related a sense of affection and respect after playing for him, and he never expressed much love the other way. Armstrong, the Leaf captain, credits Imlach with being a good bench coach with an ability to quickly see which players were having good nights and which players weren't. Most agreed he was a very hard-working coach, and at times could be a good motivator. "I liked working for Punch because you knew where you stood," said Bobby Haggert, the club's trainer throughout the 1960s. "He wasn't a backstabber, and none of the players can say that he was. I think it was a case of familiarity breeding contempt. Punch also felt the constant pressure to win in Toronto, and he felt he had to keep up the pressure on the team." Eddie Shack was constantly in trouble with Imlach, and remembers the coach never being able to just let the team enjoy big victories. "The first Stanley Cup we won in '62, we were in Chicago enjoying a beer shortly after the final game," he says. "I mean, the game is hardly over, and Imlach hollers, 'Hurry up and get going! The bus leaves in 15 minutes and if you're not on it, you're not on the fucking team next year!' So we celebrated our first Stanley Cup with a 15-minute beer." Shack agrees with Haggert that Imlach felt terrific pressure to keep the competitive pedal to the metal in Toronto, and found a very different man in Buffalo in the early 1970s when he played for Imlach and the Sabres. "There was no pressure to win at all. It was an expansion environment. It was much more fun and he was much more lenient," says Shack.

Imlach felt daily heat emanating from his stressful relationship with team president Stafford Smythe, who perhaps hoped in 1958 he would be named general manager of the Leafs, the same job he'd held with the very successful Marlies. Instead, his father hired Imlach, and as the years passed he couldn't bump Imlach out because of the multiple Cup wins. The two men had a terrible working relationship, and the players saw that. "Smythe resented Imlach's lack of respect for him," says Brian Conacher. "It was obvious Imlach had no use for Smythe." Despite all the reasons and rationalizations, many players talk about the pointlessness of so much that happened, particularly as Imlach neared the end of his reign in Toronto and refused to make any accommodations to the changes that were occurring in sport and society. "He was a dictator. Most of those guys around that time were," said Jimmy Keon, brother of Dave, who saw Imlach's act play out at several training camps. "He had a hard time dealing with certain types of players. It would have seemed like a failure to him to have to make adjustments to a personality like Frank Mahovlich."

Bobby Baun was a player who spent time on both Imlach's good and bad sides, leaving after the 1967 Cup bitterly resentful of Imlach. "I look back and feel that we really couldn't understand Imlach and his ways," says Baun. "And there was the knowledge how he and others were stocking up the Rochester team for their personal gain at the expense of the Leaf hockey team. I told Imlach flat out, when we were again on good terms, that his ego destroyed him." When Imlach died of a heart attack in 1987 while watching the Grey Cup on television, tributes came in from around the hockey world, but those from Leaf players lacked any sense of love and loyalty that the Packers had for Lombardi. "Punch treated the team as a team and didn't give special treatment to individuals," said Red Kelly. Keon said that Imlach "ran things his way and told you how he wanted things done. If you did them that way, you didn't have any trouble with him."

When Imlach died, Bower and Allan Stanley served as pallbearers, while sportswriter George Gross gave the eulogy. The inclusion of Gross was instructive, for it recalled the many Monday lunches during the 1960s when Imlach had habitually dined at the Town Hall on King Street with a group of media personalities that included Gross, then writing for *The Toronto Telegram*, CFRB sportscaster Bill Stephenson and *Toronto Star* hockey writer Red Burnett. These were days when reporters who travelled with the team received per diems from the team, just like the players. Clearly, Imlach played an influential role in both how events surrounding his team were reported and the manner in which his image was created and developed through his tight relationship with those who covered the team.

In September 1966, Imlach attended a dinner in Stratford, Ontario, along with Armstrong and Conn Smythe to honour *Toronto Star* sports editor and columnist Milt Dunnell, who

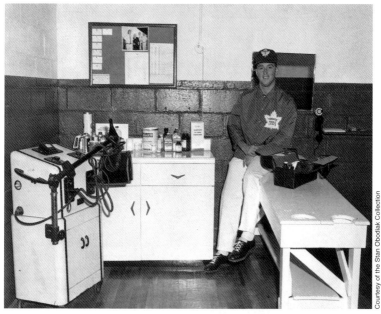

Leaf trainer Bob Haggert in the Leaf training room in the 1960s. Haggert would leverage his friendships with NHL players once he left the Leafs to represent many NHL players for promotional and endorsement opportunities. Among his clients would be the National Hockey League Player's Association.

Leaf equipment manager Tommy Nayler. Also considered the greatest skate sharpener in the world and an innovator in modifying equipment to assist injured players. Nayler joined the Leafs from their inception in 1931 and his tenure lasted almost five decades.

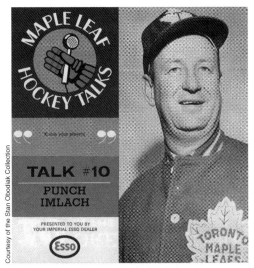

Leaf general manager and coach Punch Imlach featured as part of the "Maple Leaf Hockey Talks," a series of 45 rpm vinyl records presented by Esso.

Bench boss Punch Imlach surveys the action as Frank Mahovlich, Gerry Ehman and Ed Litzenberger hit the ice for a line change on the way to the 1964 Stanley Cup. Andy Bathgate and Allan Stanley survey the action from opposite ends of the bench.

Coach Joe Primeau, Conn Smythe and ex-coach Hapy Day in Smythe's MLG office in 1951. Fresh from another Stanley Cup win, their fourth in five years and sixth in the previous 11 years, the Leaf fortunes were about to change drastically. They would not win a playoff round for the next seven seasons, missing the playoffs on three occasions. Their fortunes would not turn around until Punch Imlach took the controls as general manager and coach in 1958.

Golden-haired Bill Barilko, pictured in 1945 as a member of the Hollywood Wolves, far from his hometown of Timmins, Ontario. He disappeared in 1951 after scoring the Stanley Cup winning goal for the Leafs. His childhood friend, Allan Stanley, was a pallbearer for Barilko when he was found in 1962 and was later a member of the '67 Leafs. Tim Horton, who replaced Barilko with the Leafs, was Stanley's defence partner.

MAPLE LEAF GARDENS
LIMITED

TORONTO 2, ONTARIO, CANADA

CORNER OF CARLTON AND CHURCH STREETS
TELEPHONE 368-1641

April 27, 1966.

The BEATLES

JOHN

PAUL

GEORGE

RINGO

News Flash:—

Help! Those Lads from Liverpool, best known as the BEATLES, are coming back to sing and play their greatest hits on the Gardens' stage Wednesday, August 17th, with shows at 4 p.m. and 8:30 p.m., presented by CHUM and After Four.

Toronto is again the only Canadian stopping spot on their North American tour and already MLG has been deluged with letters and calls. *Please, Please Me* with tickets is the general theme of them all. Out-of-town fans say they have their *Ticket to Ride* and now need the tickets to get inside. Soon our switchboard and box office will be working *Eight Days a Week* plus a few *Hard Days Night*(s)!

These BEATLE tickets will go on sale sometime in May, but between CHUM and After Four *We Can Work It Out* so that you may secure tickets now, using the mail order form on the reverse side. Preferred seat locations for both performances are set aside now for preferred MLG customers like yourself. Use this priority mail order form not later than Monday, May 9th, and you won't have to *Twist and Shout* in the box office lineup to get your tickets.

If you or somebody in your family wants to see the BEATLES and from the best seats possible, complete and return this order form like *Yesterday.* Orders will be filled on a first-come, first-served basis. Send yours in now. Don't be a *Nowhere Man!*

Yours sincerely,

MAPLE LEAF GARDENS.

HOME OF THE TORONTO MAPLE LEAF HOCKEY CLUB

Leaf subscribers for the 1966-67 season are given advance notice of their opportunity for "preferred seat locations" for the upcoming concert by the Beatles at Maple Leaf Gardens.

Stafford Smythe (foreground, left) and Harold Ballard smile for the cameras in 1969 after signing papers to buy out the Gardens shares of former partner John Bassett. The Toronto-Dominion bank loaned the two men $5,886,600 to buy out Bassett, and two bank officials flank Gardens director Don Giffin behind Smythe and Ballard. After Ballard's death, Giffin would briefly serve as president of Maple Leaf Gardens and was the man who hired Cliff Fletcher to join the team in 1991.

Broadcast voices of the Leafs, Foster Hewitt and his son Bill, with Leaf coach Red Kelly and publicity director Stan Obodiac in 1977.

A Stanley Cup victory provides an increasingly rare moment of camaraderie for Leafs' vice-president Harold Ballard and John Bassett, the chairman of the board. By the '67 Cup, their relationship had degenerated into a bitter business and personal grudge that both men would take to their grave.

Bruce Gamble played 23 games in goal for the Leafs in the 1966-67 season, one of five goalies to play for the club that year. Here, Chicago's Bobby Hull tries to deflect an incoming shot while Leaf captain George Armstrong and defenceman Jim Dorey look on in 1969.

Al Smith was the backup to Terry Sawchuk for the fourth and fifth games of the '67 Stanley Cup final. Never a regular with the Leafs, here he is shown in a 1971 photo playing for Pittsburgh with Paul Henderson in the background. Smith later sought fame as a playwright and author, driving a cab in Toronto before dying of pancreatic cancer in 2002 at age 56.

Leaf president Stafford Smythe (third from right) in June 1971 after being arrested in his Gardens office on charges of theft and fraud. He is escorted by two Metro Toronto police detectives while a female reporter tries to get a comment. Smythe died four months later, 12 days before he was scheduled to go on trial.

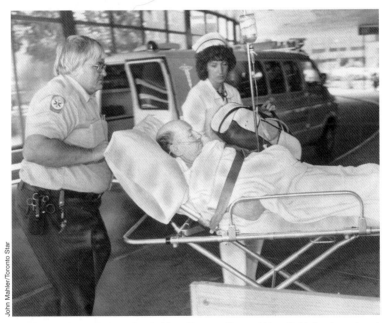

GM Punch Imlach being wheeled into Toronto General Hospital following a heart attack in 1981. He had tried to avoid publicity, but team owner Harold Ballard alerted local media to the story. When he regained his health and tried to return to his duties, Imlach found his parking spot at Maple Leaf Gardens was gone and his office phone line had been cut.

had started out in Stratford. Dunnell, the dean of Canadian sportswriters, was still covering the team, and would continue to do so for another two decades. It's nearly impossible to imagine a similar type of event and relationship between media and a team today, particularly in Toronto, where a corporate curtain has descended separating the hockey club and the city's ravenous sports media. In many ways, the reporters of the day saw the team through the eyes of Imlach, and the relationship between the powerful Leaf coach and the media was such that reporters felt beholden to Imlach. To be cut off by Punch would put a writer on the precipice of losing his job altogether.

He was a virtual cult figure, and the world of the Leafs was reported, and thus publicly understood, as the world according to Imlach. When players failed, it was because they weren't trying hard enough, or at least that was how the reports often read. "Mike Walton and Jim Pappin haven't been getting too much ice time, but when they do they just go through the motions," wrote Burnett in February 1968. "When in gear they rate in the exclusive company classed as goal-scorers. But it will take hard work and second effort to straighten them out. And that holds true for a few of the others, too." That was obviously Imlach's opinion—the players' redemption was based solely on "hard work and second effort." At least that's what he wanted circulated, and that's what hit the papers. The triumph of '67, not surprisingly, was primarily reported as another great triumph for Imlach.

For Mahovlich and others, many of the bad feelings between themselves and Imlach surrounded money. Those financial disputes were reported, generally speaking, from the point of view of the embattled manager trying to deal with greedy athletes. Holding both the general manager and coaching portfolios meant there was no separation of responsibilities in the Leaf front office, no opportunity for the GM to take a hard line on salaries without affecting the relationship between the coach and team.

Grudges that lasted for years were built up over salary disagreements, and Imlach's influence on the media meant that players were routinely projected as malcontents. Imlach, it seemed, took business concerns in a personal way. Indeed, throughout the 1960s, he often owned chunks of stock in Maple Leaf Gardens and the Leafs, as well as their farm clubs, so it's easy to understand how he might have resented any player demands that detracted from the bottom line of the company.

For Mahovlich, a salary dispute marked the genesis of his problems with Imlach. The big winger had followed up on his tremendous 48-goal effort in the 1960–61 season with 33 goals the next year plus another six in 12 playoff games as the Leafs won the Cup. He'd made $10,000 a year as part of his first contract in 1957, and figured he had demonstrated his value. He wanted a raise to $25,000 a season, and when the Leafs wouldn't budge, he left camp. As he sat, the new Leaf ownership group of Stafford Smythe, Harold Ballard and John Bassett, which had bought out Conn Smythe a year earlier, came up with the outlandish plan to sell him to Chicago for $1 million. Imlach had recommended the Leafs take the offer, and Ballard had signed off on the deal. The plan fell through in the wee hours of the morning on October 6, 1962, and Mahovlich received a call at 7 a.m. telling him to be at the Gardens in two hours. When he arrived, he was offered a new contract for $25,000 a season. "They didn't want to give me any time to react or digest what had happened so they got me in line before the news hit full bore," says Mahovlich.

From then on, Mahovlich believes, his relationship with the Leaf hockey boss deteriorated. "Toronto became a tough place for me to play in," says Mahovlich, who was appointed to the Canadian Senate in 1998. "From that point on, I always felt I was playing with a leash attached to me. Imlach always seemed to resent that I had held out that fall. I think this is where his relationship as a coach turned sour with me and some of the other players. I always thought he should have moved up to management and let someone like Bert Olmstead or Joe Crozier become the coach. I think we still would have won Stanley Cups. We may have even won more Cups." If Imlach was sour over the incident, so was Mahovlich, who had to fight to get a $25,000 salary from a team that had nearly sold him for $1 million, equivalent to a season's worth of Gardens gate receipts. "I realized how I was getting shafted with my salary," he says. "Later on, I began to realize more how we were all getting shafted as players, how Clarence Campbell had shafted us with our pension plan and his promises. I never started making good money until I played in the WHA [in 1974]." Mahovlich, an athlete who came to love art and painting, never again surpassed the 40-goal mark as a Leaf.

———— ❧ ————

Mahovlich was one of the last outstanding players the Leafs developed out of their relationship with St. Michael's College, but there were a few other special ones. The school stopped entering teams for Junior A competition following the 1961–62 season, and one of the young players on that final team was the 17-year-old Mike Walton. Born in Kirkland Lake, Walton's family had moved around a great deal, eventually settling north of Toronto while his family ran a restaurant/garage in Sutton, Ontario. He played well enough to catch the eye of St. Mike's officials and was offered a partial scholarship to the school, nothing like the red carpet that had been laid down for Mahovlich a decade earlier. He boarded with his uncle on Bathurst Street near the school and was disappointed when the hockey program shut down. The St. Mike's players were transferred to another school, Neil McNeil, and it was there that Walton began to show he might be a special player, scoring 22 goals in 38 games for the Maroons. Despite that, Leaf president Stafford Smythe, who had run the Marlies in previous years, didn't believe Walton was good enough to play for the Leafs prize junior affiliate, the Marlboros. Others did, including young executive Jim Gregory, and Walton made the Marlies. That season, the team won the Memorial Cup, and Walton soared with 92 points in 53 games, including 41 goals. He wasn't particularly big, but he was blazing fast and tricky with the puck, and after winning the '64 Cup the Leaf powerhouse seemed to have another talented forward coming.

Instead of the Leafs finding a way to develop Walton's obvious skills and groom him to be a key component of the club as other core players aged, the next six years turned into a constant battle between Walton on one side, aided by his agent Alan Eagleson, with Smythe and Imlach on the other side. Part of the relationship problem with Smythe might have been that Walton courted Smythe's niece, Candy Hoult, while playing for the Marlies and eventually married her. Imlach, meanwhile, just couldn't find a way to like the brash young forward. "I was everything he didn't like," says Walton. "I was young. I had long hair and sideburns, and he hated that. I was insecure, and I made up for it by being cocky and mouthy. He didn't like anything about me." During one training camp, Imlach paid two military men to surprise Walton, pin him down and shave off his hair and sideburns. "I'm truly thinking I'm getting mugged, but one of 'em told me that Imlach had put them up to it," says Walton. "So I look like shit and don't play in the next five exhibition games, and back then you only got paid in training camp if you played in those games. So for one of those games I was sitting with Candy in Conn Smythe's front row reds, right behind the Leaf bench. I wore a Beatle wig and sat there the whole time as Imlach paced on the bench right in front of me. He was pissed, but the guys couldn't stop laughing."

For three seasons, Walton tore up the minors with Tulsa and Rochester, but couldn't earn a full-time roster spot with the Leafs. He scored 40 goals in 68 games with Tulsa, and was convinced he'd be a Leaf in the fall of 1965. "All training camp I'm thinking I'm going to make the big team," he says. "All I've done is win, all I've done is score. But, no, they want me to go back to Tulsa. I say no way. So finally they agree to send me to Rochester." There, he notched 35 goals in 68 games with the Americans, and helped the team win the Calder Cup as the AHL's leading playoff scorer. "No question I'm ready for the NHL now," he says. "But at training camp in 1966, it was the same old shit. They told me to go back to Rochester or Tulsa. So I quit. I can remember King Clancy coming to our home in Willowdale and convincing me to go back to Rochester and that I'll get another crack with the Leafs. I reconsidered and headed back to Rochester."

Down in the minors, Walton stewed. "I mean, it's a six-team league and I know that teams like Boston and Detroit would snap me up for their NHL teams in a heartbeat. It's just bullshit the way I had been treated from the word 'go' by the Leafs." Finally, after the Leafs had lost 10 straight games during the regular season, and after Walton had potted another 19 goals in 36 games, he got the call to the NHL. Like Peter Stemkowski and Jim Pappin, his break that year came when King Clancy temporarily inherited the coaching reins of the team when Imlach was hospitalized. Suddenly, Walton began receiving huge dollops of ice time, and he began to produce, just as he always had everywhere. Without the domineering presence of Imlach, Walton's distinctive skill with the puck emerged. When Imlach returned, that ice time was cut back, and in the playoffs Walton was a spare forward, not assigned to the top three lines. As the playoffs wore on, however, the Leaf power play became more important and more productive, and those were the occasions on which Walton was sprung from the bench to work his magic. He managed four goals and three assists in 12 games, with most of those points on the power play.

As with Mahovlich and Brewer, however, Walton's pure skill wasn't enough to create a lasting link with the organization. Like those two, he was perpetually portrayed as a troublemaker, and he ultimately suffered psychological problems that contributed to his exit. After the '67 playoffs, he continued to develop, led the club with 30 goals the next season and was generally described in the hockey world as a potential superstar. "On good days this is the most exciting player in Toronto Maple Leaf history," wrote *The Toronto Star*'s Trent Frayne. He was feisty, too, getting into a celebrated brushup with Gordie Howe in the 1968 all-star game, and in late January 1968 he was named the NHL's mid-season second-team all-star behind Stan Mikita and ahead of talented players like Keon, Phil Esposito and Alex Delvecchio. Yet a week later he was in Imlach's bad books again, dropped from the regular three-line rotation and dumped in the press box after Imlach tried unsuccessfully to get Walton to agree to go voluntarily to the minors.

By the mid-point of the next season, Walton announced he wouldn't play for Imlach and demanded a trade. Even after Imlach was fired in April 1969, Walton couldn't find peace in the organization. After playing a game against Los Angeles on December 2, 1970, the 26-year-old forward withdrew and said he couldn't physically bring himself to play for the Leafs any longer. He and his agent, Eagleson, met with GM Jim Gregory and the club physician, Dr. Hugh Smythe, the brother of the team president and uncle to Walton's wife, ostensibly to discuss Walton's health. "To my astonishment, and with me sitting there, Dr. Smythe told [Walton] what bad hockey he'd been playing," said Eagleson. "'You don't pass the puck enough,' he told Mike. I mean, what the hell, he's only the bloody doctor." A week later, the Leafs suspended Walton without pay for refusing to play, and then had to backtrack when NHL president Clarence Campbell ordered the club to lift the suspension after an independent NHL-appointed doctor had diagnosed Walton as suffering from "acute depression."

Five weeks later, after countless rumours, Eagleson announced the Leafs had one week to trade his client or be sued. "Eagleson is not running the Toronto Maple Leafs," said Stafford Smythe, declining to offer any sympathy for Walton. Finally, on February 1, Walton was traded to Boston in a complicated three-way deal involving Philadelphia, which gave the Leafs the young goalie they were looking for in Bernie Parent. In Boston, Walton was united with Bobby Orr, his business partner in the Orr–Walton Sports Camp in Orillia, Ontario. "A lot of pressure will be off me in Boston," said a jubilant Walton, who was photographed walking jauntily down Bay Street wearing an ankle-length fur coat when the trade was announced. He lived up to his offensive promise with the Bruins, scoring 53 goals in two seasons and helping the club win the '72 Stanley Cup. He then jumped to the WHA and was a sensation with the Minnesota Fighting Saints, scoring 105 goals in two seasons. By the late 1990s, he was a Leaf insider again, this time in his capacity as a successful realtor helping many players find new homes. But the sour memories remained. "I was the guy who got screwed by Leaf management and ownership through my entire Leaf career," he says. "I had the life and confidence sucked out of me after all those years in the organization. It was best for everybody when I was traded."

Unlike the others, Dave Keon never suffered from clinical depression, never quit the club or demanded a trade. Yet while Walton and Mahovlich eventually declared a truce with the Leafs, forgiving past transgressions, and Brewer actually returned to play for the club again at age 41, Keon's alienation has been the longest lasting. He stubbornly refused any and all entreaties to attend the closing of historic Maple Leaf Gardens in 1999. "The Toronto Maple Leafs are a distant memory, and not a good one," said Keon in a newspaper interview two years earlier. His bitter estrangement from the team he joined as a 16-year-old in 1956 came mostly in the wake of the '67 Cup triumph, and was fuelled by a variety of events that followed the success of that year. Philosophically, however, it was rooted in earlier years when he began to believe the Leafs had abandoned the principles, standards and traditions that had made the franchise great.

He had come through the St. Mike's system, and took great pride in the Catholic school as a reflection of his belief in the single-minded dedication it took to be a Leaf. He was moody and intense, and when the Leafs shipped out two of his contemporaries, Dick Duff and Bob Nevin, in a 1964 deal with the New York Rangers, he saw it in classic religious terms, a betrayal of basic and fundamental beliefs that underpinned the entire organization. He had believed in the Smythe tradition, saw honour in the way that Conn Smythe had developed the organization and featured men like Syl Apps and Ted Kennedy. To Keon, Ron Ellis was the last of the true Leafs, a player developed and sculpted in the Marlboro junior organization and the last product of the old sponsorship system. New York Yankee star Joe DiMaggio had been his hero, entrancing young Keon with his professionalism, class and, above all, his sense of dignity.

Keon wasn't picked on by Imlach like Mahovlich or Walton, but he felt disrespected by management after being named MVP of the playoffs in 1967. Early on he detected the sickness within the organization as Harold Ballard gradually assumed control, and that awareness stoked the fires of his growing disenchantment. His personal life was difficult; one of his five children, a son named Richard, died at eight months of age. In the early 1970s, his marriage dissolved; it was a tortuous process for him, as a devout Catholic. He was enraged when Gardens executives maintained connections with his former wife and his children as though it were a form of betrayal. Finally, in 1975, after 15 terrific seasons as a Leaf and six as team captain, he left to join the WHA's Fighting Saints, a team coached by an old junior hockey opponent, Harry Neale. Keon had played only briefly in the minors, four games for Sudbury of the Eastern Pro League, and had maintained a high standard of quality over his 1,062-game Leaf career, accumulating only 75 penalty minutes over that time along with four Stanley Cup rings, a Calder Trophy, a Conn Smythe Trophy and two Lady Byng Trophies. He always played with class and skill, competing like a demon but behaving like a gentleman at all times.

He left for $300,000 over two years, more money than the Leafs wanted to pay, or perhaps more money than Ballard could afford with the hockey club leveraged to the hilt. At age 35, Keon also wanted the security of a no-trade contract, and Ballard wouldn't budge on that, either, although hockey people believe Keon still had three or four good years to give the Leafs if they had kept him. Other NHL teams inquired about his availability, but while Ballard wouldn't give Keon a no-trade deal, he wasn't prepared to deal him either. Two years earlier, Parent had bolted the Leafs for the WHA, and the Leafs had traded his rights to Philly for draft picks and net-minder Doug Favell. By 1975, Parent was the best goalie in hockey, so when the New York Islanders came calling about Keon, Ballard demanded a first-round pick.

With no place else to go and no contract from the Leafs, Keon left for the Fighting Saints. It was easy to see how the accumulation of indignities, real and perceived, had driven the proud Keon away. His hurt was deeper, more personal perhaps, than that of Mahovlich or Walton, his skilful, high-strung teammates on the '67 championship team. "I left the Leafs because I had a disagreement over a business matter," said Keon in 2003. "That's all I'm prepared to say." That said, there is a sense among old colleagues that Keon would like to find his way back, but doesn't quite know how. His son, Dave Jr., became a fixture at Leaf games as the off-ice crew supervisor at the Air Canada Centre. After an estrangement of several years in the 1990s, the two men, father and son, repaired their differences and grew closer. The spitting image of his father, Keon Jr. is often announced as the goal judge before games, while his father remains distanced from the organization despite direct appeals from senior Leaf officials.

At the same time, Keon has tried to repair old relationships. Bobby Haggert, the trainer on the '67 Leafs, recalled that when his wife died in 2001, he was surprised to pick up the phone and hear Keon's voice at the other end. "I don't even know how he got my number," said Haggert. "I hadn't talked to him in 20 years. But it meant the world to me." To Haggert, Keon was the "best of them all," the quintessential Leaf. "I think he got bad advice, that he listened to the wrong people and that hurt him in his professional life and to a degree in his personal life," says Haggert. "They convinced him to stand up to Harold Ballard rather than working at crafting a successful deal. You're not going to win a game of brinksmanship with Ballard." Keon actually did return to the Gardens for an old-timers exhibition game in the early 1990s when Don Giffin was briefly in charge of the team, but the reconciliation didn't last. "After that, I figured out the ownership was no different than Ballard and I had no use for it," he said.

As of 2004, the reasons why Keon still refused to return to the Leaf fold are highly personal and varied. But in an interview for this book, Keon emphasized that he was appalled by the manner in which the Leafs decided to acknowledge players of the past in the mid-1990s by "honouring" their numbers, but not retiring them. Only two players in Leaf history, Bill Barilko and Ace Bailey, had ever had their numbers retired. Barilko's Number 5 was taken out of circulation after he disappeared in a 1951 plane crash, and Bailey's Number 6 was eliminated from use after he was permanently disabled in a 1933 stick-swinging incident with Eddie Shore. Bailey did volunteer to let his number be worn by Ellis, a player he admired, during the 1970s.

During the 1990s, a series of players, from Bower to Mahovlich to Apps to Kennedy, had banners with their names and numbers raised to the rafters at Maple Leafs Gardens and later transferred to the Air Canada Centre. But the numbers themselves—Mahovlich's Number 27, Apps' Number 10—stayed in circulation, often worn by mediocre players. Keon's Number 14 wasn't similarly honoured, largely because he refused to participate in any special ceremonies. As he watched from a distance, one average player after another, from Stan Weir to Mike Kaszycki to Rob Cimetta to Dave Reid to Darby Hendrickson to Jonas Hoglund, donned the Leaf jersey he made famous. Dave Andreychuk, at least, restored some honour to the number with 120 goals in 223 regular season games from 1992 to 1996. By contrast, Jean Beliveau never had to watch any other player wear Number 4 with the Montreal Canadiens.

Keon found the process of "honouring" numbers disgusting, particularly when it involved two of the Leaf captains who had preceded him, Apps and Kennedy. "I was embarrassed for them. I told Johnny [Bower] I thought it was embarrassing. He said, 'Well, Mr. [Conn] Smythe didn't retire numbers.' I told him Mr. Smythe wouldn't hold such an embarrassing ceremony. What does honouring a number mean? Johnny told me that's the way they do things," said Keon. "I told him it was a pretty chickenshit way to do things. I'm embarrassed for them all. I confronted [Leaf president Ken] Dryden and said, 'Do you think the Montreal Canadiens would just honour The Rocket's number?' He couldn't give me a good answer." By 2004, it seemed unlikely Keon would ever again appear at a Leaf game unless the club's policy on jersey retirement were changed, not just for him but for all those who have banners in their names hovering over the ice surface at the Air Canada Centre.

To Keon, the proud, sensitive and skilful artist on skates, the honour of being a Leaf meant everything. He considered being a Leaf a vocation as opposed to merely employment. He saw it all slipping away as early as 1964 with the Andy Bathgate trade and watched the process accelerate through the years, as the Smythe family gave way to Ballard. Once that honour and tradition was gone, the Leafs he had known were gone forever. He long remained the loose end that could never be tied up.

Stanley Cup Final, Game Three
Montreal at Maple Leafs, April 25, 1967

To comprehend the ties that bound a team like the '67 Maple Leafs, you have to understand the collective history and background they shared and the relatively small universe that was professional hockey in those days.

On that Leaf team, there were 11 players who had come up through the Leaf development chain by playing junior hockey with either St. Mike's or the Toronto Marlboros, or both. They had no experience playing with any other professional organization, and had only ever drawn paycheques from the Smythe-owned Leafs. Six of those players— George Armstrong, Bob Pulford, Dave Keon, Frank Mahovlich, Bobby Baun and Tim Horton—had played on the 1962, '63 and '64 Leaf teams that had won the Stanley Cup, and had never skated for any other NHL club. Horton and Armstrong had been Leaf regulars for 15 seasons. As a group, these were men who had known each other for years and had played together, both as amateurs and pros. They knew each other's families and favourite watering holes and had been taught to play the game the same way by the same mentors. They were bred and sculpted to be Leafs and had become Leafs.

The rest of the '67 team had come from outside the Leaf organization, but few were truly outsiders. Four players—Terry Sawchuk, Red Kelly, Marcel Pronovost and Larry Hillman—had played together on the

1955 Detroit Red Wings championship team, and all had been Leafs for
at least two years. Winger Larry Jeffrey had arrived with Pronovost in a '65
trade with the Red Wings. Allan Stanley had played first for the Rangers
and then Boston, but he had been Horton's defence partner since 1958.
Netminder Johnny Bower had been Ranger property until 1958 when he
joined the Leafs, and he too had been part of the three-Cup teams in the
earlier 1960s. Eddie Shack hadn't come through the St. Mike's/Marlie
system, but even he'd been a Leaf for six years by the 1967 playoffs. Every
player on the team was Canadian-born, and all had come up through
the ranks of Canadian junior hockey. Their coach, Punch Imlach, had run
the team since 1958 and lived east of the city in Scarborough, near the
Tam O'Shanter rink, where the team frequently practised if the downtown Ted Reeve Arena wasn't available.

To understand how different that world was from that of the mod-
ern game, consider the 2004 Maple Leaf playoff roster, a squad construct-
ed of athletes from eight different countries. Only five of the players—
Nik Antropov, Tomas Kaberle, Karel Pilar, Alexei Ponikarovsky and Matt
Stajan—were drafted by the Leafs and had played all of their NHL games
to that point with the club. Kaberle and Pilar were from the Czech
Republic, Antropov from Kazakhstan, Ponikarovsky from Ukraine, and
Stajan grew up in Mississauga, just outside Toronto. Thirteen players—
Stajan, Owen Nolan, Darcy Tucker, Bryan McCabe, Gary Roberts, Tie
Domi, Ron Francis, Chad Kilger, Nathan Perrott, Drake Berehowsky,
Bryan Marchment, Wade Belak and Trevor Kidd—competed in the
Canadian junior leagues, but none together on the same team or even in
different years with the same junior organizations. There were five
U.S. college-trained players. Three—Brian Leetch, Ken Klee and Tom
Fitzgerald—were American-born athletes. Goalie Ed Belfour of Carmen,

Manitoba, tended goal for the University of North Dakota, while Joe Nieuwendyk of Whitby, Ontario, starred for Cornell University.

The roster also included Russian Alexander Mogilny, who was playing for his fourth NHL club, and captain Mats Sundin from Bromma, Sweden, who had played for the team since 1994 and was at that time the longest-serving Leaf. Two of Sundin's countrymen, Mikael Renberg and Calle Johansson, were also on the club, but both spent their NHL careers mostly with other teams. Rookie goalie Mikael Tellqvist, also from Sweden, was the third-string goalie. Finnish-born Aki Berg manned the Leaf blueline, while a third Czech, centre Robert Reichel, filled out the roster.

By comparison to their '67 Leaf ancestors, the 2003-04 team was a scattered, diverse and loosely related group of professionals, a team of mercenaries with only passing ties to the city, who were paid a collective $63 million—averaging more than $2.5 million a year per player—to challenge for the Cup. Only Stajan, Berehowsky and Marchment grew up in the Greater Toronto Area or played minor hockey in the city, and only a handful owned houses in the city or spent their summer months in southern Ontario. By the winter of 2004, only two players who had played in the first game at the Air Canada Centre when it opened in 1999 were still with the club. The head coach, Pat Quinn, spent his off-seasons in Vancouver, closer to his varied business interests. The GM was John Ferguson Jr., the son of the former Montreal great, who was born in Winnipeg and attended Providence College. Like Quinn, he held a law degree.

Of the '67 Leafs, the average salary was about $20,000 when it took more than that to buy a comfortable house in a nice neighbourhood like Leaside or the Kingsway, and far more to live in Rosedale or Forest Hill. Most were married with homes in the city, although Sawchuk rented and left his family in Detroit. Brian Conacher and Bobby Baun were born in Toronto, and the rest came from five provinces, no farther east than Shawinigan Falls, Quebec, and no farther west than Lethbridge, Alberta. More than half were born in Ontario. They cared about Toronto housing prices and property taxes, took the subway at a time when it only went north–south to Eglinton Avenue before the east–west Bloor Line was constructed. They had jobs and business interests in the city that occupied them in the summer months and enhanced their incomes.

It's not hard to understand, then, that when Pulford scored at 8:26 of the second overtime before a deafening audience at Maple Leaf Gardens to win Game Three of the 1967 Stanley Cup final against the Montreal Canadiens, it was more than just a big goal. It was the kind of moment that Pulford, born in Newton Robinson, Ontario, had been trained for since he was lured to Toronto 14 years earlier to play for the Weston Dukes Junior B team, and then the Junior A Toronto Marlboros. With the Marlies, he had played with Baun and against Keon and St. Mike's, all the time knowing they would likely one day be Leafs together. Not every player on that '67 Leaf team got along, and certainly the vast majority despised the dictatorial Imlach. But when Pulford collected Jim Pappin's pass and guided it into the open net to give the Leafs a 3–2 victory and a two-games-to-one lead in the Cup final, it was as though a family member had done the deed. At the time, Pulford said it was "the greatest goal of my life." Thirty-seven years later as the president and general manager of the Chicago Blackhawks, he called it "the biggest goal of my NHL career."

It had been an extraordinary night at the Gardens, a night filled with athletic drama and multiple moments of uncertainty. The Leafs had led 2–1 late in the second period on goals by Pulford's linemates, Peter Stemkowski and Pappin, but had seen that lead erased with 50 seconds left before intermission on an ugly defensive miscue in their own zone.

The sequence began with Imlach's peculiar strategy of using a defence-man to take defensive zone faceoffs, a scheme that other teams no longer used since it yielded inconsistent results. Pronovost took the draw and won it from Beliveau, but the Leafs broke down from there, with Stemkowski handing the puck to John Ferguson, father of the future Leaf GM, who rapped a backhander past Bower to tie the game. "That was a bad goof," admitted Stemkowski.

The match had also included a rare playoff fight, a dandy between Conacher and Montreal's Claude Larose that ended with Larose cut for seven stitches. "If I had known the game was going to last four hours, I might have had other thoughts. My arms feel as if I have sandbags in them," said Conacher, whose father, Lionel, had played in the NHL's longest game (116 minutes, 30 seconds of overtime) between the Montreal Maroons and Detroit Red Wings 31 years earlier. In the final seconds of the third it momentarily appeared as though Keon might prevent overtime on a break down the right wing, but his shot hit the right post behind Rogie Vachon with one second on the clock.

There were two significant moments in overtime before Pulford ended the game. In the first OT period, J.C. Tremblay headmanned the puck out of the Montreal zone to Beliveau at the red line. With Pronovost stranded up ice, Yvan Cournoyer took a pass from Believeau with more open ice than he'd seen all night. He sliced inside of Keon and around a stumbling Hillman to cut towards the net from left to right. Bower, figuring Cournoyer was going to try to move right across the crease and make him commit, instead flicked out his goal-stick in one of his patented poke-checks to knock the puck off the Montreal winger's stick. "I knew if I missed he would go right by me and have an open net for the game-winning goal and I would look terribly foolish," said Bower.

Early in the second overtime period, a far less effective pass from Tremblay exiting the Montreal zone hit Henri Richard in the skates, forcing the 5-foot-7 centre to look down and try to gain control as he crossed his own blueline and headed up ice. Stanley, lined up on the other side of the ice, saw the Montreal pivot in that vulnerable position and came across hard, decking Richard with a thunderous blow that appeared to momentarily knock him cold and eventually forced him to leave the game. Richard, the scoring star of Game One, did not reappear and was not a factor for the remainder of the series.

Just past the eight-minute mark of the second OT session, the line of Peter Stemkowski between Pulford and Jim Pappin hit the ice one more time for a faceoff in the Montreal zone. With Richard out, Habs coach Toe Blake chose not to put out Beliveau or Ralph Backstrom, but instead assigned winger Bobby Rousseau to take the draw as part of a makeshift forward unit with Dick Duff and Claude Provost. Stemkowski won the faceoff cleanly back to the left point and the stick of Stanley, whose shot was blocked. The puck skittered to the other side of the ice—deep into the right corner, where Stemkowski and Jacques Laperriere battled for possession. Terry Harper had Pulford locked up beside the net, and Provost seemed to be in position to check Pappin. But Stemkowski beat Laperriere out of the corner, and Provost moved too slowly to take Pappin when the puck moved to the right faceoff circle. Harper, meanwhile, had let Pulford go, and Pappin's goalmouth pass was quickly rapped into the open side for the game winner.

The combination of Bower's critical save, the Stanley hit on Richard and Blake's coaching decision had helped create another important goal by the Stemkowski unit. Vachon, who had made 51 saves to that point, lost his second straight to Bower, a man twice his age. "C'est la guerre," said a weary Vachon afterwards. Pulford's goal ended the longest overtime game at the Gardens in 34 years and gave his line 11 goals in nine playoff games. "Not bad for three guys who were on the scrap heap all season," cracked Pappin, who had been in the minors while both Stemkowski and Pulford had figured in trade rumours. Montreal, winners of 16 straight regular-season and playoff games after capturing Game One, had lost its swagger after dropping the next two games. "What do we have to do to put the puck in the net?" wondered winger Gilles Tremblay after he and his mates had put just two of 93 shots past Bower in more than seven periods of playoff competition.

Just as with the Chicago series, the Leafs looked to be poised to be destroyed after one game; instead, they bounced back with gusto. The ties that bound them together were still holding.

8 *The Family Way*

There would have been days in the mid-1960s when being around for the unofficial, off-hour workouts at Maple Leaf Gardens would have been more intriguing than watching the Maple Leafs themselves go through their paces.

On any given day, you might have had Johnny Bower working himself back from his latest injury, fielding drives from shooters like Terry Clancy, son of King, and Brent Imlach, son of Punch. Or you might have Tommy Smythe, son of team president Stafford Smythe and grandson of the legendary Conn Smythe, directing volleys at Bower. Some days Stafford's brother, team physician Hugh Smythe, might join in, as would Bill Ballard and his brother Harold Jr., the children of Harold Ballard, vice-president and part owner of the famous Leafs. All that would be missing would be Foster Hewitt and his son, Bill, doing the play-by-play from the gondola.

The workouts would get intense, Bower recalled, and sometimes the kids would furiously scrimmage amongst themselves, symbolic, perhaps, of the struggle all felt as the supposed next in line to the glory and heritage of their famous names. The reality was that none were able to match the accomplishments or notoriety of the family members that had come before. To be around the Gardens in those days meant many things, one of which was to get a sense of the various family entanglements, and the pervasive sense of nepotism that made the Leaf environment a complex and compelling study in the positive and negative dynamics of human relationships.

———— ✿ ————

If there was a member of the '67 Leafs who understood the weight of ancestry, it was winger Brian Conacher. He was the offspring of Toronto's first family of sports, and one of Canada's most famous clans. Ben and Liz Conacher, Brian's grandparents, had produced a remarkable group of children, growing from their roots at Jesse Ketchum school on Davenport Road in downtown Toronto to achieve startling successes in sports and life. Brian Conacher's father was none other than The Big Train, Lionel Conacher, an extraordinary, almost superhuman athlete. He played in the NHL, the Canadian Football League, minor pro baseball and was the country's light-heavyweight boxing champion, all reasons why he was named in 1950 as Canada's athlete of the half-century. His brother, Charlie, was young Brian's uncle, as well as being arguably the most dashing player ever to play for the Leafs. He led the NHL in goal scoring five times, and was a fixture for years on The Kid Line with Gentleman Joe Primeau and Busher Jackson. "When I was a kid in Toronto in the 1930s, I thought Charlie Conacher was God," said renowned Toronto sports eye specialist Dr. Tom Pashby. There was Roy Conacher, who played 11 seasons in the NHL, and a younger brother, Bert, might well have made it too if he hadn't suffered a serious eye injury playing shinny with his brothers. Even so, he played for a Toronto team that won the Memorial Cup in 1936.

This was the ancestral baggage that Brian Conacher carried when he tried to make a name for himself as a professional hockey player in the 1960s. His father had died when Brian was only 12. Conacher Sr. was a Member of Parliament for the Toronto riding of Trinity, when he collapsed and died of a heart attack at age 54 while playing a softball game on Parliament Hill. "We always thought that he really hadn't died young because he accomplished so much," says Brian. "But when my sister Connie turned 54 she called me and said, 'You know, we always thought Dad lived a long and full life, but now that I'm 54, I realize how young he was.'"

In the winter of 2004, 62-year-old Brian, still lean and angular and 10 pounds above his playing weight, looked back upon his family history as he strolled through Lionel Conacher Park, about two blocks from his home in Toronto's affluent Rosedale neighbourhood in central Toronto. The park, named in honour of The Big Train in 1967, contains a children's baseball diamond, two sets of playground equipment and borders onto Cottingham Public School, the city's smallest elementary school. A large plaque reads, "Lionel Pretoria Conacher. Affectionately known as 'Big Train.' Received his early education in this area. Truly remarkable in football, baseball, hockey, lacrosse. Outstanding in boxing, swimming and track and field. Voted by the press as Canada's greatest all-around athlete and greatest football player for first 50 years of the century."

Lionel Conacher grew up on Scollard Street, about 500 feet from the park that bears his name. "His true love was lacrosse," says Brian of his father. "But he got more into hockey later, mainly because you could make money at it."

If there was pressure to add more legends to the family name, Brian never felt it. His father pushed family members to take advantage of their athletic gifts as a means of getting ahead in life. "We'll take the cuts and bruises so our kids can get an education," Lionel often said. That meant for Brian, and his four siblings, the emphasis wasn't on the pursuit of athletic glory but on achieving a university education. "I lost my dad when I was only 12 years old, and his athletic feats were behind him," says Brian. "I loved years later catching up on some of those stories in the Hot Stove Lounge at the Gardens with [former Toronto mayor] Allan Lamport, who had known my dad well." A family favourite was the time when Lionel, playing for the Montreal Maroons, and Charlie, skating for the

Leafs, engaged in a rock 'em, sock 'em fight. "It was the night my sister Connie was born," says Brian with a laugh. "My dad obviously had a bit of pent-up emotion. They say it was an unbelievable fight."

Three Conachers—Lionel, Charlie and Roy—are in the Hockey Hall of Fame, and while Brian did not have the kind of career that would qualify him for enshrinement, he did make the NHL on merit. If his career wasn't brilliant, it did include one impressive season, that of the 1966–67 campaign when he was a Rookie-of-the-Year candidate all season and an important part of the Leafs' drive to the Stanley Cup. He only just made the team at training camp, beating out 1966 NHL Rookie-of-the-Year Brit Selby. "I never really had any idea of the aura of the Conacher name until that season in the NHL," says Brian. "It was a learning experience. It gave me great pride what the name meant to the Leaf organization and Leaf fans. I was one of the guys on the bubble at training camp. I'm sure my name didn't hurt in the decision."

Just days before the clinching victory on May 2, Charlie Conacher was released from hospital, where he had been fighting his latest battle with throat cancer. "His first public appearance when he got out was my wedding on May 15, 1967, at Upper Canada College," says Brian. "He was all decked out in his white suit. He was so pleased to attend and we were so honoured to have him there. That was his best moment. After that, the throat cancer got a hold of him and he just went downhill fast. But I have very fond memories of him at our wedding." Charlie Conacher died the following December at age 57, living just three years longer than his big brother.

— ⚜ —

If Conacher understood living under the shadow of legends, so too did Bill Hewitt, who both benefited from having an influential father and found his life's work pale in comparison to his dad, a Canadian original. Son of the great Foster Hewitt, arguably the greatest name in Canadian broadcasting history, Bill Hewitt called the Toronto-based games of the '67 final against Montreal for *Hockey Night in Canada* and counted down the final seconds on television when the Leafs captured the Cup at the Gardens. His father was on the radio for that game, a one-two family punch that described the Leafs and their games to millions of listeners and viewers for decades.

Foster had called games for the Leafs in pre-Gardens times, and in 1951 he founded the CKFH radio station, with the "FH" standing for his initials. His son did news and sports broadcasts, even dabbling in a fishing show, and eventually started broadcasting junior games. As television became popular, it was decided Foster would stick to radio while his only son, Bill, would do the television. Foster's influence was so great that, given his son's interest in broadcasting, there was little question that Bill would move into the Leaf orbit. For six years, beginning in 1961 and ending in 1967, a third Hewitt, Bill's son Bruce, would join his father's broadcast once a season on *Young Canada Night* and do the play-by-play for a few minutes. Bill Hewitt was never seen as the innovator and colourful announcer his father was; he was widely regarded as an average broadcaster.

The Hewitt influence on the Leafs might have been even greater had Foster not turned down overtures from Stafford Smythe in 1961 to join his new ownership group with Harold Ballard and John Bassett, which was prepared to buy out Conn Smythe's majority control. Instead, Foster sold his sizeable piece of Gardens stock and invested in Bassett's Baton Broadcasting, a decision that made the Hewitt family millions of dollars.

By the 1966–67 season, the Hewitts had their game day down to a science. Bill would leave his North Toronto home and arrive at the Gardens at the same time Foster was arriving from his Forest Hill house. They were rarely more than two or three minutes apart. They would hold a brief production meeting in the TV room across from the Leaf dressing room. Soon after, they would make their way up the west staircase of the Gardens and leave their coats in the radio room at the north-west corner of the building where public address announcer Paul Morris worked. Father and son would then venture out on the catwalk and make their way to the famous gondola, which looked precarious and unsteady from the seats. It was small, but contained several partitioned-off areas. Bill and Brian McFarlane would sit at the far left end that was designated for TV. In the next booth was Foster, often with young Bruce as his statistician.

The relationship between Foster and Bill Hewitt is a subject of some debate. "They were great friends," says Bruce Hewitt. "They just had different personalities and interests." Foster, a geologist by trade, liked to travel and investigate his business interests first-hand, including his shares in various mining concerns. Bill enjoyed the quiet life, especially retreating to his farm in Sunderland, Ontario, which eventually became his home. Many, however, who were around the two men in the 1970s and early 1980s say Foster would often belittle his son in front of others, criticizing his contributions to CKFH. Foster was seen as controlling of his son's life to the point that Bill's dreams of taking flying lessons were quickly put to rest by his father.

Bill Hewitt never had a chance to measure up to the immortal status of his father, which was sealed by his play-by-play of the 1972 Summit Series between Canada and the Soviet Union and his call on Paul Henderson's dramatic, series-winning goal. As the Leafs struggled in the 1970s, Bill also struggled to keep up with the changing demands of television. With his father retired, he continued to operate as a loner, a difficult approach in the atmosphere of the TV world, where so much of what an announcer does is in collaboration with others on the technical and creative side. To TV execs, Bill wasn't very good at doing much else than straight play-by-play, describing the basic movement of the puck around the rink. Those in the production truck would joke that if McFarlane told him the end blues were on fire and had collapsed, Bill's next line would be, "Faceoff in the Chicago end to the left of Esposito ...."

Bill Hewitt's broadcasting career came to an abrupt and rather mysterious conclusion in September 1981 when, while broadcasting a pre-season game between the Leafs and Montreal Canadiens, he became hopelessly confused. At one point he failed to recognize for a lengthy period that Toronto coach Mike Nykoluk had replaced starting goaltender Bob Parent with Jiri Crha. The night had started with the rest of the crew thinking it was just another night with Bill making the same errors he usually made, but gradually it became clear this was something very different. Hewitt's play-by-play descriptions were filled with gibberish and names of players who hadn't skated in the NHL for years. It was handled quietly in the media, but the truth was it was the last straw for Canadian Sports Network executives Don Wallace and Ted Hough, both of whom had grown increasingly frustrated with Hewitt's play-by-play abilities.

The night was publicly explained as a bad reaction to cold medication, but that was plainly not true: Hewitt would have returned to work once his "cold" had subsided. There were quiet suggestions of an ongoing problem with pills and perhaps alcohol, but suggestions that Hewitt had done games while inebriated were dismissed as pure myth by others. What really went wrong that night was never revealed. Hewitt, who had seen his workload on *Hockey Night in Canada* slashed two years earlier, was forced out of the Leafs' midweek broadcasts altogether. A year later, with that sad, pathetic night standing as his final NHL game, Hewitt retired to his

Sunderland property at age 53, citing a blood disorder as his reason for leaving broadcasting.

To those who knew him well, he was upbeat and at peace with his life in his post-broadcast days, and he established another long-term relationship after his first marriage had failed years earlier. If TV had decided Hewitt had nothing more to contribute, it seems likely he was just as happy to wave farewell. Perhaps he was relieved he no longer had to work under the immense shadow of his father. He stayed away from the Gardens for nine years until returning in 1991, six years after the death of his father at age 82. Front page headlines accompanied the news of Foster Hewitt's passing on April 21, 1985, extolling the inventiveness of the man who was the dominant voice of hockey for Canadians for three decades before the advent of television. At his funeral, hockey luminaries from Johnny Bower, Red Kelly and George Armstrong to Jean Beliveau and Danny Gallivan filled the church. On Christmas Day, 1996, his son Bill died in obscurity, an event quietly noted in the Toronto dailies.

—— ✤ ——

If, as his son Bruce suggests, Bill Hewitt was comfortable living in the shadow of his father, the same could never be said of Stafford Smythe. Like Foster Hewitt, Conn Smythe was a pioneer, and young Stafford seemed obsessed with being every bit the powerful, intimidating character that many regarded his father to be. By the 1966–67 season, father and son were at each other's throats after years of problems. By the time the Leafs were in the midst of their improbable run to the '67 Cup, Stafford was drinking seriously and involved in shady business dealings that would eventually plunge him into serious legal troubles. The battle of the Smythes became a very complicated relationship for those around the Gardens to understand and manage, particularly Stafford's son, Tommy, who was in many ways being groomed to take over the hockey club some day.

Tommy too had felt the strains of family pressure while playing for the Junior B Marlies. An average player, Tommy had been foisted on the team's coach, Alex Davidson, the brother of Leaf chief scout Bob Davidson. One late fall evening the entire Smythe clan journeyed to North York Centennial Arena to see Tommy play. As his grandparents, parents and sisters watched, he didn't play a shift. The next morning, Stafford called the team's manager, Len Heath, to find out how much it was costing the Leafs to fund the Junior B operation. Heath gave him a figure of $23,000. Stafford's next call was to Jim Gregory, who at that time oversaw the entire Marlboro operation. "Do you expect everybody on that team to make it to the NHL?" asked Stafford. "Of course not," responded Gregory. "Okay, then will five or six players make it?" queried Smythe. "Boy, five or six of them making it to the NHL would be fabulous," said Gregory, feeling that two or three would be a more accurate number. "Then for twenty-three thousand fucking dollars, let my son be one of the 12 who doesn't make it but plays anyways," bellowed Stafford. Gregory was forced to order Davidson to play Tommy, but soon after, the young man solved the problem by leaving the team.

In his book *Centre Ice*, Tommy Smythe described his years of being trained to be a hockey man. "During my two years of high school at Upper Canada College, my alarm went off at 3:30 a.m. each morning," he wrote. I was picked up at 4 a.m. and taken to Woodbine race track, where I worked in my grandfather's stable exercising his two-year-old horses. A car dropped me off at school for 9 o'clock … A quick shower at 5 p.m., and then it was off scouting hockey players somewhere in southern Ontario with the scouting staff of the Toronto Maple Leafs and their junior affiliate, the Toronto Marlboros. When the final buzzer of the game rang, the scouting party headed for a meal. My head never hit the pillow before 1 a.m.

in the morning only to be jolted awake once again in a few hours time. I don't know how I did it, but I know why; it was the price I had to pay to gain access to the world in which I wanted to live, the world of running the Toronto Maple Leafs and Maple Leaf Gardens."

Ballard's takeover of the Leafs in the wake of Stafford's death in 1971 meant Tommy Smythe would never realize his dream. But in the spring of 1967, Tommy felt he brokered an uneasy peace between his grandfather and father, with a new office for his grandfather, Conn, at the Gardens helping to break the ice. The spring turned into a glorious one for the Smythe family. The Leafs, with Stafford as president, won the Stanley Cup. With 21-year-old Tommy as assistant general manager, the Marlboros won the Memorial Cup, emblematic of Canadian junior hockey supremacy. In June, Conn Smythe's three-year-old filly, Jammed Lovely, raced past 13 other horses to win the 108th Queen's Plate at Woodbine, Canada's biggest horse race. Conn would continue to race horses, but the Smythe hockey empire would soon be lost.

⸻ ❧ ⸻

For Brent Imlach, the hockey-playing son of Punch, carrying a famous family name meant constant teasing from teammates and opponents. But it also meant a brief chance to play in the NHL, an opportunity young Imlach almost certainly would never have enjoyed if not for his father's position of influence and power. When the Imlach family moved to Toronto in the fall of 1958, 11-year-old Brent didn't yet know how to skate. But he learned quickly and progressed, landing a spot with the Junior B Neil McNeil Maroons in the early 1960s, where, despite his small 5-foot-8, 150-pound frame, he was a solid scorer as a centre. One of the benefits to having his father coach the Leafs was that Brent would sometimes travel with the team and sometimes even get to participate in practice. "Dad has come out to one game this season and when I got home he gave it to me for a thousand different mistakes I made—and I knew he was right," Brent told *The Toronto Star* in December 1964. "For the most part, though, he leaves me on my own and we never discuss my hockey career." At that time, Imlach wore Number 14 out of admiration for Leaf centre Dave Keon. "I think hockey is a great life," said Brent. "Because I've seen what it can do for a man, and I wanted to be part of it."

By the 1965–66 season, young Imlach was with the Junior A Marlboros, a team that sported future NHLers like Jim McKenny, Brad Park, Gerry Meehan, Wayne Carleton and Brian Glennie. Jim Davidson, son of Leaf chief scout Bob Davidson, also played for that team. On January 16, 1966, after forward Wally Boyer went down with an injury before a game in Detroit, Punch Imlach summoned his son, known as "Pinch" to needling friends, for his first NHL game. Then a Grade 13 student at Cedarbrae High School in Toronto, Imlach wore Number 24 for his debut, skated on a line with Orland Kurtenbach and superstar winger Frank Mahovlich and was paid the standard $100 for an unsigned amateur. "My kid is the Marlboros' best centre, so he's the guy," said the elder Imlach. Three nights later, Imlach dressed again as the Leafs played at home, but he didn't skate a single shift. His mother, Dodo, wasn't very happy with her husband. "She opened the conversation by saying, 'You're mean,'" Punch told reporters. "Look, if I put him on and something went wrong, there'd be all kinds of criticism. People would ask why I didn't bring up an experienced guy from the minors. I'd be accused of favouring my own son. For myself, I wouldn't care, but that kind of talk would be hard on Brent. And it's a difficult deal for him already. The biggest problem with Brent has been to convince him he's making it on his own merits and not because he's my son."

The reality was that Brent Imlach wasn't an NHL talent, and everybody knew it. On March 2, 1966, Leaf forward Brit

Selby fell ill before a game with the Canadiens and Brent was summoned from home, where he'd been studying for an exam. He didn't make it to the Gardens until the second period and again didn't play a shift, but he was on the overnight train to Montreal for the rematch the next night when George Armstrong, for one of the only times in his career, confronted Imlach. "I went at Punch and told him there was no fucking way his kid should be with this team, that he wasn't near good enough," says Armstrong. Imlach didn't try to argue the point with his captain. "To his credit, he just said, 'What kind of a father would I be if I didn't give him a chance?'" says Armstrong. Brent Imlach took the opening faceoff at the Forum the next night against Jean Beliveau, centring a line between Kurtenbach and defenceman Tim Horton, who would sometimes be used at forward, played a regular shift and even skated on the Leaf power play. But Punch knew the game was over. His son only played one more game for the Leafs on Christmas Day, 1966, about two weeks before the club went into a terrible 10-game losing streak.

The next season, after the Leafs had won the '67 Cup, Brent Imlach moved on to London to play briefly for the Junior A team and to attend the University of Western Ontario. From then on, he was a university player, competing for Western, the University of Toronto and York University before his eligibility expired. In a tiny footnote to family history, he was actually acquired by his father in August 1970, in a trade between the Leafs and Buffalo Sabres in which Floyd Smith went to the Sabres as well for cash. In one of the stranger twists, Brent Imlach went on to become a player agent for a time, doing the kind of work that drove his father crazy when the NHL Players Association first emerged in 1967. In 1977, Brent tried to convince his father, then GM of the Buffalo Sabres, to sign one of his clients—a player who Brent felt was a diamond in the rough, despite the fact he had been released by the woeful Cleveland Barons. Punch Imlach passed, and two years later, the player in question, Charlie Simmer, scored 56 goals in 64 games for the Los Angeles Kings as part of the famed Triple Crown Line with Dave Taylor and Marcel Dionne. "Should've listened to Brent," said Imlach often.

That said, the father wasn't done doing favours for the son. Back with the Leafs for another run in 1981, Punch Imlach received a call from his son in the dying moments before the NHL trade deadline in March to make a deal for a client, Ron Zanussi, who desperately wanted out of the Minnesota North Stars organization. The Leafs made the deal for a draft pick, and Zanussi went on to score three goals in 55 games before disappearing into the minors forever.

— ⚜ —

Tommy Smythe was never close to being an NHLer, and Brent Imlach likely should never have skated in any of the three games with which he is officially credited. Terry Clancy, son of King, was a more capable player than either, and he also had to pursue his career as the child of a hockey figure known throughout Canada. Over the course of an 11-year pro career spent mostly in the minors, Terry Clancy skated in 93 NHL games, 86 of them with the Leafs in the 1970s after first being lost in the 1967 expansion draft and then later reclaimed. If Imlach's best moment was facing off against Beliveau in Montreal in March 1966, Clancy had a better one in the same city a little more than four years later. The Leafs lost, 5–2, to the Canadiens, but Clancy scored both Toronto goals and was named one of the game's three stars.

He grew up in Ottawa, the city where King Clancy first became famous as a player, and was childhood buddies with goaltender Gary Smith. Clancy, a winger, skated for St. Mike's and then played a year for the Montreal Junior Canadiens while attending Carleton University in Ottawa. Sam Pollock, who would go on to fame as the general manager of the Habs, was the man assigned to drive young Clancy back and forth from Ottawa to Montreal for games. "He was the worst driver I ever met, probably still is," Clancy laughs. "He drove all over the road. I can't believe I'm alive today."

Clancy played for Canada at the 1964 Winter Olympics, then turned pro in the Leaf chain, spending time with Rochester and Tulsa. While the Leafs were going through the rollercoaster season of 1966–67 that would produce the 11th Stanley Cup in team history, Clancy was happy as a minor-leaguer in Rochester. "We were loaded with veterans because Punch and [head coach Joe] Crozier wanted a team that could win it all," says Clancy, referring to the equity Imlach and Crozier held in the Rochester team. By Clancy's estimation, the Leafs would call up inferior players from Rochester to help that team keep winning. "We had guys like Darryl Sly and Gerry Ehman who were better players, but we didn't care," he says. "We all knew how everyone hated the environment in Toronto, and we all loved the environment in Rochester." Part of the Leaf picture that Clancy wanted no part of, of course, was his father, who jumped in to coach the Leafs for 10 games that season when Punch Imlach was hospitalized. "He could barely talk to the guys, he was so nervous," said Clancy. "So he just kept it simple and made it fun. He was extremely nervous, but nobody saw that side." Unlike Punch Imlach, King Clancy did little to actively aid his son's career. In fact, immediately after the Leafs won the '67 Cup, Terry Clancy was left unprotected in the expansion draft and was lost to Oakland.

— ❧ —

Of all those caught in this unique predicament, Jimmy Keon was one who dipped his toe into the pond warmed by the brilliance of a famous relative, and then retreated to other pursuits. Had he stayed in the game, some believe he might have realized his brother Dave's dream—that the two boys from Noranda would skate together on the same forward line for the Leafs. But Jimmy, however much he worshipped his brother, just didn't share the dream.

Jimmy Keon loved the game and was a good, honest player, the kind of grinder the Leafs produced in great numbers and fit easily into Punch Imlach's system of defensive hockey. Six years younger than Dave, he wasn't the same elegant skater and didn't possess quite the same single-mindedness, but he was reliable and useful and able to be a good teammate. Too good, perhaps. As a member of the Marlie Juniors, he'd started to run with a crew some dubbed the "Rat Pack," a group that included Al Smith, Bob Whidden and Jim Cassidy, and the party continued all the way to minor pro in Tulsa. They drank, they caroused, they chased skirts and lived hard. "I didn't handle the life all that well," says Jimmy Keon. "I found it very tedious, and I found myself carousing and living a lively single life. I didn't handle it well." He'd been a good student at St. Mike's earlier, good enough that his angry mother hauled him home halfway through a school year when his grades dropped. Even then he already had other notions running around in his head.

He was making $5,500 a year playing in Tulsa, and had played in a couple of exhibitions with the Leafs, once on a line in the fall of 1967 with his famous brother, who would soon become captain of the Leafs. "Dave was trying to break in a curved stick. He tried to make a pass to me and it went right past my nose," says Jimmy. "We got to the bench, and he was yelling at me, and Armstrong leans over, with no teeth, and says, 'Nice fucking pass. Kid's trying to make the team and you almost took his eye out.'" Undeterred, Dave kept barking orders at his brother, trying to make him look good so he could stick. "I'd be along the boards, and he'd be yelling at me to get into the middle. Then I'd be in the middle, and he'd be yelling at me to get on the boards. At the end, he came up to me and said, 'You played really well,'" says Jimmy. "That meant a lot."

Partway through that season, however, Jimmy Keon packed it in. He'd had enough of the life and was heading home; he was finished with pro hockey. His instincts told him his path had to be different. "I guess there was pressure, but not from my brother. He wanted me to be a player, and he wanted to play with me. He was really upset by my decision. He thought it was a great life, and it was very difficult for him to see me leave." Jimmy had lived with the ribbing and the friendly jibes as well as the more mean-spirited verbal shots that he wasn't anywhere near as good as his older brother. "I'd say, well, there aren't that many who are," he says. In retrospect, he wonders if Peter Mahovlich hadn't had an easier path, playing in Hamilton with the Red Wing organization and not joining forces with his famous older brother until the 1970s when both played for Montreal and with Team Canada '72.

Fortunately for Jimmy Keon, the pressure of his name was not matched by equal pressure within his family. In fact, his older brother was the exception, a professional athlete harvested from a family that valued education more than sport. His father, David Sr., never skated in his life. He worked in the mines around Noranda at a time when it was a 50/50 anglophone/francophone split. The managers were mostly English-speaking and the workers, while from a variety of cultures, were largely French-speaking. His mother, Laura, was the oldest of 10 children from an Ottawa Valley clan; she became a teacher and had taught natives on Manitoulin Island. Her marriage to David Sr. was unusual, for it came when he was 49 and Laura was 32. Undaunted by their relatively late marital rendezvous, they forged ahead and had a family of six children, including the two boys. In fact, they were so ambitious that there would have been eight children had Laura not miscarried twice. By the early 1950s, young David had gone south to play for St. Mike's. "But she pushed me differently," says Jimmy. "She wanted me to be the first in our family to get a college or university education."

The tug on the younger boy, then, was just as strong to go in another direction from hockey. While his older brother was disappointed when Jimmy left Tulsa in 1968, his decision was met with encouragement from the family. He immediately enrolled in Carleton University in Ottawa, sometimes playing for the Canadian national team stationed there. Later he acquired his MBA from the University of Western Ontario and became a high-ranking executive with Corby's Distilleries. His hockey achievements were limited to several seasons spent playing senior hockey in Orillia, where he won the Allan Cup with that club. Jimmy never looked back and never regretted missing the opportunity to skate for the Leafs alongside his brother as Dennis Hull did with his superstar brother, Bobby. "It was a very different decision than the one the world expected of me," he says.

———— ❦ ————

For the Conachers, Hewitts, Smythes, Imlachs, Clancys and Keons, having their families associated with the Leafs and Maple Leaf Gardens was both a blessing and a curse. They were all part of the fabric that formed the '67 Leafs, a multi-layered, complex culture that produced one last gasp of brilliance that unforgettable spring.

Stanley Cup Final, Game Four
Montreal at Maple Leafs, April 27, 1967

Thursday. Again.

On three previous playoff occasions in the spring of 1967, the Maple Leafs played on a Thursday evening and lost. Badly. On April 6, they opened the post-season in Chicago and were blown out 5–2. On April 13, they watched helplessly as a two-games-to-one series lead over the Hawks evaporated on home ice in a 4–3 defeat. On April 20, the Leafs opened the Stanley Cup final against Montreal with a 6–2 pratfall at the Forum.

Now here it was again. Thursday, April 27. Damn.

The Leafs had picked up their game since getting spanked by the Habs a week earlier, of course, using 42-year-old Johnny Bower's net-minding to steal two from the hotshot Canadiens. But it was Thursday again, and 24 hours before game time—the bad omens were piling up. At the NHL awards ceremony in Toronto, no Leaf had come remotely close to winning a trophy, with Dave Keon a distant second to Stan Mikita in the voting for the Lady Byng Trophy. Boston defenceman Bobby Orr, meanwhile, the same youngster from Parry Sound the Leafs had dismissed as "too young" to consider seven years earlier, had won sil-verware as the league's best rookie and been crowned by Norris Trophy winner Harry Howell as the NHL's next special defenceman. Also that week, the Central Hockey League had announced its awards, and the best goaltender had been 26-year-old Gerry Cheevers, the same netminder the Leafs had lost for nothing two years earlier when they decided to keep two aging goalies, Bower and Terry Sawchuk.

That omen seemed downright spooky by game time the next night. Sawchuk, on the day off, had declined to lament his sudden relegation to backup as he watched Bower swarmed by reporters. "John loves every minute of it," he said. "I'd sooner be over here enjoying peace and quiet." Not for long. It was Thursday again and time for bad things to happen to the '67 Leafs. Bower had taken the warm-up, but when the game started, it was Sawchuk between the pipes with no backup goaltender on the bench. To make matters worse, legend has it Sawchuk was also nursing a wicked hangover. By the time the second period rolled around, young netminder Al Smith had taken up the extra spot on the bench, and rumours were running wild around Maple Leaf Gardens as to the where-abouts and condition of Bower. As it turned out, there was nothing mys-terious about it, but it was not good news. Bower had seriously pulled his groin in the warm-up while blocking a shot by Larry Hillman. Nobody knew it at that moment, but the aged wonder would not appear again for the Leafs that spring.

That last-minute change may have knocked the Leafs off balance, or the Canadiens may simply have been the more desperate team on that night. Sawchuk struggled mightily in his return to the net since being blast-ed by the Habs in Game One. In the words of columnist Milt Dunnell, he played "like a barefoot boy on a burning deck," jittery and uncertain from the start, ultimately surrendering all the goals to the visitors in a dispiriting 6–2 defeat. Mike Walton and Tim Horton had scored for the Leafs, but in addition to Bower's absence, the top line, centred by Peter Stemkowski, had gone cold. Just as in Game One, meanwhile, the defensive pair of Tim Horton and Allan Stanley was ripped to shreds. After being on the ice for three goals, Stanley was benched in favour of Bobby Baun. Horton, meanwhile, was caught on the ice for five of the six Montreal goals. In four playoff games played on Thursday, the tight-checking, defence-minded Leafs had coughed up a mind-boggling 21 goals.

The next day, Bower didn't even bother taking the train to Montreal for Game Five. Smith, just 21 years old, would be the backup to Sawchuk. Vachon made 35 saves in Game Four and looked to be back on his game again as the emotional pendulum had swung back in favour of Les Habitants. The script had unfolded exactly as it had with the opening-round series against Chicago, with the Leafs losing the opener, winning the next two, dropping the fourth game and now headed into the enemy's rink for a critical Game Five match. The euphoria of Pulford's overtime winner in Game Three had vanished. The margin of error for the Leafs had again shrunk. The best news for the Leafs? Unless the series went to a seventh game, there would be no more Thursday games.

9 *The Unsung Heroes*

In 2003, a friend asked Larry Hillman if 37 years wasn't enough, if it wasn't finally time to lift the little-known Hillman Hex from the Toronto Maple Leafs.

"I looked at him and said, 'I think maybe 50 years sounds like a nice round number,'" says Hillman with a grin.

As the years passed, the Hillman Hex seemed powerful enough to anyone who believed, and a worthy symbol of the disaffection felt by many members of the 1967 team for the organization, an alienation unusual in its depth. That season, and those memorable playoffs, marked the best hockey Hillman ever played, yet he viewed them in retrospect through a prism of bitterness and anger. He had his own, specific reasons, but it's fair to say that in the retelling of that surprise '67 championship by a Leaf team that wasn't supposed to be nearly good enough to win, Hillman has been one of several pivotal individuals who have been all but robbed of recognition for their crucial contributions.

Most historical versions have focused on the presence of a group of over-the-hill athletes, the goaltending exploits of Johnny Bower and Terry Sawchuk and the coaching of the legendary Punch Imlach. Those were all factors, to be sure, and they were the dominant elements of the three previous Cup wins in 1962, 1963 and 1964. But 1967 was different. Specifically, the roles played by Larry Hillman and Marcel Pronovost on defence, and Peter Stemkowski, Jim Pappin and Brian Conacher up front, have been badly underplayed over the years. Most of that group were treated shoddily by the organization despite their efforts and dumped from the roster soon after that spring as part of the remarkably swift demolition of a championship team. It was almost as if the Leaf organization wanted to destroy the evidence of the contributions of those individuals to ensure history, always written by the victors, would read a certain way. There were famous players on that team, and a surprisingly and arguably disproportionate number of individuals who ultimately were inducted into the Hockey Hall of Fame. But in many ways, they received too much of the credit, with versions of that season pure hagiography and distortions of the facts, designed more to venerate Leaf hockey saints rather than accurately depict the events that occurred.

At the time, Leaf fans well understood how Pappin had led the league in playoff scoring that spring, and how Stemkowski had been such a ruthless, punishing force on the forecheck while serving as Pappin's centreman. They had cheered Conacher for his relentless physical play and his dazzling two-goal performance in Game Six of the opening-round series against Chicago, arguably the most important game of the entire playoffs. They had watched in awe as the Hillman–Pronovost combination had proved utterly impenetrable and given up only one even-strength goal against in the entire playoffs. They were significantly superior to the more heralded pair of Tim Horton and Allan Stanley. Hillman, in particular, logged extraordinary amounts of ice time and directed the Leaf power play. Yet today, many have to be reminded that any of those players were part of that '67 team, partly because of the years that have passed, and partly because of the way in which that season has been documented. They were the unsung heroes of '67, men whose talents shone brightly but have since been all but forgotten.

Hillman and Pronovost were hardly a known defence commodity as the 1967 Stanley Cup playoffs loomed. They hadn't played much together that season, and certainly their collaboration for the opening game of the playoffs was anything but the result of careful design. They had known each other for years, as both had been part of the excellent Detroit teams of the early 1950s that had captured four Stanley Cups in six years. Hillman, a raw-boned, square-shouldered lad from Kirkland Lake, Ontario, managed to sneak into three playoff games on the 1955 Red Wing champions, thus becoming the youngest player ever to have his name engraved on the Stanley Cup at 18 years and two months of age. He had been drawn to the Red Wings rather naturally through his worship of Ted Lindsay, who would arrive in the gold mining town in northeastern Ontario every summer for a visit, often with Gordie Howe in tow. Lindsay would take some of the more promising lads to Timmins for a skate, and Hillman was included. In 1952, the Wings heeded Lindsay's recommendation and invited Hillman to try out for their affiliated junior team in Windsor. The next year, the team moved to Hamilton, and in his third year under the Wings control Hillman played 49 games in Hamilton and six for the parent Detroit squad, which was gunning for its third championship in four seasons. Hillman ended up being part of that team, which also included the more established Pronovost, then in his fourth full NHL season.

Despite his early success with the Wings, Hillman moved on two years later to Boston in the intra-league draft at the same time his younger brother, Wayne, was moving through the Chicago system. The Bruins sent Hillman to Providence, where he played with his older brother, Floyd, who had skated in the six games for the NHL Bruins the previous season, the only games in the big leagues he would ever see. For a long time thereafter, it appeared that Larry Hillman was to be sentenced to a similar career, always close to staying in the NHL for good, but never quite sticking. He moved to the Leafs via that same intra-league draft process in 1960, and immediately became mired behind others on the Leaf defence depth chart. In particular, the pairs of Horton with Stanley and Bobby

Baun with Carl Brewer became entrenched in those years as the Leafs charged to Cups in 1962, '63 and '64. In the '64 play-offs, Hillman did get into 11 of the 14 Leaf playoff games, but the next year he was again designated for the minors and only appeared briefly in the NHL. After a decade as a pro, Hillman seemed to be treading water and was heading nowhere.

Brewer's retirement in September 1965, significantly altered the Leaf depth chart on defence. Hillman started to earn an edge over Kent Douglas, another veteran defenceman, but there were others still ahead of him, specifically Pronovost, who had been picked up in a deal with Detroit. When the 1966–67 season began, the Leafs also were excited about young blue-liner Jim McKenny, an offensive-minded stylist out of Ottawa who had put up big numbers with the Marlboro Juniors at the same time Bobby Orr was demonstrating with the Oshawa Generals that defence could be played in a far more flamboyant way than had previously been seen. McKenny was only 20, but there was a roster spot for him if he could take it, and he had signed a two-year contract that summer that included a $7,000 signing bonus and salaries of $7,000 and $8,000. The Leafs were excited about McKenny's potential, and assigned him Number 2, the number Brewer had left behind. Imlach was determined to make it appear as though the club could easily fill the void left by the mercurial Brewer. McKenny, sadly, was an alcoholic, and within a matter of days he'd broken team rules and been exiled to the minor league team. Brewer's old jersey was then assigned to Hillman. McKenny was sent to Tulsa, but when team officials decided his behaviour wasn't helpful to the young players on that team, he was sent to the older club in Rochester, where he roomed with the inimitable Don Cherry. "I was the only one who would room with him," says Cherry. "It was like he was trying to destroy himself."

Even then, McKenny was given another opportunity dur-ing the season in a six-game stint that coincided with Imlach's hospitalization, but he couldn't grab a roster position for keeps. "I couldn't stand the pressure of being with the Leafs," McKenny recalls. "It was horrible and oppressive. I couldn't figure out their systems and the way they wanted me to play and my style of carrying the puck didn't fit with them. I just didn't want to be there. The players were nice to me, but it was just too intimidating to break into the inner group. I don't care what any player says now — they all hated Imlach back then, every one of them. I knew that I would never be able to play on a Leaf team as long as Imlach was the coach." McKenny did play for Rochester in their run to the Calder Cup final in '67, and ultimately cracked the Leaf lineup for good in 1969 when Imlach was no longer in charge.

More than two decades later, McKenny conquered his drinking problem, and didn't look back to lament not taking advantage of the chance to be part of history with the Leafs in '67. "If all you play for is the Cup, then you're missing out on the daily life experience and that's what it's all about," he says. "I'm able to help people out now with alcohol problems because of my life experiences. What good would a Stanley Cup ring do for me in real life today?"

Brewer was gone, McKenny couldn't make the grade and Hillman, after serving such a long apprenticeship, was ready to jump into the void. He'd injured his left shoulder on multiple occasions earlier in his career, most seriously when he was hammered by Moose Vasko in a game against Chicago six years earlier. Surgery had improved the joint but it hadn't healed perfectly, so when he was given a chance to move to the right side on defence to play with Pronovost, it meshed with his physical limitations. "I shot left, so moving to the right side was perfect for me because I had more range of motion with my right arm, the one closest to the boards," he says. When the playoffs began, he and Pronovost were together, with Baun, the overtime hero of the '64 playoffs, anchored to the bench after an injury-plagued season. Hillman, to that point regarded as a journeyman, was a revelation in the post-season. "I think I logged the most ice time outside of the goaltenders," he said. "I started every period, played the power play, took faceoffs and was out there in most critical situations." His long, backhand flips relieved pressure in the Leaf zone time after time, and his smart positional play allowed the more adventuresome Pronovost to stray without costing the team goals.

If Hillman believed that his fine play would finally earn him a full-time job in the NHL the following season and a corresponding increase in pay, however, he was very wrong. In the weeks that followed the Stanley Cup parade, he tried to negotiate an increase from his $15,000 salary. "I asked for $21,000 and Imlach offered $19,000," he recalls. "I then had it in my mind that I wouldn't settle for anything less than $20,000. I knew through my brother [Wayne] what other guys were making. On the Rangers, my brother was making $21,000, Arnie Brown was making $23,000 and Jim Neilson $24,000. That summer, Bobby Baun had signed with Oakland for $35,000. Al Arbour, who had played for the Leafs in Rochester the previous season, had signed a three-year contract with St. Louis for $25,000 a season. I couldn't believe it. I had been with the Leaf organization for seven seasons. I could barely do a push-up after my shoulder surgery in 1961 and I had worked at it and continued to do hundreds of push-ups a week to build up my shoulder. Seven years with the organization and the best hockey of my life the previous spring. And three guys on a team who were eliminated in the first round were going to make more? And a guy who was our fifth defenceman and another guy who had played for our minor-league team were going to make more?"

The players association was now established and there were six more teams in the league and more than 100 new jobs, but Hillman was still locked in by the rules of the old order. His teammates commiserated with him, and captain George Armstrong suggested that he sign for the $19,000, and his teammates would make up the difference by chipping in $100 each. Mike Walton even gave him a cheque, but Hillman stood fast on principle. On opening day of the 1967–68 season, Hillman sat morosely in the stands at Maple Leaf Gardens with his wife and children, waiting for a final meeting with Imlach as the other players watched Leaf management put the proud defenceman on the griddle. Imlach upped his offer to $19,500, but Hillman said $20,000 was his bottom line. Imlach left, and sent word with trainer Bobby Haggert that if Hillman didn't take his final offer, he would be fined $100 a day. It had become a war of attrition that neither side could win, and a pointless, petty dispute that undermined all that had been accomplished just five months earlier.

Hillman went to a salary arbitration hearing with NHL president Clarence Campbell 24 days later, having lost $100 each day. On behalf of the union, Alan Eagleson presented Hillman's case, but the system did not provide for an independent body or individual to resolve the dispute. Instead, Campbell, a man hired by NHL owners, held the hearing at the Gardens and ruled in favour of the Leafs and the deduction of $2,400 in fines. Now Hillman was in big trouble with nowhere to turn unless he capitulated. "Over the summer, I had invested in $50,000 worth of land in the Niagara Peninsula and I was starting to get in a financial bind," said Hillman. Eventually, he agreed to join Rochester after coach Joe Crozier agreed to pay half of his $2,400 in fines. While skating for $18,300, Hillman was eventually called up and played 55 games for the Leafs that season, but remained bitter over his treatment at the hands of the Leaf organization. At the end of the season he moved on to Minnesota, and eventually played for Montreal in their successful run to the

1969 Stanley Cup. But he never forgave the Leafs. "After the way I was treated, I put the Hillman Hex on 'em," he says.

———————— ❧ ————————

In comparison to his defence partner, Pronovost was treated like a king. Indeed, he earned a salary of $32,000 for the 1966–67 season and received a bonus of $15,000—the total amount of Hillman's contract—when the Leafs won the Cup. To be fair, his resume was a great deal more impressive than his partner's, which is how he'd worked his way up the salary scale with a Detroit club that generally paid better than the Leafs. Pronovost had played 14 seasons for Detroit and had been named a first-team NHL all-star twice and a second-teamer twice. He'd actually first moved on to the Detroit defence in the 1950 playoffs against the Leafs as a replacement for Red Kelly, who had been moved to the forward lines because of injuries.

No longer fleet afoot by the spring of '67, the deep crevices and lines on Pronovost's face hinted at his smarts and resourcefulness, plus the 14 broken noses he'd suffered during his career. By then, he had an uncanny ability to bail himself out of trouble against young, faster men by relying on his guile and experience. On December 4, 1966, he tracked down a young Bobby Orr and delivered a heavy hit that inflicted the first of what would be a long, destructive series of knee injuries that would ultimately bring a premature conclusion to Orr's career. The 36-year-old Quebecer loved to take unpredictable trips up ice as well, occasionally coming up with big goals. He was an unusual character who teammates dubbed "Doc" behind his back, because he had an answer for everything. Tight with Sawchuk, he nonetheless was careful not to run afoul with management by being viewed as a drinking partner of the temperamental goaltender. "Marcel had a rule that he would never sign an autograph in a bar so he wouldn't be associated with being in any bars," recalls Stemkowski. "So whenever we signed something in a bar and Marcel was there, we'd say to the person, 'Hey, there's Marcel Pronovost. Better go and get his autograph.' That would really bug Marcel."

After the Leafs won the Cup, Imlach chose to protect Pronovost in the expansion draft despite his age, losing Baun instead. It was a sign of the close bond that had developed between the two men, and a decade later when Imlach was running the Buffalo Sabres, he hired Pronovost to be his coach. Imlach was in his final months of running the Sabres then, and he undoubtedly remembered how Pronovost had come through so effectively for him 10 years earlier. A year and a half later, they were fired on the same day by the Sabres.

———————— ♣ ————————

Hillman and Pronovost were, by the time the Leafs lunged for the Cup in 1967, grizzled veterans of the NHL wars. By comparison, Conacher was a virtual neophyte who had all but wandered his way to the Leafs. A tall, angular fellow, bigger than most NHLers at 6-foot-3 and almost 200 pounds, Conacher started through the ranks in straightforward enough fashion, playing well for the Marlie juniors in the late 1950s and early 1960s, but then he took a few different turns. First he played a few minor pro games with Rochester and one NHL contest with the Leafs in the 1961–62 season, and then took a direction that wasn't that uncommon for good young hockey players in those days—he went to school. Conacher played a season for the University of Western Ontario and then joined Canada's national team for the 1964 Winter Olympics, and then for another full season. By then, he had veered far from the pre-determined path to NHL stardom, but in the fall of 1965, at the same time Brewer was leaving the Leafs to play for the Canadian national team, Conacher decided to take a second look at the pro game.

He skated mostly in Rochester that year, playing only his second and third NHL games with the Leafs, but by

September 1966, he was able to grab a full-time job in the NHL. It would be the only pro season Conacher would play in which he didn't skate a portion of the campaign in the minors. His goal totals during the regular season, 14 goals in 66 games, weren't eye-catching by modern standards. But they were good enough at the time; Conacher was considered a solid Calder Trophy candidate all season. It was in the playoffs, however, that he transformed his game for a four-week-long stint that, like Hillman, was probably the best hockey he ever played. It was as though for that short duration it all clicked for Conacher. He was able to mesh his ancestry with his abilities and the needs of his team. The makeup of the Leafs meant they needed a rambunctious forward—somebody who could skate and play with more common sense than Eddie Shack but make a difference in a hockey game by taking the body with intelligence and force. That Conacher did more than just throw a few good bodychecks is what made him special for the Leafs that spring.

He started the playoffs as an extra forward along with Mike Walton and Shack. As long as the regulars stayed healthy, Imlach had no particular use for the tall kid with the famous name, but the regulars didn't stay healthy long. In the second playoff game against Chicago, George Armstrong suffered a knee injury, and Conacher took his place alongside Dave Keon and Frank Mahovlich. Like McKenny, he found the atmosphere with the Leafs under Imlach oppressive, but when he went in for Armstrong he looked like he'd been sprung from a slingshot, playing an energetic disturber role similar to that which John Tonelli would fill for the outstanding New York Islander teams of the 1980s. Conacher began dishing out the hits right away, with Hawks forward Stan Mikita a special target. Keon and Mahovlich would do all the fancy stuff, and Conacher would just play his position, use his size to get in people's faces and wait for any chances that might arise. Two big ones arose in Game Six against the Hawks. Conacher cashed in on both, scoring twice as the Leafs eliminated the heavily favoured Chicagoans. The insertion of Conacher added youth and speed up front for the Leafs, a team that needed some of both in those playoffs. When the final began, Armstrong was ready, but Larry Jeffrey wasn't, having suffered a season-ending knee injury in that final game against Chicago. So Conacher bumped over to the left side in Jeffrey's place beside Red Kelly and Ron Ellis, and again gave the club that burst of energy at key moments. "If I could be on only one Stanley Cup team in my career, I feel fortunate it was the 1967 team," he says.

That there was no next act to Conacher's NHL career is part of the reason his role on the '67 champs has been so easily forgotten. The next season he played 64 regular-season games with the Leafs but also a couple in the minors. He squabbled with Imlach over money and felt he was the target of Imlach's anti-union vendetta along with teammates like Stemkowski and Walton, young guys who had dared trade in their loyalty to the Leafs for a union membership. He was the kind of useful grinder Imlach liked and he had youth on his side, but nonetheless, like Hillman, he was left unprotected in the 1968 intra-league when the Leafs instead protected Bryan Hextall, who would never skate in a single game for the club. The Leafs, in fact, lost three regulars that day in Conacher, Hillman and defenceman Duane Rupp, getting nothing of value in return except cash.

After mulling over his future during the summer months, Conacher surprised the hockey world by retiring at age 27 in a move reminiscent of Brewer's departure. "I reached a decision it would be better to earn my living with my brain, rather than my body," he told reporters. He seemed to be of a mixed mind about his career, musing that he'd turned pro mostly for the money, but hinting that his family legacy had motivated him to prove to himself that he could play in the big leagues like other members of his famous family tree. "Punch Imlach had made me a very cynical young man," says Conacher, who eventually became president of the NHL Alumni Association. "I was headstrong to begin with, and I thought another Punch Imlach awaited me if I went to Detroit. I was also ambivalent about whether hockey was the right career for me. I had other options. So I got my real estate licence and did some broadcasting, and I also played a little with the Canadian national team including the 1969 Izvestia Cup when we had Ken Dryden as our goaltender."

Conacher gave the NHL one last look in 1971 with the Red Wings, but found himself in the minors when owner Bruce Norris decided he didn't like the way Conacher skated. He turned down a chance at the end of that season to play in St. Louis and instead joined the Ottawa Nationals of the WHA for a year before quitting. In the fall of 1972, between leaving the Wings and joining Ottawa, he made good on his broadcasting training by being part of one of the greatest series of all times, providing colour commentary alongside Foster Hewitt for the 1972 Summit Series between Canada and the Soviet Union.

Conacher had given the Leafs a terrific spring in 1967, bashing bodies and scoring important goals, and his compatriot in the mucking and grinding had been Stemkowski, a Marlboro grad who also emerged during that run to the Cup as a figure who promised to be a standout Leaf for years. Indeed, before Game Four of the Stanley Cup final against Montreal, Imlach had paid the Winnipeg native high praise by comparing him to one of the greatest Leafs ever. "He could become as important to the Leafs as Ted Kennedy was when he played for Hap Day," said Imlach. "And Teeder was a great one." Stemkowski had come to Toronto to prove his high school girlfriend wrong—she'd said he'd never move that far away—and survived terrible homesickness to eventually be part of the '64 Marlie team that won the Memorial Cup. To deal with missing Winnipeg, he'd wander down to Eaton's after practice to look around, then go to a local eatery named Basil's, where the cook would send along extra portions for the strapping young athlete. He'd then hit the movie theatre. It was a routine he'd repeat many times, both as a Marlie and as a Leaf, to cope with the homesickness that came with being a young man in a strange, big city.

He worked his way up through the Leaf system, getting a chance to play in early 1965 when the very popular Billy Harris had been demoted to Rochester after being on the Cup winners of '62, '63 and '64. "The team didn't make me feel all that welcome," he recalls. "I wasn't real comfortable. I never really thought much about it at the time, but no wonder we didn't click—we were a generation apart." He played 56 games in the 1965–66 season, and by the next year was a regular on the roster and one of the young Leafs who hated their boss. "We all couldn't stand Imlach," he says. "He had no special relationship with anybody, but I was one of his whipping boys, being one of the few younger players. We had no systems, no breakout strategy. He had two theories with his coaching. One, get the team in good shape. Two, get the team as mad as possible at him so they would be an angry and passionate team on the ice. I remember one or two occasions we got back from Montreal at Union Station at 8 a.m. and Imlach would announce we had to be on the ice by 9:15. So we would head up to the Honey Dew on Carlton Street to grab a quick breakfast before we had to hit the ice for this practice that had just been announced."

Just 23 at the start of the 1966–67 season, Stemkowski was still the lonely kid from The 'Peg, boarding with a chiropractor and his wife near Greenwood race track close to the Beaches area in the east end of the city. He was plugging along, playing on the third and fourth line behind established pivots Keon and

Red Kelly, as the club played in fits and starts. Then came Imlach's illness in mid-February, and Stemkowski's big break followed. "Clancy was a messiah," he says. A new line was created with Stemkowski at centre, another former Marlboro junior, Jim Pappin, on the right side and veteran Bob Pulford on the left. If not for the creation of this line, the Leafs probably would not have had the firepower to capture the Cup. In their first 12 games together, the three forwards combined for 15 goals. When the playoffs came, they were the team's undisputed Number 1 line. Stemkowski was the top centre on English Canada's most famous team, just four years after leaving Winnipeg and his Ukrainian-born parents, immigrants who spoke only broken English, and heading east to Ontario.

He gave the club a different look; he was a big, physical centre with a penchant for using his body to create loose pucks and scoring opportunities. Like Conacher, it seemed as though Stemkowski had finally figured it all out. "I got more aggressive using my weight and forechecking to dig the puck out," he says. "We just seemed to complement each other so well." None of the three were Imlach favourites, but the Leaf coach had no choice but to lean on the trio more and more. Pulford was the union agitator, the quiet veteran who was notorious for bumming smokes off his teammates between periods. Stemkowski, the big kid from the West, would hide a garlic sausage in his stall and sneak a nibble between periods when Imlach wasn't looking. Pappin was the lean winger with a chip on his shoulder who could set up plays and score. Pappin and Pulford were already friends, and Pappin was Stemkowski's one friend on a team where he still felt like an outsider. "I remember one shift when one of them, Pappin or Pulford, didn't pass to the other," says Stemkowski. "When we got back to the bench they got in a heated argument. I thought, cripes, and these guys are great friends and they're tearing a strip off each other like that."

During Game Three of the final against Montreal, the CBC arranged to have a camera in Stemkowski's family home in Winnipeg to watch the reaction of his family to his success. "First shift, I got speared by Ted Harris and all I can think of is, I'm lying on the ice and my family is worried about me back home in Winnipeg," he says. "At the end of the game, we won, I'd scored a goal and I'd been speared." Stemkowski had also engineered Pulford's winning goal in overtime by out-muscling Jacques Laperriere in the corner, the kind of play he'd made time and time again that spring. Against Chicago in the first round, he'd terrorized the Blackhawk defence, particularly all-star veteran Pierre Pilote. By the time the Leafs claimed the Cup, "Stemmer" had scored five times and assisted on seven others in 12 playoff games. It appeared the Leafs created a strong top forward line that would be productive for years, and had the successor to the aging Kelly up the middle.

By the following March, however, Stemkowski was gone, part of the disastrous deal with Detroit that had also sent Mahovlich, youngster Garry Unger and the rights to Brewer to the Wings. Like Conacher and Hillman, he'd run afoul of Imlach in contract negotiations following the Cup win, and had been part of the anti-union crusade being waged by Imlach and Leaf ownership. "I supported the union when it started," says Stemkowski. "Some of the older guys like [George] Armstrong, [Johnny] Bower and [Allan] Stanley weren't all that interested in getting too involved knowing how Imlach felt. He blamed everything on the players association." Stemkowski had made a paltry $9,000 that season and, with the union just starting to make its presence felt, asked for $20,000 at training camp in 1967. "Imlach had a look in his eye like I'd asked for every single cent he had," says Stemkowski. "He was livid. He told me he wasn't going to waste his time with me and he'd let Clancy handle it. I talked with Clancy over the next few weeks and signed for $17,000."

Later, Stemkowski wasn't as happy as Mahovlich to join the Red Wings, but scored 46 goals in two seasons and then went on to a long, productive career with the Rangers, finishing his NHL career with Los Angeles in 1978. By the end, Stemkowski had played 967 NHL games plus another 83 post-season matches. But less than a quarter of that total had been with the Leafs, a team that had once proclaimed him as the successor to one of the most celebrated players in team history.

———— ✿ ————

Four months before the 1967 NHL playoffs began, Pappin was stuck in Rochester again, the fourth straight season he'd bounced between the NHL and the minors, despite his obvious talents as a goal scorer. He'd even played defence with Rochester at one point, and Pappin figured his time was up as a Leaf. When he was recalled to the big club on January 30, 1967, he arrived with one goal in mind—to play well enough to catch the attention of one of the six expansion teams that would be joining the NHL the following fall. He'd met some of the expansion folks the previous summer at a golf tournament, owners like Bill Putnam of Philadelphia and Sid Salomon of St. Louis, men who might be able to help him escape the Leafs.

Already an ex-Leaf in spirit, Pappin returned for a last stint with the club and began to play with a looseness and confidence he'd never had before. Placed on the line with Stemkowski and Pulford, he started scoring with regularity, which continued into the playoffs. Game after game against Chicago and Montreal, Pappin was consistently the club's most dangerous attacker. When the Leafs enjoyed a power play, Pappin often found himself on the right point, proving his brief fling as a defenceman in Rochester had actually been a profitable experience. In all, he scored seven goals and added eight assists in 12 games, leading the playoffs in scoring. In those days, the NHL board of governors voted on the Conn

Smythe Trophy to acknowledge the MVP of the playoffs, and Pappin was surprised when teammate Dave Keon won the award for his strong two-way play. Pappin's mother never forgot that slight until the day she died, and Pappin remembers resenting Keon for a long while. "I thought he was one of Imlach's boys," he says. "But later I found out that he hated Imlach as much as the rest of us."

That productive spring should have cemented Pappin's future role with the Leafs, particularly with Mahovlich on his way out. Instead, like Hillman, Conacher and Stemkowski, he found himself embroiled in a contract dispute with the Leafs in the off-season. He'd earned $14,500 in the 1966–67 season, with a $1,000 bonus for 20 goals and another $1,000 for 25 goals. He'd scored 21 goals with the Leafs and four with Rochester, plus another seven in the playoffs, so he figured he was owed both bonuses. The Leafs, however, said they would only pay the first $1,000 bonus. "I came from Sudbury where people would fuck you all the time," says Pappin grimly. Pappin figured he could even it all out with his new contract, and asked for $22,000 plus a $1,000 signing bonus. One day in training camp, he was joined by Horton on the walk back to the hotel from the practice rink, something Pappin found unusual. "What are they offering you?" said Horton, who was aware of the ongoing salary impasse. Pappin gave him the $22,000 figure, and Horton asked if it would help if Pappin knew what he was making. He then told the young right winger he was making $28,000. Pappin never understood Horton's motivation, but to a player still looking to establish himself, the comparison to a player of Horton's longevity and status would have been intimidating. Pappin signed, getting a little less than he'd asked for, but never again played with Pulford and Stemkowski, and in fact was again sent to the minors the next season and refused to report for several weeks, bitterly shocked at his treatment by the Leafs.

In May 1968, two months after Stemkowski had been traded and 12 months after the two young forwards had made up
two-thirds of the line that had delivered the Leafs another Cup,
Pappin was sent to Chicago in another ridiculous, vindictive
trade, this time for a washed-up Pilote. "Pappin had one great
playoff set for us," snapped Imlach. "He didn't measure up last
season and he didn't figure in our plans for next year, so I'm not
losing a member of my team. He had made it clear he didn't
want to play here and I had said he wouldn't be back. So I guess
we're both happy." Imlach didn't bother telling Pappin in person; he called his wife and gave her the news instead. The
Pappins celebrated by going out to dinner, and then Pappin
went out and scored 216 goals from 1968 to 1975 for the
Hawks. Over that time, no Leaf player scored as often.

Stanley Cup Final, Game Five
Maple Leafs at Montreal, April 29, 1967

Frank Mahovlich could barely wait for the season to end, to conclude another nine months of torture under the sneering Punch Imlach before being able to retreat to his family and friends, and thus escape the pressures of wearing a Maple Leaf uniform, which he felt far more than his teammates.

Mahovlich certainly didn't arrive at the Montreal Forum for Game Five of the 1967 Stanley Cup final with a stirring speech in mind. That wasn't his role on the team. He'd only delivered average performances throughout the post-season and didn't feel like he was the one who could rally his teammates with the series tied two games apiece. He'd been eclipsed as the club's top offensive threat by winger Jim Pappin, and Dave Keon was the forward drawing raves from writers and broadcasters as a potential MVP choice if the Leafs were able to upset the Canadiens. As he sat in his stall at the Forum in the final moments before taking the ice for the fifth game, however, something stirred in the sensitive giant. The Leafs were a quiet team, which meant a vocal fringe forward like Eddie Shack could find all kinds of time to chatter and chirp before a big game. This time, however, The Big M didn't like what he was hearing. "I was sitting getting ready for the game quietly as I normally do," recalls Mahovlich. "Shack was mouthing off about how our goal scorers had to get scoring, and something just came over me. I yelled back that we all had to contribute, that every one of us was capable of scoring a big goal." For a moment, Mahovlich's teammates sat stunned, shocked that the sensitive star had raised his voice in such a way. Then, as quickly as the moment had arisen, Terry Sawchuk was up and out the dressing room door heading to the ice. Mahovlich jumped up immediately and followed Sawchuk, who had provided the perfect punctuation on his surprise speech to his suddenly energized teammates

On the day of Game Five, Canadians were preparing to move their clocks ahead one hour for Daylight Savings Time, and so too was the entire country looking forward as never before. The day before, the doors to Expo '67 in Montreal had been flung open to the world, and the crush of bodies that crammed inside the world's fair that day overwhelmed even the most optimistic organizers. More than 400,000 people arrived on opening day, double the expected crowds. The computers installed to count attendance broke, there was a breakdown on the futuristic Gyratron ride, huge lineups for food and exhibitions clogged the grounds and a Vietnam protest added political undertones to the day. Over the first three days, 1.5 million patrons poured through the gates, smashing previous records for other global gatherings. To many, Expo was to mark the turning point for the entire country, a six-month period that would transform the nation and make Canadians think of themselves in a different way as the rest of the world took a second look. If the 1919 Paris peace conference had redrawn the maps of Europe and the Middle East and set the stage for many of the successes and disasters of the 20th century, Expo '67 was heralded, promoted and envisioned as a similarly pivotal event in history, a peaceful event that would transform the world.

It was, as the world was contemplating space travel and unexplored frontiers, designed to be a peaceful gathering that would cap a tumultuous decade and mark the beginning of an era that would introduce new methods of solving world problems and ameliorating international tensions. It seems almost silly in retrospect, but that's how people viewed the event then. Vietnam was tearing America to shreds, yet many saw the future in unique, ambitious terms. "Computers will soon eliminate war as an evolutionary function by providing enough wealth to supply all mankind," proclaimed U.S. architect and visionary Buckminster Fuller. Fuller's designs and ideas dominated Expo, particularly the grand geodesic dome of the American pavilion. His concepts and lofty notions were similarly prevalent and appealing, creating an almost giddy sense of progress and possibilities in a city some described as "a Canadian Venice." "By 1985, almost anything you can dream of can and will have happened … man will be living in an entirely new, responsibly conscious relationship to the universe," said Fuller.

The fact that the world fair had almost collapsed three years earlier because it was so fraught with logistical problems, but had been rescued by the Pearson government and delivered to the world on schedule, seemed to legitimize the notion that Expo represented more of humanity's aspirations than any similar gathering in history. It was to be an unofficial, international peace conference, an effort to create a compelling climate of understanding and diplomacy that would overwhelm Cold War tensions. At least, that's what the dreamers thought.

Sixty-two nations, more than any other world's fair, organized exhibitions and pavilions under the general theme Terre des Hommes, the title of a book by Antoine de Saint-Exupery, which translated into English as Man and His World. Millions of tonnes of landfill had created a new island in the St. Lawrence River to host the gathering, and Canadian journalist Peter C. Newman underscored the sense of history in the making. "This may in retrospect turn out to have been one of those rare moments that change the direction of a nation's history," he wrote. "This is the greatest thing we have ever done as a nation and surely the modernization of Canada—of its skylines, its style, its institutions—will be dated from this occasion and this fair."

Expo '67 was a grand success in many ways, but also a grand illusion. It did not, in the end, dictate the future of the country or influence the international community. It was a wonderful party, but not a cataclysmic cultural and social event. In fact, the events that followed suggested the excited enthusiasm of the time masked an underlying sense of national immaturity and insecurity, for Canadians had much to understand and experience about their own country. Indeed, the glamour and glare of Expo had served to put a happy face over the multiple signs of obvious fractiousness within the country. "Nothing better illustrated the innate sturdiness of Canada's character than the spirit in which she approached her jubilee," wrote acclaimed novelist and humorist Hugh MacLennan about the months that preceded Expo. "In those days we out-Scotched the Scotch in our determination to look on the worst side of everything and make the nation appear unworthy in the eyes of a jealous and wrathful Providence. If it be true that God turns his back on a people that falls in love with itself, there seems no immediate danger that He will turn his back on Canada."

Toronto journalist Robert Fulford covered Expo '67 for *The Toronto Star*, living at the fair for four months and producing "This Was Expo," a collection of words and pictures that beautifully encapsulated the vision and events of those heady days. "In a sense, it was the quality of Canada's part in it that was special. It was as good as any of the stuff from the rest of the world," he says. "Canadian architecture, the site plan, it was all superb. We'd never done anything that good before. It was certainly a bracing event for Canadian architecture and design. I was rather surprised it didn't have the same effect on the institutions of Canada, on government, and so forth."

In the end, the heat of Expo was a short-term phenomenon. Indeed, as Fulford notes, when Vancouver hosted a world fair in 1986, none of those who had been instrumental in Expo '67 were involved. "They were unconnected," said Fulford. Post-Expo, Montreal was almost immediately plunged into political, social and economic uncertainty, as separatist forces spawned by the "Quiet Revolution" of 1960 exploded with a fury never before seen in modern Canadian history, creating the October Crisis of 1970 and the imposition of martial law under the War Measures Act by Prime Minister Pierre Trudeau. Expo also turned out be a financial mess, as even before the fair began the federal government was reporting that its commitment to assume 50 per cent of the Expo '67 deficit was going to cost $68 million. "If you were going to hold a world's fair in order to make your city an economically great city, Expo '67 would not be a good example to follow," said Fulford. "Montreal went into a period of decline after Expo because of the rise of separatism."

As the 1970s progressed, Montreal lost one corporate headquarters after another to Toronto. Yet Montreal had received Canada's first Major League Baseball franchise in 1969, the Expos, and Hugh Hefner thought the city so noteworthy he located the first Playboy club outside the U.S. on the banks of the St. Lawrence. The spectacular excesses of the 1976 Montreal Olympics, which carried the grandiose signature of Montreal mayor Jean Drapeau, as did Expo, served to distract attention from the problems that were beginning to plague the Canadian Venice. Expo had been a dream, but for Montreal, it failed to mark a glorious new epoch. For the country, it was the big promise that proved empty: Canada had much more growing up to do.

For the cities of Montreal and Toronto and their respective hockey teams, it marked a fork in the road, but in opposite ways. As Montreal declined, the Habs were in the midst of arguably the greatest era in team history, a period in which they would capture the Stanley Cup 10 times in 15 years. The sun would not set on the Canadiens' empire until the team won its 21st Cup in 1979, and even after that the club managed two more Cup victories in 1986 and 1993. For the Leafs, meanwhile, the time of Expo marked the end of an empire, and the beginning of decades of losing, which would at various times make the franchise—and, by extension, the city—a national laughingstock. The city of Toronto, however, was about to boom, ultimately drawing in all the ambitions of Montreal and then surpassing it as Canada's most powerful and influential city. Montreal was the centre of national attention in '67, but Toronto became the much envied, or much hated, "centre of the universe" to the rest of the country. As Toronto rose, the Leafs fell. As Montreal slumped, the Habs shone anew.

In 1967, Canadian author Joseph Schull contemplated Canada on its 100th birthday, looking back to its beginnings. "It was a world that seems to us now incredibly small, incredibly self-complacent and self-deceived," he wrote. By the year 2000, it was possible to look back at Canada's centennial year in the same fashion, and to see the final year of the six-team National Hockey League in a similar way. The NHL was a tiny sports and business society that existed in a relatively small geographic area and employed, almost without exception, young Canadian men in the cities of Toronto, Montreal, Detroit, Chicago, New York and Boston. There were only about 150 players in the league, and the teams had been established and unchanged since the Brooklyn Americans had gone bust and quit the league on September 28, 1942, dropping the NHL's membership to just six teams—a group that became known as the Original Six. The NHL was not like major league baseball, which during the 1950s had seen the Philadelphia Athletics move to Kansas City, the Boston Braves shift to Milwaukee, the New York Giants uprooted to San Francisco and the Brooklyn Dodgers of Jackie Robinson, Pee Wee Reese and Roy Campanella relocated to Los Angeles. The relentless pull westward had altered baseball's foundations, but hockey had been an unchanging, quaint little club for a quarter-century until it finally agreed to include six new clubs, including two in California, for the 1967–68 season. Until then, Foster Hewitt had never required a program to announce NHL games because there were so few players to remember.

The NHL existed within limited boundaries, but to be a Leaf was to exist in the national consciousness of Canada. The players were celebrities and heroes, but not rich men. They lived in ordinary houses in ordinary neighbourhoods, taking summer jobs at hockey camps to supplement their income and happily accepting invitations to appear on intermission interviews with *Hockey Night in Canada* because it meant an extra $100 in their hip pocket. When Captain George Armstrong bought his home in Leaside for $22,000 after a decade as a pro athlete, he still needed a first and second mortgage.

The players were loved, but it was the owners, specifically the legendary Conn Smythe and his heirs, who were the giants. They were the men who controlled the means of production. It was symbolic and telling that well into the 1960s, Leaf players would work for the Smythe family as goalies, defencemen and forwards during the winter months and then supply labour for the Smythe gravel pit in the summers. "The Leafs are now terribly important in Toronto," said Fulford. "But in 1967, they were the national team of Canada. Maple Leaf Gardens itself was the focus of the imagination for a lot of people. When a hockey player got to play on the ice at Maple Leaf Gardens, it was an ecstatic moment. But I don't think any of the Leaf players then were movie-star celebrities. They were spoken about and admired, but they were not what they are now."

A policeman might earn $7,000 or $8,000 a year in 1967, the same as a young player on the Leafs. Mahovlich, the closest thing to a superstar the franchise ever had, was making $32,000 a year at a time when a good, solid home in the west end would go for $25,000. They had perks and freebies galore, of course. Car dealerships on Yonge Street and on the Golden Mile in Scarborough would make sure they didn't have to worry about car payments. But they didn't live in swanky Forest Hill or the Bridle Path; they lived in Islington, Leaside and Don Mills, where their neighbours were teachers, subway drivers and salesmen. It was the franchise that was obscenely wealthy, paying only a small portion of its revenues to the hockey players that won the games. The Leafs made even more off junior players, who earned only $60 a week but could draw sellout crowds to the Gardens. Leafs players wanted to be paid better, to be sure, but it was the proprietors of the team that greedily stole to feather their own nests and build exclusive, multi-million-dollar homes.

To be a Leaf player was to have reached the pinnacle of the Canadian hockey dream, but it was not the proverbial pot of gold for young men from Winnipeg, Kirkland Lake and the streets of Toronto. The camaraderie made it special—the ability to travel around large North American cities with similarly minded young men while playing a sport most understood better than anything else in their lives. The stories were numerous and legendary, such as the time a well-lubricated Tim Horton and Allan Stanley hung little Dick Duff out of the window at George's Spaghetti house when Duff got a little too yappy for their liking.

By 1967, Toronto was poised to shed its image of Hogtown, of Toronto the Good, of the Queen City where entire neighbourhoods were still dry. Soon, being a Leaf would be more like being a rock star than being a working man and a good neighbour. The perception would change, and so too would the reality.

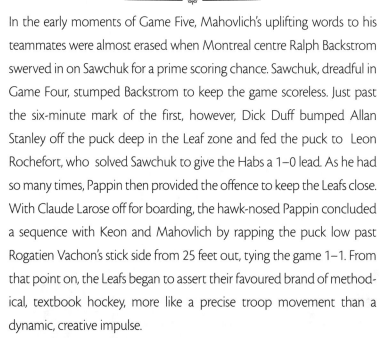

In the early moments of Game Five, Mahovlich's uplifting words to his teammates were almost erased when Montreal centre Ralph Backstrom swerved in on Sawchuk for a prime scoring chance. Sawchuk, dreadful in Game Four, stumped Backstrom to keep the game scoreless. Just past the six-minute mark of the first, however, Dick Duff bumped Allan Stanley off the puck deep in the Leaf zone and fed the puck to Leon Rochefort, who solved Sawchuk to give the Habs a 1–0 lead. As he had so many times, Pappin then provided the offence to keep the Leafs close. With Claude Larose off for boarding, the hawk-nosed Pappin concluded a sequence with Keon and Mahovlich by rapping the puck low past Rogatien Vachon's stick side from 25 feet out, tying the game 1–1. From that point on, the Leafs began to assert their favoured brand of methodical, textbook hockey, more like a precise troop movement than a dynamic, creative impulse.

Mahovlich's words of encouragement, suggesting any Leaf could be a hero, proved prophetic. First, Brian Conacher continued his surprising spring by beating Vachon on a rebound at 3:07 of the second, a play created by some diligent corner work by Red Kelly. Conacher had been a physical presence throughout the post-season and the scoring hero of Game Six against Chicago in the first round, a more influential performer than some of his more famous teammates. He was out eight minutes later killing an interference penalty to Red Kelly when he jarred the puck loose from Montreal forward Bobby Rousseau at centre ice. Out of nowhere swooped the bulky frame of defenceman Marcel Pronovost, one of 12 children born to a hockey family in Lac à la Tortue, Quebec, and a player always on the lookout for the big chance to move forward and join the attack. Pronovost charged down the wing, with Ron Ellis joining him on a two-on-one break and only Montreal defenceman J.C. Tremblay back. Ellis had led the Leafs in goals during the regular season and expected Pronovost to slide the puck to him, as did every pair of eyes in the stands and on both benches. But Pronovost held the puck, stickhandling and waiting. He had no plans to pass the puck at all. He looked up, cocked his wrists and fired a wrist shot that struck twine behind the stunned Vachon. The Leaf bench erupted as Vachon slumped. The visitors had a 3–1 lead, and with Sawchuk looking rejuvenated again, it would be more than enough.

Just as Mahovlich had predicted, if only to deflect the pressure from himself, one of the least likely Leafs had provided the most important goal of the season, a shorthanded goal, no less. "Frank Mahovlich won the fifth game for us," says Pronovost. Keon would add one more to make the final 4–1, a crushing blow to the Habs in a city high on Expo. "Home ice won't be a factor until the seventh game," said a defiant Montreal coach Toe Blake. "That's right—only in the seventh game, when we win the Cup." The truth was the spirit of the Habs was broken, as was the team's confidence in Vachon, the young goaltender strategically highlighted by Imlach at the beginning of the series. Gump Worsley,

37 years of age and inactive since March 12, had replaced Vachon for the third period, stopping all 10 shots he faced. Jacques Plante, the former Montreal goaltender, had been watching from the press box, and told reporters he would have gone to Worsley much earlier. The Canadiens had played virtually flawless hockey for six weeks going into the Stanley Cup final, but now they'd fallen behind three games to two, losing twice on home ice. "Let's just say we made a helluva down payment on the Cup tonight," said Leaf captain George Armstrong.

Stanley Cup Final, Game Six
Montreal at Maple Leafs, May 2, 1967

It was May 2, unseasonably warm with a hint of rain, and the smell of green—as in money—was in the air.

For Game Six of the 1967 Stanley Cup final, the Leafs were going in goal with Terry Sawchuk, arguably the greatest "money" goaltender in NHL history. They had captain George Armstrong, long in the tooth and long a winner, a fellow who would nervously tap his legs in the dressing room before a big game saying, "C'mon, money-makers." Defenceman Marcel Pronovost knew that he would receive a $15,000 bonus if the club went all the way, and he could already feel the friendly bulge in his wallet. Scattered on the Leaf dressing room floor at Maple Leaf Gardens were $3,000 in Canadian one-dollar bills, spread there by coach Punch Imlach—a superstitious sort who wouldn't touch a two-dollar bill—as a reminder to his team that more than pride and bragging rights to Canadian hockey supremacy was on the line.

They probably didn't need the reminder. This was a collection of seasoned pros who were very well aware it had been three long years since they'd received the Stanley Cup winners' share. Many of these players had grown fat on those post-season bonuses in 1962, 1963 and one more time in 1964. For winning the Cup in '67, each Leaf would receive a hefty $5,250, including $750 for finishing third in the regular season, $1,500 for winning the opening round and another $3,000 for knocking off Montreal for the

Cup. For some of the younger Leafs, that cheque would be more than 50 per cent of their wages for the year, a huge windfall. For Sawchuk, who made a relatively paltry $18,500 that season, it would relieve some of the pressure he was feeling about supporting his large family of six children back home in Detroit. Such an infusion of cash would be timely for Jim Pappin, as well, taking a little of the urgency out of his summer work effort. For $69, a hockey fan could "Ride Horses—Play Hockey" with Pappin at the Holiday Hockey Ranch in Pickering. Pappin was in need of a little extra income—his daughter, Arne, had been born after the fourth game of the Chicago series. Frank Mahovlich, meanwhile, was making $32,000, but he had a new travel agency to cultivate and the extra cash would be welcome. The playoff bonus was, in those days, a far greater proportion of a player's income. When the New Jersey Devils captured the 2003 Stanley Cup, they split a winner's purse of $2,381,500 among more than two dozen players and support staff, netting each player between $75,000 and $80,000. With the average NHL salary at $1.8 million, the bonus represented less than a week's pay to some.

For the '67 Leafs, however, the money on the table represented a big payday. These were hardened pros, many of whom had gone to war with the organization over their salaries in previous years, scraping to get a $500 raise out of the club. Cold cash meant something to them, and losing the series would cost each man $1,500. Imlach knew how to get them focused.

Temperatures soared as high as 70 degrees Fahrenheit on the humid day, which meant the Gardens, filled with 15,977 fans, would be a sweat-box. The face value of tickets was $7, $6, $4.50 and $2.50, with a few $1.50 standing-room spots available for what Leaf fans hoped would be the final game of the season. Even the pre-game warm-up included tension and uncertainty. Gump Worsley, 37, was expected to start for the Canadiens after relieving Rogie Vachon for the third period of Game Five. Worsley, a game and well-liked veteran, hadn't started in almost two months. At the other end was Sawchuk, but he was joined on the ice by two colleagues, Johnny Bower and Al Smith. Bower hadn't played since suffering a groin injury in the warm-up to Game Four, and Smith had been perched on the end of the Leaf bench in the previous two games. When Game Six began, there was Bower on the bench in uniform, but he was actually a straw goaltender, with Smith watching on television from a room nearby in case he was needed. "If Terry had been hurt, Bower would have re-injured his groin on the way to the net and the kid would have come out of hiding," said Imlach later. Perhaps Imlach wanted to use a little psychology against the Habs, who had been stumped by Bower's work in Games Two and Three or perhaps, as he later claimed, he just wanted all his old warriors with him for this battle.

The Canadiens, with coach Toe Blake having already predicted a victory in seven games, knew they could still even the series if they could get their high-powered offence rolling. They'd won the fourth game in Toronto 6–2, after all, and the previous spring they'd won both games at the Gardens en route to a first-round sweep. So it wasn't as though the famous building on its own intimidated the men from Montreal, winners of 12 previous Stanley Cups. In the series, the Habs had scored 15 goals, but 12 had come in two games. In their three losses, players like Yvan Cournoyer, Henri Richard, Ralph Backstrom and Bobby Rousseau had gone silent, while speedy ex-Leaf Dick Duff, to the confusion of many, hadn't been used much. Early in Game Six, it appeared the visitors might have brought their firepower with them, but Sawchuk made a good stop on a Jean Beliveau slapshot. At the other end, Worsley did the same to Frank Mahovlich, and the two teams settled into a tight-checking contest of wills. With Brian Conacher off for interference early, Imlach twice used his peculiar strategy of employing defencemen to take faceoffs in the Leaf zone. Both Tim Horton and Larry Hillman lost those draws, creating Montreal opportunities. When the Leafs went on the power play, they deployed Bob Pulford, Pete Stemkowski and specialist Mike Walton up front, with Hillman on the left point and Pappin on the right point. By this juncture of the playoffs, Hillman had clearly supplant-ed his better known blueline mates as the club's Number 1 defenceman, logging enormous amounts of ice time, while Pappin was playing ahead of the likes of Mahovlich, Armstrong, Ron Ellis and Dave Keon in impor-tant offensive situations.

Ties and jackets dominated the crowd as players with no names on their jerseys flashed past white boards, absent the advertisements they display in modern NHL times. Only two players, Montreal's J.C. Tremblay and Rousseau, wore helmets. The lone helmet-wearing Leaf at that time, Larry Jeffrey, had suffered a season-ending knee injury in the final game of the first round against Chicago and watched this game on crutches. Sawchuk wore a mask, while Worsley didn't. The Leaf fans who had booed Sawchuk for his leaky performance in Game Four were now turn-ing their attention to the classy Beliveau, who received hoots and catcalls for what was perceived to be overly rough play. Midway through the first, Beliveau brought his stick up on Allan Stanley after a whistle, and moments later he was sent off for taking a wild run at Horton. It was clear the Canadiens had brought a new sense of urgency to the game. With Conacher off for the second time in the period for boarding Richard, Imlach again used Horton on a defensive zone draw, and again he lost the faceoff, but the Leafs defended seamlessly.

Neither club scored in the first, adding to the obvious tension. With six minutes gone in the second, Ellis changed that by driving to the net to bang in a rebound off a shot by Red Kelly. The chance had been created at the other end when Stanley had blocked a weak shot by Jacques Laperriere and flipped the puck out to centre where Kelly had corralled it to create a two-on-one break with only Montreal blueliner Terry Harper back to defend. Worsley had made the first save, but the rebound was big and dangerous, perhaps a sign of rust on the part of the veteran goalie, and Ellis had lifted it high. Sawchuk, meanwhile, continued to play perfectly. After Stanley, this time, had become the latest Leaf defenceman to lose a defensive zone draw, Sawchuk stoned Duff from 10 feet out to keep the Leafs ahead 1–0. Playing his best game of the playoffs, Sawchuk made a brilliant save on Beliveau minutes later, and then another on John Ferguson as the visitors took the play to the home side.

In the final minute of the second period, Pappin and Stemkowski headed up ice on an innocent-looking two-on-two rush, with Harper and Laperriere retreating to defend. Stanley had started the play by taking a diagonal run to hit Claude Larose in the Leaf zone, the same kind of play he'd used to nearly decapitate the Pocket Rocket, Richard, earlier in the series. The two Leaf forwards criss-crossed as they moved into the Montreal zone, with Pappin ending up past the faceoff circle on his wrong wing as the offensive thrust appeared to fizzle.

In desperation, Pappin lifted a backhand towards the front of the Montreal net where Harper and Stemkowski battled for position, and the puck glanced off Harper's skate past an astonished Worsley. The Leafs had a 2–0 lead on a back-breaking score with only 36 seconds left before intermission. Once again, as they had so many times in the playoffs, it was

Pappin and Stemkowski who had delivered an important goal, albeit a fluke—Pappin's league-leading seventh of the playoffs.

During the intermission, the half-dozen Leaf players who had never been on a Cup-winning team nervously prepared for one more period. Ellis, meanwhile, was surprised to look across the room and see Horton and Kelly, with 11 championships between them, leaning shoulder-to-shoulder, snoozing. Early in the third, Duff woke his team up with a dazzling rush, beating Horton to the outside and then sneaking inside of Stanley to sweep the puck past Sawchuk while falling to the ice. "One thing I'll always wonder about this series," said Boom Boom Geoffrion afterwards, "is why Toe didn't use Duff more." Using only 13 players, with Walton appearing solely for power plays and Bobby Baun, Eddie Shack, Aut Erickson and Milan Marcetta all nailed to the bench, the Leafs set out to make that slender one-goal lead stand up. Sawchuk almost made a terrible mistake with less than six minutes to play as he fielded a flip shot from centre off the stick of Richard. The puck bounced and then appeared to hit Sawchuk's knee, bouncing to his left and just wide of the post.

With four minutes left, Imlach stubbornly stuck to his plan of using defencemen to take defensive zone faceoffs rather than Keon, Kelly or Stemkowski. Horton took the draw against Beliveau, who simply drove the puck at the Leaf net, forcing Sawchuk to make a save. With 2:23 left in a similar situation on the other side of the ice, it was Pronovost's turn to take the faceoff, and after a brief scramble, the Habs again gained possession but could not get a clear shot.

As public address announcer Paul Morris announced the final minute of play, Hillman relieved pressure in the Leaf zone by slamming the puck the length of the rink for an icing call. With 55 seconds left, Worsley was pulled from the Montreal net for an extra attacker and the faceoff was set to the left of Sawchuk. "Kelly, Armstrong, Horton and Pulford," bellowed Imlach. "And Stanley, you take the faceoff." While the decision to use the 41-year-old Stanley on the draw has frequently been erroneously portrayed as a brilliant spur-of-the-moment decision by the Leaf coach, it was anything but. Imlach had used the strategy over and over throughout the playoffs and on a number of times that night, despite the fact it had rarely been successful. In that situation, he simply chose Stanley because the right-handed Horton took the faceoffs on the other side of the ice when that defence tandem was on duty. Still, the story was retold and embellished so many times over the years that even Stanley came to believe it, suggesting he had not taken a faceoff "in six years" when he was sent out in the final minute of Game Six. He'd actually taken a faceoff earlier that game and many over the course of the '67 playoffs. It was classic Leaf myth-making, designed mostly to make Imlach look like a genius.

The truth was that years earlier, players had frequently just bulled ahead on the drop of the puck, shoving the enemy centre out of the way, but the rules had been changed to make that faceoff interference. Imlach, however, had never gotten out of the habit of using defencemen in this way. Stanley, who had been in countless similar situations since turning pro immediately after the conclusion of the Second World War, correctly guessed that referee John Ashley would be very unlikely to call interference on such a play now.

Pulford, meanwhile, came to see symbolism in the players Imlach chose to put on the ice—five veterans who had played on the three previous Cup champions of the decade. "I think he knew at that moment that was our swan song," says Pulford. "That was the swan song of his dynasty." As the players milled about preparing for the critical faceoff,

Gardens workers cleaned eggs off the ice and the hit song "Tijuana Taxi" by Herb Alpert and the Tijuana Brass played over the arena speakers, Stanley prepared to take the draw, then stepped away to have one last word with Kelly. Kelly then moved from a position directly behind Stanley, the place Leaf centres played when defencemen took defensive zone draws, to a spot on the faceoff circle in the slot directly to Stanley's right. The moment the puck was dropped, Stanley swiped at it, then charged into Beliveau. Kelly jumped into the faceoff circle to grab the loose puck ahead of Cournoyer and tapped a 10-foot pass up ice to Pulford. Pulford took two strides, then flipped a long cross-ice backhand pass to Armstrong on the right boards. The Leaf captain crossed centre and, with Laperriere the only Montreal player back, took a hard wrist shot from 65 feet that flew into the unguarded Habs net to make it 3–1 with 47 seconds left to play. Kelly was unfairly robbed of an assist on the play, but in his final NHL game he had set up two important goals and been a member of his eighth championship effort. The Leafs had their Cup, six months and 12 days after beginning what had been a long, arduous and often contradictory season.

At game's end, Bower was the first off the bench to congratulate Sawchuk. Walton and Pappin weren't far behind. The post-game celebrations seemed like a blur, mostly because they happened so quickly—far more quickly than today when television cameras and dignitaries flood the ice and turn the revelry into a marathon. Within 25 seconds of the final whistle, the traditional handshakes between the Habs and Leafs had already begun, with Pronovost, Bower and Kelly leading the way for the Leafs and Stemkowski grabbing Imlach's fedora and tossing it high into the air. Within 90 seconds, Baun had bolted the ice with Sawchuk close behind and Clarence Campbell was presenting the Cup. "Ladies and gentlemen," said the patrician NHL president, stumbling over his words, "it is now my very pleasant duty and responsibility to present the Stanley Cup to the Maple Leaf hockey club.... for the 11th time!" Armstrong skated over to accept the trophy with his young son, Brian, and together they lifted the Cup. After, Armstrong waved his teammates over for a few photos. Then the triumphant Leafs skated off the ice, less than five minutes after the conclusion of the game.

There were two moments from the final portion of the contest and the post-game celebrations that could easily be viewed, in retrospect, as spooky omens. Duff's spectacular goal in a losing effort was oddly symbolic, for he had been traded away by the Leafs three years earlier and represented the short-term fixes and costly personnel moves that had been made to position the Leafs for one last Cup challenge.

Armstrong, meanwhile, stumbled on a TV cord and very nearly dropped the Cup as he left the ice. He was saved this near embarrassment only by the quick hands of Pappin, a player whose superb contributions to the Leaf victory would soon be forgotten by management and the fans. Indeed, many still recall Armstrong's empty-netter, but few remember that it was Pappin who scored the winning goal to capture the Cup.

In the jubilant Leaf dressing room, champagne corks flew, Hillman sucked on a beer to quench his thirst and word leaked out that Keon had won the Conn Smythe Trophy as MVP of the playoffs. Imlach and King Clancy, who had rescued the club with his successful pinch-hit coaching efforts in mid-season, were tossed into the showers while fully-clothed. With no set plans, the players agreed to convene at Pappin's for a celebratory party, with the Leaf forward scribbling his address on the dressing room chalkboard before stepping out into the rainy night.

The next morning at 8 a.m., a groggy Pappin was roused by the sound of the doorbell at his home on Blaydell Court in the west end of the city. The party had gone on until 4 a.m. and Pappin hadn't gone to bed until 5 a.m. after driving trainer Tommy Nayler home. The house still reeked of beer and cigarettes. When Pappin answered the door, he was greeted by men he didn't know, but who quickly explained themselves. They were there to take measurements for the swimming pool that Pappin's horse pal, Jimmy Black, had promised to build him before the opening game of the final if the Leafs could knock off the Habs and help Black make $30,000 on a 15–1 long-shot bet. Two weeks later, as the Leaf hockey empire officially came to a close, the $3,200 pool was complete—a generous perk for a surprise hero.

10 *The Dismantling*

The end appeared to come quickly for Punch Imlach, less than 15 minutes after his Maple Leafs had been swept in utterly humiliating fashion from the 1969 Stanley Cup playoffs by the young, brash Boston Bruins. In the two games played in Boston, the Leafs had lost outrageously, 10–0 in the opener and 7–0 in the second contest. As part of the humiliating Game One result, Leaf forward Forbes Kennedy had gone on a one-man rampage, incurring 38 minutes in penalties as he fought one Bruin after another. Kennedy was fined and suspended for the rest of the series, adding to the sense of total embarrassment for the once proud Leafs. When the series ended in Toronto with two one-goal contests, the decision by team president Stafford Smythe to fire Imlach, the team's general manager and coach since 1958, seemed almost a fit of pique. Smythe appeared to be an embarrassed executive caught up in the emotion of the moment, and canning his coach outside the loser's dressing room seemed anything but a carefully considered decision.

But the decision really wasn't of the knee-jerk variety at all. Smythe had been thinking about it for at least three years, but the 1967 Cup victory had forestalled any move to replace Imlach as GM or coach. Smythe's father, Conn, thought Imlach a "good"—not great—coach and a "lousy manager." The younger Smythe had fought with his father over many hockey and non-hockey issues, but on this the two men were of a single mind.

Moreover, Imlach's demise had been anything but abrupt. It had been slow and steady, something akin to creeping mildew.

Losing to the Bruins was, in fact, both instructive and symbolic. In goal for all four Boston victories was Gerry Cheevers, a netminder groomed as the Leafs' goalie-of-the-future in the early 1960s, but eventually a player lost for no return on waivers four years earlier because Imlach preferred to emphasize the short-term advantages of his aged puckstoppers, Johnny Bower and Terry Sawchuk. The Leafs had developed and trained Cheevers, and now he was on his way to the Hall of Fame wearing a Boston uniform. Bobby Orr played parts of that series, but had been the victim of a heavy, controversial bodycheck by Leaf blueliner Pat Quinn. Orr would eventually lead the B's to a pair of Stanley Cups and win the Norris Trophy as the NHL's best defenceman for eight straight years. He could have done all of that for the Leafs, but an inquiry on behalf of the young Parry Sound defenceman to the Leafs in 1960 had been arrogantly dismissed by Imlach and his staff.

But despite all the personnel errors made by Imlach and the organization between 1960 and 1966, there was no reason the Leafs had to fall into such disrepair and become a team that could be embarrassed so handily by Boston. They had, after all, won the Cup just two years earlier. Moreover, the team they'd knocked off in '67, the Montreal Canadiens, had gone on to greater heights, winning the '68 and '69 championships. What had happened was nothing less than the haphazard, reckless demolition of a champion, and Imlach had been the architect of that, too. If he had intentionally set out to destroy the Leafs after that glorious spring of '67—a team that was old but had 10 players who would later be voted into Hockey's Hall of Fame—he could not have done a more thorough job than what he accomplished by basic mismanagement.

The dressing room had been so stable for so many years until the summer of '67 that those who were there can vividly remember where individual players sat, and even how the room usually smelled of damp wool from the heavy jerseys they wore in those days. The goalies, Bower and Sawchuk, had shared the wall directly to the right of the entrance for three years. Farther down were the defencemen, where men like Tim Horton and Allan Stanley had been sitting together for almost a decade. The forwards sat to the left of the entrance, near trainer Bobby Haggert, sometimes sitting together in the forwards units that were together at the time.

Imlach himself didn't have an office adjoining the dressing room. He would arrive for practice in his shirt, tie and jacket, and hang his overcoat and fedora in Haggert's office. He would don a Leaf windbreaker and ball cap before heading onto the ice. He usually didn't wear hockey gloves or carry a stick, and he almost always left his tie on during the workout. The scene and the procedure had remained the same, virtually unchanged, ever since Imlach had arrived in the fall of 1958, and Imlach had profited from that stability. He had benefited greatly from the rich Leaf farm and junior system of the 1950s, but was unable to find ways to sustain the growth of the team by developing a system of his own to keep the Leafs competitive when the league's culture and methods began changing in the early 1960s.

By the fall of 1969, however, there was almost nothing left of the '67 Leaf team. In terms of players in their prime, the club still owned centre Dave Keon, winger Ron Ellis, veteran forward Bob Pulford and stylish scorer Mike Walton. That was it. Only four players from that championship team still capable of playing at a high level were left, and two of those, Pulford and Walton, would soon be gone as well. Bower was still around but ready to retire, and the same went for captain George Armstrong. On defence, Tim Horton and Marcel Pronovost were still under contract, but both were finished as prime-time players. Pronovost would soon be sent to the minors, and Horton would be gone in a trade to New York within months.

The Canadiens, on the other, hand, had just won the '69 Cup with a team that looked remarkably similar to the one the Leafs had faced two years earlier in Canada's centennial year. Fourteen players from that team were still in Montreal uniforms. The only significant players missing from the '67 Habs were forwards Gilles Tremblay and Dave Balon, and neither were stars. The defence corps was still intact, a group that included Ted Harris, Terry Harper, J.C. Tremblay and Jacques Laperriere. The goalies, Rogie Vachon and Gump Worsley, remained in place, as did all the firepower up front led by Jean Beliveau, Henri Richard and Yvan Cournoyer. The Habs had added good young players like Serge Savard, Mickey Redmond, Jacques Lemaire and Christian Bordeleau, setting the stage for more dominance in the 1970s. In fact, eight players from the '67 finalists were still on the team when it won the Cup in 1972. Sam Pollock had done a masterful job of protecting the club's assets from the potentially destructive effects of expansion, and he would soon engineer a deal that would deliver Guy Lafleur to the franchise.

Had the Habs beaten the Leafs in '67, they would have won five in a row in the second half of that decade. To Yvan Cournoyer, the defeat taught the Canadiens a lesson. "That loss was the toughest of my career," he says. "We learned the series is never over until it is over." In 11 subsequent Cup final appearances over the next three decades, the Canadiens would win 10 times. Never again were they upset, losing only to the favoured Calgary Flames in 1989.

— ❧ —

So what had happened to the Leafs? How had the team been so recklessly dismantled in comparison to the team they'd beaten in '67? For starters, the Leafs botched the expansion draft in June 1967 that was organized to provide the new franchises in Los Angeles, Oakland, Minnesota, Pittsburgh, St. Louis and Philadelphia with competitive rosters. Foolishly, Imlach had protected Bower and Pronovost, even though the 42-year-old Bower had been hurt over and over in the 1966–67 season and would not likely be taken, and Pronovost was both high-salaried and near the end of his career. In the goalie portion of the draft, the Leafs lost Sawchuk to L.A. They also lost Gary Smith, the best young goalie left in the withered farm system, to Oakland. Bobby Baun, at age 30 the youngest member of the Leaf defence corps, was also left unprotected and was taken by the Seals. Larry Jeffrey, a regular in the playoffs before being hurt, went to Pittsburgh. Two good young minor-league forwards, Bill Flett and Eddie Joyal, were also lost to Los Angeles. Defencemen Al Arbour and Darryl Edestrand, experienced types who would have helped ease the transition from the '67 champions to a younger team, went to St. Louis.

The following season, the carnage continued. In the same deal with Detroit that sent Frank Mahovlich packing, the Leafs gave up forward prospect Garry Unger, 24-year-old centre Peter Stemkowski and the rights to 30-year-old defenceman Carl Brewer. At the end of the season, 28-year-old Jim Pappin was traded to Chicago. More players, including Brian Conacher, Larry Hillman and defenceman Duane Rupp, were lost for nothing in the waiver draft after that season. In all, the Leafs had squandered a good core of capable and promising players, including Gary Smith, Baun, Hillman, Rupp, Arbour, Edestrand, Brewer, Mahovlich, Unger, Stemkowski, Jeffrey, Conacher, Pappin, Flett and Joyal, in the 12 months after winning the Cup, receiving only Norm Ullman, Floyd Smith and Paul Henderson in return.

All of this, of course, had come at the same time many of the key players on the '67 team had grown too old to contribute, and at the same time demand for NHL-calibre players had doubled. By April 1969, Imlach was gone as well, leaving only scorched earth behind. What had taken 20 years to build, Imlach had plundered in less than two years. It took another decade for the Leafs to get back on track with a team that made it to the 1978 semifinals, only to be dumped by Montreal in four straight. Imlach returned a year later and destroyed that team as well.

Other than Mahovlich, Imlach had hardly rid the team of stars. But the rest ranged from viable NHLers to good players who contributed at the NHL level for another decade. The club did have some young talent coming, particularly in defencemen Jim Dorey, Rick Ley, Jim McKenny and Brad Selwood, but there was no structure around which those players could learn and develop. The foundation had been destroyed. The residue of Imlach's abusive style meant Walton would also soon demand to leave. The Leafs did manage to land Bernie Parent from Philadelphia in that transaction, but then threw that asset away by allowing Parent to jump to the WHA over a salary difference of $8,000.

Smythe, meanwhile, didn't put a great deal of consideration into Imlach's replacement, nor did he carefully search the ranks of available GMs and coaches. The day Imlach was fired, Leaf executive Jim Gregory was in the stands in Oklahoma City watching the Tulsa Oilers, still the Leafs' top farm club, play against the local Blazers in the sixth game of a best-of-seven Central Hockey League playoff series. The Oklahoma City GM, Bill Leavens, came to Gregory with a message that Smythe was looking for him and was on the phone. Gregory looked around at his colleagues in the stands, men like Ray Miron, Doug Barkley and Gerry Blair, and assumed someone was playing a practical joke. So he ignored the message. Ten minutes later, Leavens returned again with the same message, this time with Smythe's phone number and the suggestion that the Leaf president wasn't too pleased his underling wasn't calling him back. Gregory called, and Smythe told him to get back to Toronto immediately. Gregory briefly protested, suggesting he might as well stay for the conclusion of the series. Smythe told him to get back immediately because he was the new GM of the Leafs. No interview, no search. Gregory looked down at the Tulsa bench and coach John McLellan, the man he would take to Toronto with him to be the first new coach of the Leafs in 11 years.

Even with Imlach gone and new figures of authority in place, however, the poisonous final months of the old regime continued to leech into the Toronto hockey department. In September 1970, 18 months after Imlach's firing, Bob Pulford was traded to the Los Angeles Kings for winger Garry Monahan. Pulford, the final member of the team's top line in the '67 Cup run to leave, said the old feud between Imlach and Smythe fueled his departure. "Stafford and I had been through a lot together," he recalled. "We had won the Memorial Cup with the Marlies together. We had socialized together. But as his relationship with Imlach deteriorated, for some strange reason he became more and more convinced that I had become an Imlach guy, and that upset him greatly." Even though Gregory was now the team's GM, Smythe made the deal to send Pulford to the Kings. "[Gregory] told me that Smythe made that trade himself with [L.A. owner] Jack Kent Cooke," said Pulford. "Jimmy called Cooke the next day to try and reverse the trade, but Cooke wouldn't go for it."

Of that '67 Leaf team, three men—Bower, Armstrong and Ellis—were allowed to retire in Leaf uniforms, while one other, Red Kelly, eventually returned to coach the team. The lovable Bower quit in 1970 and worked for more than two decades as a scout. Armstrong, so respected as a captain that he had been touted in '67 by some as a natural successor to Imlach, hung 'em up in 1971 and was also given work as a scout. After one year, and with Harold Ballard now fully in charge, Armstrong was hired to coach the Junior Marlboros, essentially against his will. The Leafs didn't automatically own any of the Marlie players anymore, but Ballard could still make money off the team and so wanted somebody he viewed as high-profile and qualified behind the bench. "It wasn't that I didn't think I was any good at coaching," says Armstrong. "I just never really enjoyed it like I enjoyed scouting." Nonetheless, the Marlies won two national championships under his guidance.

Kelly was hired to coach the Leafs in 1973 and did fairly well, conjuring up the whacky "pyramid power" theme in 1975 in which he placed the supposedly energy-drawing pyramids under the Leaf bench during games. After the 1976–77 season, he was fired, and Ballard and his sidekick, the always adaptable King Clancy, wanted to hire Armstrong. With no obvious other choice, the Leafs went ahead and drafted two players from Armstrong's Marlie roster, Trevor Johansen and John Anderson, with their first two picks in the 1977 draft. To Ballard and Clancy, drafting those players was a means of paving the way for Armstrong to take over. "I'll consider it as long as Jim Gregory or McLellan [by then the assistant GM] are with me every day on the road," Armstrong told Ballard. "I need someone with their expertise or I can't do it." "No problem," said Ballard. A few days later, however, Gregory told Armstrong that he shouldn't count on the arrangement he wanted. "Fuck what the Chief wants," Ballard had told Gregory. "We'll do it for a few trips and then he'll be all right on his own." Hearing that, Armstrong turned down the job. Ballard hired Roger Neilson from the club's Dallas farm team but had become unhappy with Armstrong, who just wanted to scout but was told he had to keep coaching the Marlies. In the middle of the 1977–78 season, he quit the Marlies and left the Leaf organization entirely, ultimately hooking up with the Quebec Nordiques as a scout.

There was to be, however, more to come in the Ballard–Armstrong saga. Armstrong returned to the Leafs as a scout in 1988 after being let go by the Nordiques. Much had changed. Ballard was in a wheelchair after a quintuple heart bypass, and his ability to effectively run the hockey club was deteriorating with equal speed as that of his general health. Still, he was happy to have Armstrong, a member of the '67 champs, returning to the fold after the Leafs had gone through two decades of near constant losing. In the impaired judgement of his declining health, Ballard was uncharacteristically sentimental about Armstrong, so much so that when John Brophy was fired in December 1988, Ballard went along with the decision—as long as Armstrong would be Brophy's replacement. This time, Armstrong took the job. "But I knew after three games that I was in so far over my head that I just turned things over to [assistant coach] Garry Lariviere," says Armstrong. "I was the figurehead and I looked forward to the end of the season and the end of my coaching career."

Ballard, however, had grown content with Armstrong. The following summer, after Armstrong had won only 17 of 47 games, and with Armstrong telling anyone willing to listen that he no longer wished to coach, Ballard still insisted that he had to stay. In a column written by *The Toronto Star*'s Milt Dunnell, the Leaf owner decreed that Armstrong was now the "chief bottle-washer" at the Gardens, and at the June draft he insisted Armstrong should take the microphone to make the team's selections, an embarrassment for the rest of the organization. Armstrong, secure in his new popularity but unwilling to tell Ballard he didn't want to coach, received a new three-year contract from team management without Ballard's approval. That fall, Ballard hired another old Leaf, Floyd Smith, to manage the team, and Smith got Armstrong off the hook by hiring Doug Carpenter to coach. A few days later, a letter arrived at Armstrong's house from Leaf treasurer Don Crump advising Armstrong that he had been terminated. Armstrong, however, turned up at the Gardens the next day waving his new contract, and he stayed on. The following

April, Ballard died. For Armstrong, one of the most respected Leafs of all time and the leader of that '67 team, it had been an absurd, embarrassing process caused partly by his own unwillingness to stand up to Ballard. The episode had, two decades after the fact, sullied the memory of the '67 champions by turning that team's captain, one of the most respected players in team history, into the object of farce.

Armstrong did keep working for the Leafs and was still scouting for the club on a part-time basis in the 2003–04 season. He took his 96-year-old mother to a junior game in Sudbury and regularly appeared at Leaf home games. Ellis, meanwhile, was the final member of that small group of '67 players to hang up his skates and to retire as a member of the Leafs. To men like Keon, Ellis was the last of the true Leafs, the last product of a system designed to carefully nurture promising young hockey players and produce members of the NHL club. He had arrived in the wake of the 1964 championship, signing his first contract for $19,000 over two years. In September 1966, he was bumped up to $12,000 in the first year of a two-year arrangement, with a salary of $14,000 in the second year. He became part of the team's "Quiet Line" with Kelly and Jeffrey, and led the team in regular season goals with 22 and was a solid third line forward for the Leafs throughout the drive to the '67 Cup. In the final game against Montreal, he scored the first goal of the game after a scoreless opening period, an important goal under any circumstances, but enormous that night. Still, he recalls not being able to fully enjoy the celebrations that year because of worries over his place on the team and whether he'd be able to stick in the NHL.

As the years passed, player after player from the '67 team left, and Ellis, after being a very good player for Team Canada at the '72 Summit Series, retired himself for two years in the mid-1970s after turning down the chance to succeed Keon as team captain in 1975. He figured the pressures of the job would be too much. "I wish I'd just taken the 'C' for one season," he says. Darryl Sittler refused to take the Leaf captaincy until he was certain Ellis would not. Instead, Ellis retired, but came out of retirement in 1977 and was by then the last remaining player from the team that had won it all a decade earlier.

---------- ❦ ----------

By 1979, Imlach had returned as Leaf GM to replace Gregory, the man who had replaced him. After the 1979–80 season, Ellis considered an offer to wind down his career in Europe, but Imlach convinced him to return for one more season. "I want you here to help with the young kids," said Imlach, and Ellis accepted the role. The season, however, quickly turned into a disaster, and Ellis found himself sitting in the press box. Told he would play on a Saturday night against Montreal, Ellis was primed to return to action—until he arrived at the Gardens to find his equipment packed up and no sweater hanging in his stall to indicate he would be playing. He was told Imlach wanted to see him. He fell into a state of shock when Imlach abruptly told him he could either accept a buy-out of his contract that would be less than the going rate of the standard NHL players contract, or he could report to the minors in Moncton, New Brunswick. Instead, Ellis went home and arranged for his agent, Alan Eagleson, to work out a settlement with the Leafs. Despite the way he'd been dumped, Ellis signed his release form with a classy note for Imlach. "Punch, I started my career with you, and I'm pleased that I finished with you," he wrote.

After 14 years, all traces of that distinctive '67 team had finally vanished from the Leaf roster. The process started 13 days after the Leafs had won the Cup, when spare forward Eddie Shack was traded to Boston, and it ended with the curt dismissal of the proud Ellis. The dismantling had been thorough and utterly heartless. Until more than a quarter century had passed, not a single member of that team received a special evening or noteworthy celebration for being part of Leaf history.

In hindsight, Imlach would have been wise to have either retired after the '67 Cup, or at least handed over the coaching reins and continued only as GM. Kelly immediately moved to Los Angeles to coach. He would have been a perfect replacement in the wake of the Leafs' fourth Cup of the decade. Imlach was only 49, but men in other sports recognized when it was time to go. Red Auerbach had retired as coach of the Boston Celtics a year earlier after winning eight straight NBA championships. Vince Lombardi, meanwhile, stepped down as coach of the Green Bay Packers after winning a second consecutive Super Bowl in 1968. Over nine seasons, from 1958 to 1967, Imlach had managed and coached the Leafs to a 302–225–103 record (.561 winning percentage) and four Cups. Had he chosen to leave then, he would have soared into the sunset like Scotty Bowman, who quit after guiding the Detroit Red Wings to the 2002 Stanley Cup.

It wasn't as if Imlach had nothing left to give as a hockey man. In fact, when he moved on to take over the Buffalo Sabres in 1970, he quickly molded that franchise into a winner and took the Sabres to the 1975 Stanley Cup final, losing to Philadelphia. After doing a poor job of developing young talent in Toronto in the final years, he drafted very well in Buffalo, selecting players like Gilbert Perreault, Richard Martin, Craig Ramsay, Jim Schoenfeld, Danny Gare and Don Edwards. Sabres players liked and respected Imlach, who got along with his best player, Perreault, in a way he never did with Mahovlich.

But if Imlach could reinvent himself in Buffalo, he certainly couldn't maintain the momentum in Toronto, where his poisonous relationship with team president Stafford Smythe and the continuous pressure to win brought out his worst instincts. That was demonstrated after his successes with the

Sabres; when he returned to Toronto he was a disaster again, just as he had been for two seasons after the '67 Cup win. His ego, history and business entanglements fogged his judgement. All told, in his final five seasons of running the Leafs, spread over 14 years, Imlach's teams won only 46 per cent of their regular season games. In the playoffs, they went 0–10, outscored 61 to 17. May 2, 1967, was indeed Imlach's last great day with the Leafs, and all that followed while in the employ of the the hockey club injured his legacy.

————— ❧ —————

Ultimately, Imlach received the same kind of graceless final farewell others had received under his watch. In fact, it was decidedly uglier than the first time around in 1969. In early September 1981, Imlach suffered a heart attack at the Leafs training camp in St. Catharines, Ontario, and the next day was rushed by ambulance to Toronto General Hospital. The team had suffered badly under his leadership in the previous two seasons, and Ballard had soured on him, but for public consumption maintained that he would stand by Imlach. "If it comes down to friendship or winning, it's friendship," he declared. But Ballard, in his heart, wanted to get rid of Imlach, and the heart attack, the second in 13 months, was his chance. After telling all of his employees to keep Imlach's illness quiet, Ballard let the information slip to his media friends, and a picture of the frail, 63-year-old Imlach on a stretcher being carried into Toronto General was published in local newspapers. Three weeks later, Imlach had heart surgery, and his future with the Leafs was up in the air as Mike Nykoluk, the same Toronto lad who had agreed to try out for the Leafs three decades earlier on the condition he could bring his pal Bobby Baun with him, ran the team.

On October 26, Ballard announced Imlach was out as GM, but he didn't name a replacement and hadn't even talked to Imlach. By early November, Imlach's status was entirely unclear, and he showed up for work expecting to resume his duties despite everything that had been written and said. He found to his dismay, however, that the sign for his private parking spot on Wood Street at the back of the Gardens had been taken down. And when he climbed the stairs to his office, he found his private line had been disconnected. When he approached Ballard, he received no explanation or assurances about his future. "I just don't want to put you in a box," said Ballard, feigning concern for Imlach's health. Imlach responded, "Well, call me when you need a manager." He walked upstairs to settle any expenses he was owed, and left the Gardens forever.

Every two weeks for the rest of that season, a Leaf employee delivered a paycheque to the former commander-in-chief, who, at the designated time, would be waiting in his idling car behind the Gardens. It was as close to an official farewell as he ever received.

Index